Edwin Othello Excell

**Triumphant Songs**

nos. 3 & 4 Combined

Edwin Othello Excell

**Triumphant Songs**
*nos. 3 & 4 Combined*

ISBN/EAN: 9783337815455

Printed in Europe, USA, Canada, Australia, Japan

Cover: Foto ©Lupo / pixelio.de

More available books at **www.hansebooks.com**

# PREFACE.

### SOMETHING SELDOM EVER READ.

# TRIUMPHANT SONGS

## SUNG THE WORLD OVER.

CAUTION.—The words and music of almost all the pieces in "Triumphant Songs Nos. 3 and 4 Combined," are copyright property. All rights of republication of either the words or music, separate or combined, are reserved, and will be defended by the owners of the copyright.

Triumphant Songs No. 3, Copyrighted, 1892, by E. O. EXCELL.
Triumphant Songs No. 4, Copyrighted, 1894, by E. O. EXCELL.

Meredith, Music Typographer, Chicago.

# Orders of Worship

## For the Sabbath School.

### NO. 1.
By G. W. Barnett, Sup't.
Wesley M. E. S. S. Chicago.

1. **Bell.**—Order.
2. **Roll Call.**—Teachers and officers.
3. **Hymn.**—No. 168. O Day of Rest and Gladness. (Or selected.)
4. **All.**—O come, let us worship and bow down; let us kneel before the Lord, our Maker.
5. **Prayer.**—Concluding with Lord's Prayer in concert.
6. **Hymn** to suit the lesson.
7. **Class Wants.**—Marking attendance of scholars, and collections.
8. **Show Bibles.**
9. **Supt.**—Where is the lesson.
10. **Reading Scriptures** alternately, sometimes Supt. first, sometimes school first.
11. **Study Hour.**
12. **Bell** for closing exercise.
13. **Hymn** to suit the lesson.
14. **Review.**—4 to 7 minutes.
15. **Announcements.**
16. **Secretary's Report.**
17. **Librarian** distributes books.
18. **Bell.**—Rise and sing. No. 428. Guide Me. (Or selected.)
19. **Apostles' Creed.**
20. **Gloria.**—No. 460.
21. **Silence.**
22. **Bell.**
23. **Dismission.**

### NO. 2.
By Samuel H. Bloom. Supt.
Second Baptist S. S., Chicago.

1. **Chant.**—No. 90. I will lift up mine eyes.
2. **Prayer.**
3. **Orchestra** play to Chorus No. 83. Take my life and let it be.
4. **All** rise and sing No. 83. Take my life and let it be.
5. **Scholars** having their own bibles repeat John v: 39. "Search the scriptures, for in them ye think ye have eternal life: and they are they which testify of me."
6. **Responsive Reading.**
Psalm cxxv : 1 to 5.
   1. *Girls.*—They that trust in the Lord shall be as Mount Zion, which cannot be removed, but abideth forever.
   2. *Boys.*—As the mountains are round about Jerusalem, so the Lord is round about his people from henceforth even forever.
   3. *Girls.*—For the rod of the wicked shall not rest upon the lot of the righteous, lest the righteous put forth their hands unto iniquity.
   4. *Boys.*—Do good, O Lord, unto those that be good, and to them that are upright in their hearts.
   5. *Girls*—As for such as turn aside unto their crooked ways, the Lord shall lead them forth with the workers of iniquity; but peace shall be upon Israel.
7. **School** repeat mottoes
8. **Lesson Hour.**
9. **Closing Exercises.** (Selected.)

### NO. 3.
By H. B. Wheeler, Supt.
Presbyterian S. S. 41st. St., Chicago.

1. **Signal Bell.**—School opens.
2. **Ten minutes** musical recital.
3. **Second Bell.**—Perfect attention.
4. **Opening Song.** No. 3. All the Day.
5. **Prayer.**—Perfect silence, and all heads bowed.
6. **Chant.**—Lord's prayer. No. 260.
7. **Song.**—(Selected.)
8. **Distribution** of class books and collection envelopes.
9. **Adjournment** of bible classes to their rooms.
10. **Outline** of lesson.
11. **Reading of lesson** by Supt. and school.
12. **Study** of lesson without interruption.
13. **Bell** for closing exercises.
14. **Song.**—(Selected.)
15. **Subject and Golden Text** by school.

[Over.

## Orders of Worship. Continued.

16. **Review** by Supt.
17. **Notices.**
18. **Secty. and Treas.** report.
19. **Closing Hymn.**—All standing.
20. **Closing Prayer.**—Followed by school repeating: "Let the words of my mouth, and the meditation of my heart be acceptable in thy sight, O Lord, my Strength, and my Redeemer. (*Chanting.*) Amen.

## No. 4.

By G. E. HIGHLEY, Supt.
Hyde Park M. E. S. S. Chicago.

1. **Piano.**—A few strains to secure order.
2. **Silent prayer.**—One minute.
3. **Responsive Service.**—No. 401. Revive us again.
4. **Announcements** of the day and week.
5. **Hymn** to suit the lesson.
6. **Prayer.**
7. **Sing** (*Softly.*) No. 414. Jesus, lover of my soul.
8. **Who** have their bibles?
9. **Golden Text.**—Lesson, and location of same.
10. **Reading Scriptures** alternately.
11. **Class Study.**
12. **Hymn.**—(Selected.)
13. **Application** of lesson.
14. **Secretary's Report.**
15. **Closing Hymn.**—(Selected.)
16. **Closing Prayer.**

## No. 5.

By E. O. EXCELL.

1. **Opening Anthem.**—No. 74. Rock of Ages.
2. **Responsive Reading.**
   1. *Supt.*—Worthy is the Lamb that was slain to receive power, and riches, and wisdom, and strength, and honor, and glory, and blessing.
   2. *School.*—My soul shall make her boast in the Lord; the humble shall hear thereof, and be glad.
   3. *Teachers.*—Let the floods clap their hands; let the hills be joyful together.
   4. *Supt.*—O magnify the Lord with me, and let us exalt his name together.
3. **Sing** No. 18. Let him in.
4. **Silent Prayer** followed by the XXIII Psalm in concert.
5. **Lesson Hour.**
6. **Review.**
7. **Hymn** to suit the lesson.
8. **Notices.** Secretary's report, distribution of books, etc.
9. **Sing.** No. 338. My Happy Home.
10. **Closing.** The Lord watch between me and thee, when we are absent, one from another.

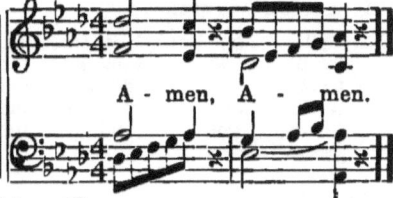

## No. 6.

By W. P. FREEMAN, Ass't. Supt.
First Presbt. S. S. of Austin, Ill.

### WORSHIP.

1. **Responsive Reading.**
   1. *Leader.*—Truly God is good to Israel, even to such as are of a clean heart.
   2. *School.*—Blessed be the Lord God, the God of Israel, who only doeth wondrous things.
   3. *Leader.*—Oh, that men would praise the Lord for his goodness, and for his wonderful works to the children of men.
   4. *School.*—Lord God of Israel, there is no God like thee, in heaven above, or in earth beneath, who keepeth covenant and mercy with thy servants that walk before thee with all their heart.
   5. *All.*—The Lord is in his holy temple, let all the earth keep silence before him.
2. **Silent prayer** followed by the Lord's prayer in concert.
3. **All sing** (unannounced,) No. 444. Savior, like a Shepherd lead us.
4. **Prayer.** (All heads bowed.)
5. **Song** to suit the lesson.

### INSTRUCTION.

6. **Apostles' Creed**, or Beatitudes.
7. **Scripture Lesson**, read responsively, from Bibles so far as possible.

# Orders of Worship. Continued.

8. **Recitation** of golden text.
9. **Lesson Study.**

### BUSINESS.

10. **Secty's Report. Notices.**

### CLOSING SERVICE.

11. **Desk** or Blackboard review, followed by short prayer from the desk.
12. **Lesson Hymn.**
13. **All**—"The Lord bless thee and keep thee; the Lord make his face to shine upon thee, and be gracious to thee; the Lord lift up his countenance upon thee and give thee peace." Amen.

## No. 7.

By W. G. SHERER, Supt.
Memorial Baptist S. S. Chicago.

1. **Order.**—Signal. Chords on Piano.
2. **Invocation.**
3. **Responsive Service.**— No. 407. Holy, Holy, Holy.
4. **Notices.**
5. **New memory verse.**— Learn a new verse every Sunday.
6. **Sing.**
7. **Sing.**
8. **Review** last ten memory verses.
9. **Present Bibles.**
10. **Read Lesson.**
11. **Prayer.**
12. **Response.**—No. 178.
13. **Lesson** —30 minutes.
14. **Singing** to suit the lesson.
15. **Secretary's Report.**
16. **Parting words.**
17. **Sing** Savior, like a Shepherd. No. 444.

## No. 8.

By C. M. HOTCHKIN, Supt.
Plymouth Congregational S. S. Chicago.

1. **Sing** two selections; beginning on time. Doors closed; perfect order.
2. **All** *Repeat softly.* The Lord is in his holy temple, Let all the earth keep silence, keep silence before him.

### Christ Promised.

1. *Supt.*—Behold the days come saith the Lord that I will raise unto David a Righteous Branch.
2. *School.*—And the government shall be upon his shoulders, and his name shall be called Wonderful, Counsellor, the Mighty God, the Everlasting Father, the Prince of Peace.
3. *Supt.*— He was wounded for our transgressions, he was bruised for our iniquities, the chastisement of our peace was upon him and with his stripes we are healed.

### Promise Fulfilled.

4. *School.*—For God so loved the world that he gave his only begotten Son that whosoever believeth on him should not perish, but have everlasting life.
5. *Supt.*—For unto you is born this day in the city of David, a Savior which is Christ the Lord.
6. *School.*—And the holy Ghost descended in bodily shape like a dove upon him, and a voice from heaven which said, "Thou art my beloved Son in whom I am well pleased."

### Christ's Mission.

7. *Supt* —The Spirit of the Lord is upon me because he hath anointed me to preach the Gospel to the poor. He hath sent me to heal the brokenhearted, to preach deliverance to the captive and recovering of sight to the blind.
8. *School.*—For the promise is unto you and to your children, and to all that are afar off.

### Christ's Words of Comfort.

9. *Supt,*—Let not your heart be troubled; ye believe in God, believe also in me.
10. *School.*—In my Father's house are many mansions; if it were not so, I would have told you. I go to prepare a place for you.
11. *Supt.*—If you love me, keep my commandments.

[*Over.*

# Orders of Worship. Concluded.

### Christ's Suffering, Death and Burial.

12. *School.*—When they were come to the place which is called Calvary, there they crucified him and the malefactors, one on the right hand, the other on the left,
13. *Supt.*—Then said Jesus, "Father, forgive them, for they know not what they do."
14. And Jesus cried with a loud voice and gave up the Ghost.
15. *Supt.*—Pilate gave the body to Joseph, and he bought fine linen and laid him in a sepulchre which was hewn out of a rock, and rolled a stone to the door of the sepulchre.

### Christ's Resurrection.

16. *School.*—Behold, there was a great earthquake, for the angel of the Lord descended from heaven, and came and rolled back the stone from the door, and sat upon it.
17. *Supt.*—His countenance was like lightning and his raiment white as snow: and for fear of him the keepers did shake and became as dead men.
18. *School.*—The angel said unto the women, "Fear not ye, for I know ye seek Jesus, which was crucified: he is not here, for he is risen as he said, Come see the place where the Lord lay."

### Christ's Commission and Ascension.

19. *Supt.*—Jesus came and spake unto the disciples, saying, "All power is given unto me in heaven and in earth, go ye therefore and teach all nations, baptizing them in the name of the Father, and of the Son, and of the Holy Ghost."
20. *School.*—So then after the Lord had spoken unto them, he was received up into heaven and sat upon the right hand of God.
3. **Singing** to suit the lesson.
4. Open **Doors.**
5. **Doors Closed.**
6. **Lesson** read responsively.
7. **Opening prayer** by one of the teachers.
8. **Sing** No. 460. Gloria Patri.

9. **Doors Open.**
10. **Take Collection,** and mark attendance.
11. **Lesson** 30 minutes.
12. **Sing.** (All standing)
13. **Lesson Reviewed.**
14. Secty's and Treas. report. Notices.
15. **Sing.**—All standing.
16. **Response** by the school. "The Lord watch between me and thee, when we are absent one from another.
17. **Very short Prayer** by Pastor or Superintendent.

## No. 9.
T. G. McCulloh, Supt.
Hyde Park 1st Pres. S. S. Chicago.

1. Supt and School recite from memory Psalm 67. Be merciful unto me, etc.
2. **Song.**
3. **Prayer.**
4. Secty's report, and notices.
5. **Selections** (from Psa. 89.)
   1. *Supt.*—I will sing of the mercies of the Lord forever; with my mouth will I make known thy faithfulness to all generations.
   2. *School.*—And the heavens shall praise thy wonders, O Lord, thy faithfulness also in the congregation of the saints.
   3. *Supt.*—God is greatly to be feared in the assembly of the saints, and to be held in reverence of all them that are about him.
   4. *School.*—In thy name shall they rejoice all the day: and in thy righteousness shall they be exalted. For the Lord is our defense: and the Holy One of Israel is our King.
   5. *All in concert.*—Blessed be the Lord for evermore. Amen and Amen.
6. **Song.**
7. **Read lesson** of the day in concert or alternately, by divisions of the school.
8. **Short prayer** about lesson.
9. **Instruction.**—30 minutes.
10. **Song.**
11. **Desk Review.**
12. **Song.**—No. 460. Gloria Patri.
13. **All.**—Lord's Prayer in concert.
14. **Dismission.**

## No. 7. Throw Out the Life-Line.

(May be sung as a Solo and Chorus.)

Rev. E. S. Ufford.     E. S. U.     Arr. by Geo. C. Stebbins.

1. Throw out the Life-Line a-cross the dark wave, There is a brother whom some one should save; Some-body's brother! oh, who then, will dare To throw out the Life-Line, his per-il to share?
2. Throw out the Life-Line with hand quick and strong; Why do you tar-ry, why lin-ger so long? See! he is sink-ing, oh, hast-en to-day And out with the Life-Boat! a-way, then, a-way!
3. Throw out the Life-Line to dan-ger-fraught men, Sinking in anguish where you've nev-er been: Winds of temp-ta-tion and bil-lows of woe, Will soon hurl them out where the dark wa-ters flow.
4. Soon will the sea-son of res-cue be o'er, Soon will they drift to e-ter-ni-ty's shore, Haste, then, my brother, no time for de-lay, But throw out the Life-Line and save them to-day.

CHORUS.

Throw out the Life-Line! Some one is drifting away; Throw out the Life-Line! Throw out the Life-Line Some one is sink-ing to-day.

Copyright, 1891, by The Biglow and Main Co. Used by per.

## No. 12. Sunshine and Shadow.

E. D. Mund, Jan. 1, 1889.  E. S. Lorenz.

1. When I walked with my Lord in the sun-shine, His com-panion-ship was sweet; Then I wan-dered with him in the shad-ow, And my joy was made complete.
2. When I stood on the mount in the sun-shine, Felt I strong to walk a-lone, Then I groped in the gloom of the val-ley, And my help-less-ness was shown.
3. When I walked with my Lord in the sun-shine, With my love was min-gled pride; When the dark shad-ows fell, I was hum-bled, And my love was pu-ri-fied.
4. Oh, how pre-cious the walk in the dark-ness! Oh, how dear the hours of pain! When the Sav-ior is walk-ing be-side me, Mak-ing loss su-prem-est gain.

CHORUS.

Ev'rywhere, dark or fair, Where my Sav-ior leads me, will I glad-ly go; Up on the mountain, down in the val-ley, Ev--'ry step he leads me, richer grace doth show.

Copyright, 1889, by E. S. Lorenz.

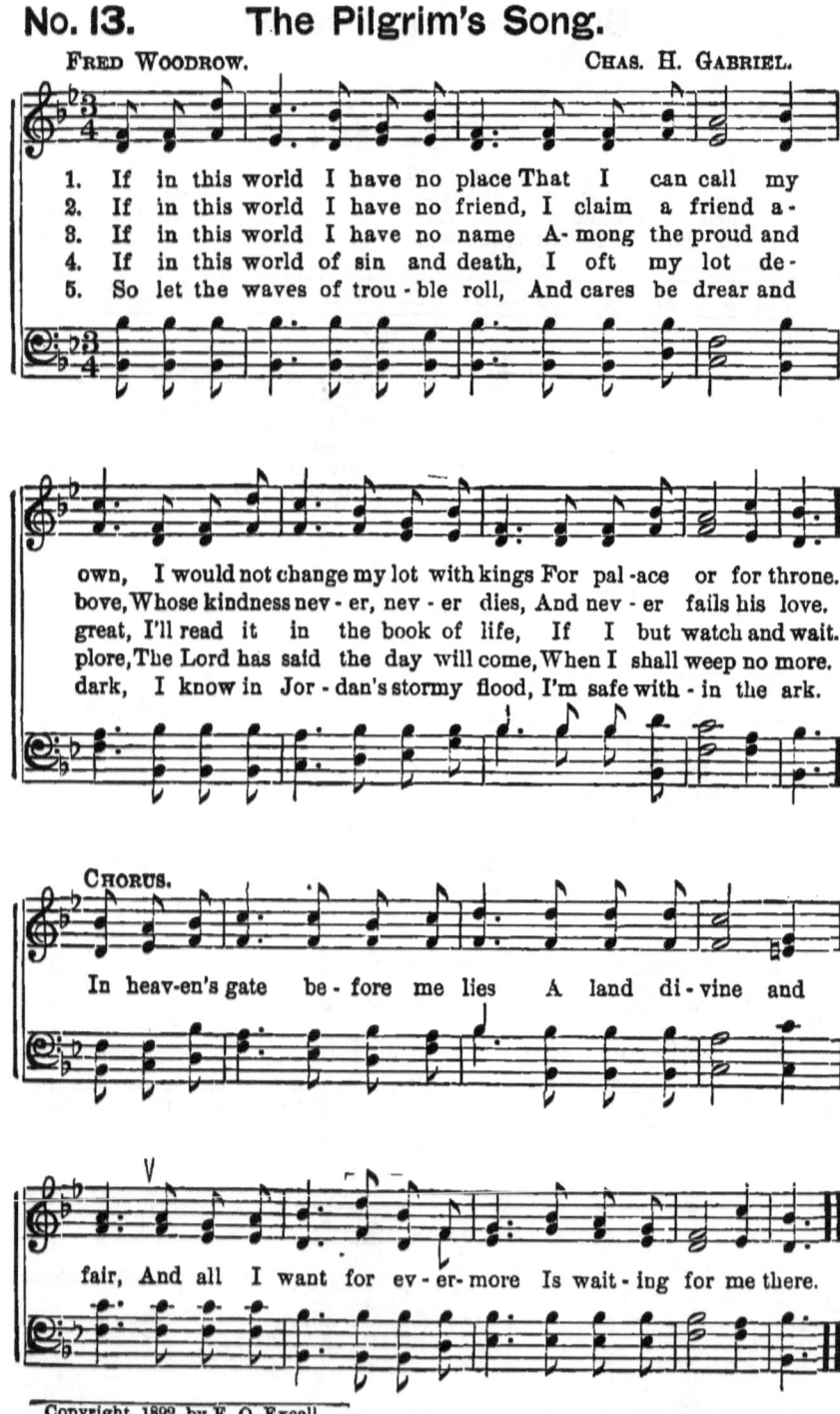

## Wondrous Grace. Concluded.

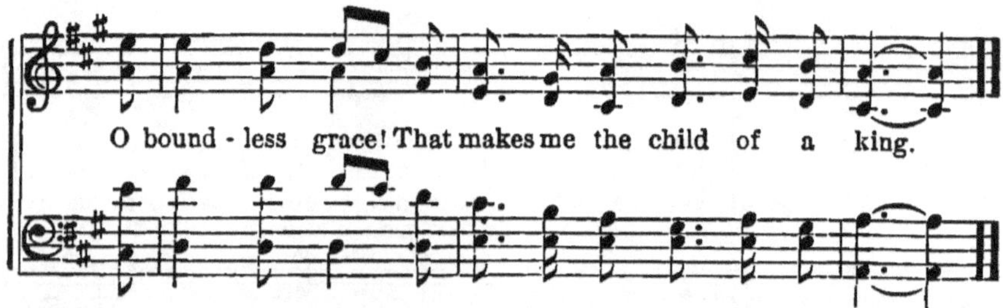

O bound-less grace! That makes me the child of a king.

3 While waiting on my Lord, the King,
My strength is made complete;
I mount on wings as eagles,
I run with tireless feet;
A thousand foes before me fall,
The days no evil bring;
The mighty God of earth and heaven,
He is my Christ, my King.

## No. 17.  Fill Me Now.

E. H. STOKES, D. D.   JNO. R. SWENEY.

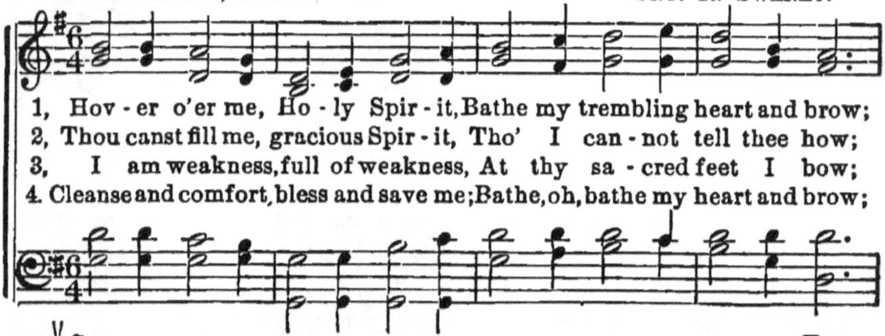

1. Hov-er o'er me, Ho-ly Spir-it, Bathe my trembling heart and brow;
2. Thou canst fill me, gracious Spir-it, Tho' I can-not tell thee how;
3. I am weakness, full of weakness, At thy sa-cred feet I bow;
4. Cleanse and comfort, bless and save me; Bathe, oh, bathe my heart and brow;

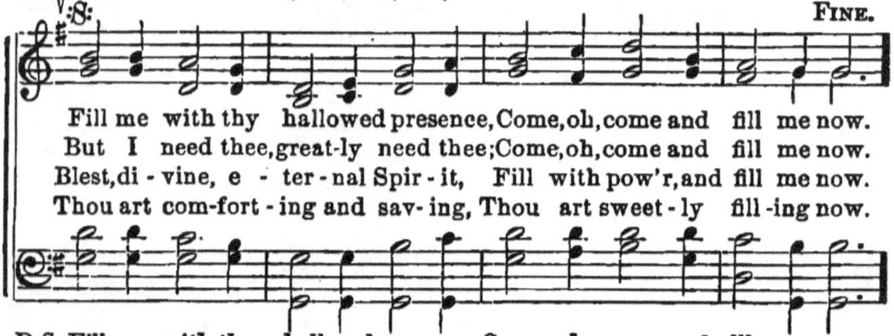

Fill me with thy hallowed presence, Come, oh, come and fill me now.
But I need thee, great-ly need thee; Come, oh, come and fill me now.
Blest, di-vine, e-ter-nal Spir-it, Fill with pow'r, and fill me now.
Thou art com-fort-ing and sav-ing, Thou art sweet-ly fill-ing now.

D.S. *Fill me with thy hallowed presence, Come, oh, come and fill me now.*

CHORUS.   D.S.

Fill me now, fill me now, Je-sus come and fill me now.

Copyright, 1879, by John J. Hood. Used by permission.

# No. 19. Calling Thee Away.

MARGARET MOODY.      W. A. OGDEN.

1. Be-yond the cares of life, and bit-ter pain, Be-yond the tho't of wealth and earthly gain, A voice is call-ing, call-ing thee to-day From sin and death to quick-ly flee a-way.
2. Be-yond the fad-ing van-i-ties of life, Be-yond the realm of pas-sion and of strife, That voice is call-ing, call-ing thee to-day From all un-right-eous-ness to turn a-way.
3. Be-yond is life and ev-er-last-ing joy, Be-yond, where naught of e-vil can an-noy, The Lord now calls thee in his bless-ed word; Oh, seek him while his lov-ing voice is heard.

**CHORUS.**

Call-ing, call-ing thee a-way, . . . . .
    a-way,
Call-ing, call-ing thee a-way, . . . . .
    a-way,
From all earthly pain and sor-row, Sweet-ly call-ing thee a-way.

Copyright, 1892, by W. A. Ogden.

## Rescue Them. Concluded.

Sav ior who died for them, Rescue the lost, and the per-ish-ing save.

## No. 23. Come, his Table is Spread.

E. R. LATTA.  J. E. HALL.

1. Come and sit down to the feast, Take of the life-giv-ing bread.
2. Come from the al-leys and streets, Come, where-so-ev-er ye tread.
3. Come, all ye need-y and faint, Come to the Lord and be fed.
4. Come, in the morning of life, Come, tho' its pleas-ures be sped.

Why will ye fam-ish-ing stand? Come, for his ta-ble is spread.
Hark to the wel-com-ing call, Come, for his ta-ble is spread.
There is e-nough and to spare, Come, for his ta-ble is spread.
Share in the gift of his grace, Come, for his ta-ble is spread.

**CHORUS.**

Come, come, hear his sweet voice, Come, come, make him your choice.

Take of the life-giv-ing bread, Come, for his ta-ble is spread.

Copyright, 1892, by E. O. Excell.

## What Little Folks Can Do. Concluded.

*Repeat pp after last stanza.*

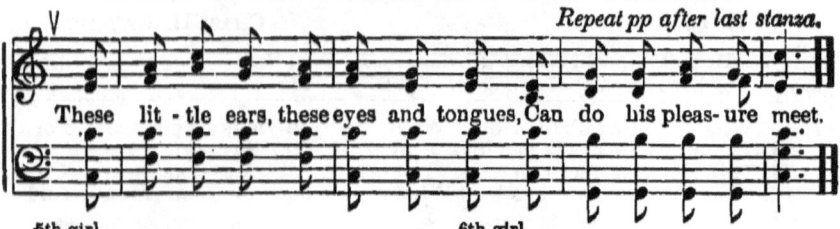

These lit-tle ears, these eyes and tongues, Can do his pleas-ure meet.

5th girl.
These little eyes can see
  The evil and the good,
They mark the passing scenes
  'Tis right indeed, they should;
They read the legends bright
  That tell of Jesus' love,
They read the sacred page that leads
  To mansions bright above.

6th girl.
These little tongues can speak
  The glory of our King,
And ever ready be
  A happy song to sing;
They shape our words of prayer,
  His message they can give
To all the world, that Jesus died,
  That all, through him, might live.

### No. 25.    He Came to Save me.

H. E. BLAIR.      WM. J. KIRKPATRICK.

1. { When Je-sus laid his crown a-side, He came to save me;
    When on the cross he bled and died, (*Omit.*) ............
2. { In my poor heart he deigns to dwell, He came to save me;
    Oh, praise his name, I know it well, (*Omit.*) ............

REFRAIN.
He came to save me. I'm so glad, I'm so glad,
I'm so glad that Je-sus came, And grace is free, (*Omit.*) ............
He (*Omit.*) ........ came to save me.

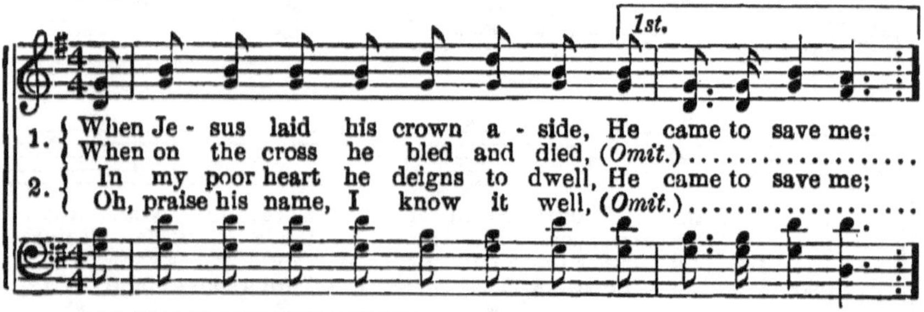

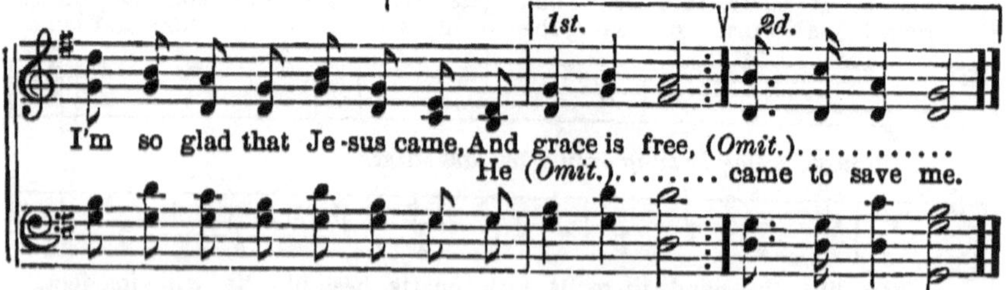

3 With gentle hand he leads me still,
  He came to save me;
And trusting him, I fear no ill,
  He came to save me.

4 To him my faith with rapture clings,
  He came to save me;
To him my heart looks up and sings,
  He came to save me.

Copyright, 1885, by Wm. J. Kirkpatrick, Used by per.

## No. 26.    'Tis Sweet to Know.

Mrs. Harriet E. Jones.      Jno. R. Bryant.

1. 'Tis sweet to know that Christ receives, The sin-ner who o'er sin-ning grieves, That he who comes, how-ev-er vile, Shall meet the Lord's for-giv-ing smile.
2. 'Tis sweet to know that on the tree, He paid the debt for you and me, That when we come with con-trite hearts, His pre-cious love our Lord im-parts.
3. 'Tis sweet to know that keep-ing grace, He will be-stow thro'-out the race, If we his dear com-mands o-bey, If we but work, and watch, and pray.

CHORUS.

'Tis sweet to know,............ yes, sweet to know,............
'Tis sweet to know, yes, sweet to know, yes, sweet to know, yes, sweet to know

That Je-sus loves............ the sin-ner so,............
That Je-sus loves the sin-ner so, that Je-sus loves the sin-ner so,

Copyright, 1892, by E. O. Excell.

## 'Tis Sweet to Know. Concluded.

That from his side............ the crimson flow,............
That from his side, that from his side the crim-son flow, the crim-son flow,

Doth wash him whit — — er than the snow,............
Doth wash him white, Doth wash him whit-er than the snow, whiter than snow.

## No. 27.  For Me and for Thee.

MARY G. CROCKER.  WM. A. MAY.

1. Christ, the Lord, on this lone-ly earth,
2. Laid he heav-en-ly glo-ry down,
3. Roy-al feet trod a wea-ry road,

For me, for me, for me, for me,

Walked a man as of low-ly birth,
King-ly head wore a thorn-y crown,
Roy-al heart bore a heav-y load,

For me, for me and for thee.

4 Mocked with smiting and cruel scorn,
   For me, for me, for me, for me;
   Feet and hands by the nailing torn,
   For me, for me and for thee.

5 Was it vain that the Lord has died?
   For me, for me, for me, for me;
   Vain the Savior was crucified?
   For me, for me and for thee.

6 At the feet of the Lamb, once slain,
   For me, for me, for me, for me.

Praise, oh praise him who lives again,
   For me, for me and for thee.

7 There, above, at the Father's throne,
   For me, for me, for me, for me;
   Jesus pleadeth his name alone
   For me, for me and for thee.

8 Jesus speaks and the work is done
   For me, for me, for me, for me;
   Full atonement thro' Christ the Son,
   For me, for me and for thee.

Copyright, 1892, by E. O. Excell.

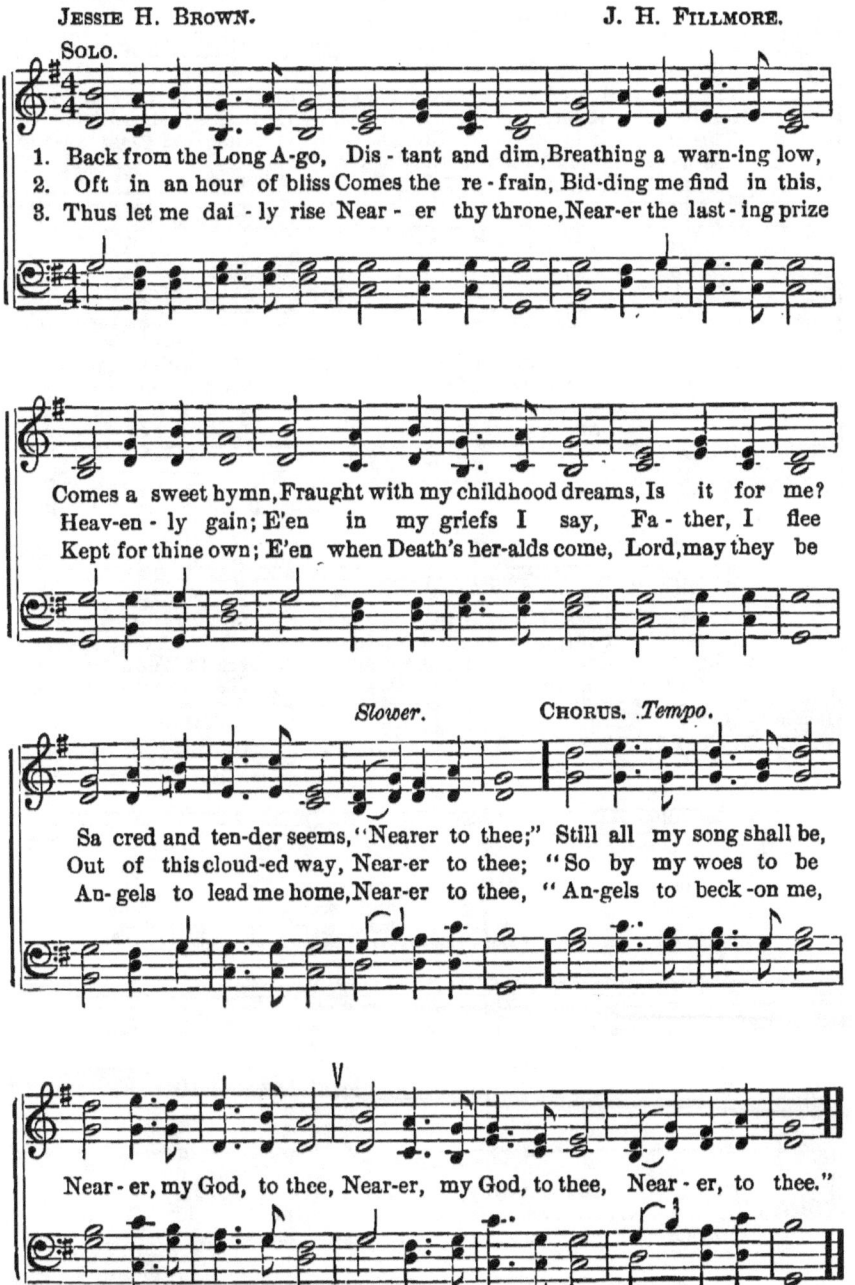

## God is Calling Yet. Concluded.

calling, calling, Call - ing, oh, hear Him, Call - ing, oh, hear Him, God is calling yet, oh, hear Him calling yet.

God is calling yet, God is calling yet,

---

### No. 35.   The Hallowed Spot.

Rev. WM. HUNTER, D. D.    ARRANGED.

1. There is a spot to me more dear Than native vale or mountain;
   A spot for which affection's tear Springs grateful from its fountain.
   *D. S. where I first my Savior found, And felt my sins forgiven.*

2. Hard was my toil to reach the shore, Long toss'd upon the ocean:
   Above me was the thunder's roar, Beneath, the waves' commotion.
   *D. S. that dark hour how did my groan Ascend for years of error.*

'Tis not where kindred souls abound, Tho' that is almost heaven, But
Darkly the pall of night was thrown Around me, faint with terror; In

3 Sinking and panting as for breath
  I knew not help was near me;
  I cried, "Oh, save me, Lord, from death,
  Immortal Jesus, hear me;"
  Then quick as thought I felt Him mine
  My Savior stood before me;
  I saw His brightness 'round me shine,
  And shouted "Glory, glory."

4 O sacred hour! O hallowed spot!
  Where love divine first found me;
  Wherever falls my distant lot
  My heart shall linger 'round thee,
  And when from earth I rise, to soar
  Up to my home in heaven,
  Down will I cast my eyes once more,
  Where I was first forgiven.

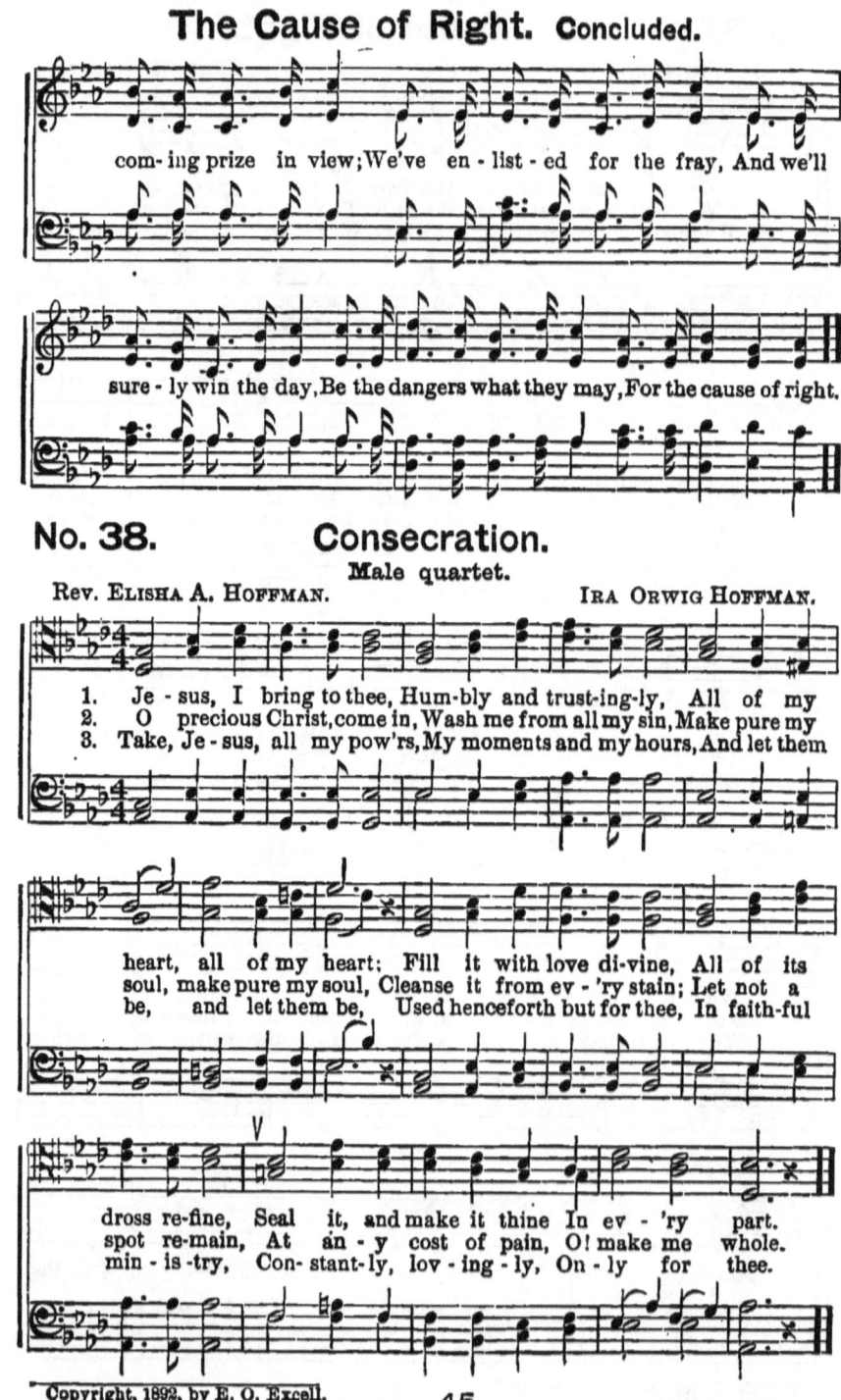

## The Beautiful Way. Concluded.

beau-ti-ful way, In that beau-ti-ful, beau-ti-ful way?

## No. 40. Sweetly Sing the Love of Jesus.

UNKNOWN.  WHARTON HOWARD.

1. Sweet-ly sing the love of Je-sus, Love for you and love for me,
2. Soft-ly sing the love of Je-sus, For our hearts are full of tears,
3. Glad-ly sing the love of Je-sus, Let us lean up-on his arm;

Heaven's light is not more cheering, Heaven's dews are not more free;
As we think how walking humbly, This low earth for ma-ny years;
If he loves us what can grieve us? If he keeps us what can harm?

As a child in pain or ter-ror, Hides him in his moth-er's breast;
With-out rich-es, with-out dwell-ing, Wounded sore by foe and friend;
Still he lays his hand in bless-ing, On each upturned ask-ing face;

*Poco rit.*

As a sail-or seeks the ha-ven, We would go to him for rest.
In the gar-den and in dy-ing, Je-sus loved us to the end.
And in heav'n his chil-dren an-gels, Near the throne have always place.

Copyright, 1892, by E. O. Excell.

3 My Father's house is built on high,
Far, far above the starry sky.

4 When from this earthly prison free,
That heavenly mansion mine shall be.

5 While here, a stranger far from home,
Affliction's waves may round me foam.

6 Although, like Lazarus, sick and poor,
My heavenly mansion is secure.

7 Let others seek a home below,
Which flames devour, or waves o'erflow.

8 Be mine the happier lot to own
A heavenly mansion near the throne.

9 Then fail the earth, let stars decline,
And sun and moon refuse to shine.

10 All nature sink and cease to be,
That heavenly mansion stands for me.

# No. 44. The Harvest.

C. D. EMERSON. CHAS. H. GABRIEL.

1. Be-hold how the fields are wav-ing, Unmeasured the ripened plain,
2. The world is the field of har-vest, And souls must be gathered in;
3. Go work, for the day is pass-ing, Go la-bor, and hope, and pray;

But few are the faith-ful glean-ers, To gath-er the gold-en grain.
Go glean from the broad, rough highways, The good from the fields of sin.
Go gath-er the price-less jew-els, Go seek for the lost to-day.

CHORUS.

Forth to the har-vest field, then, a-way! There is plen-ty for all to do,.......... The Lord of the har-vest is call-ing, But the reap-ers, a-las! are few.

Copyright, 1892, by E. O. Excell.

## How Sweet is the Bible! Concluded.

like-ness is there, And the hearts of his chil-dren are glad.
mes-sage of grace, And words that shall guide me to heav'n.

### No. 49. Recruits for Jesus.

ADELINE HOHF BEERY.     T. MARTIN TOWNE.

1. We come with ban-ners wav-ing, The her-alds of a King!
2. We come with heav'n-ly ar-mor, With shield and sword to win,
3. We march to bring sal-va-tion, To all the troubled earth;

He rules with love and mer-cy, And we his prais-es sing.
From Sa-tan and his ar-my, The souls he bound in sin.
We spread the fame of Je-sus, Our King of peer-less birth.

**CHORUS.**

Re-ceive our gra-cious Mas-ter, We bring his word to you;
Shake off the sins that bind you, And yield him ser-vice true.

Copyright, 1892, by E. O. Excell.

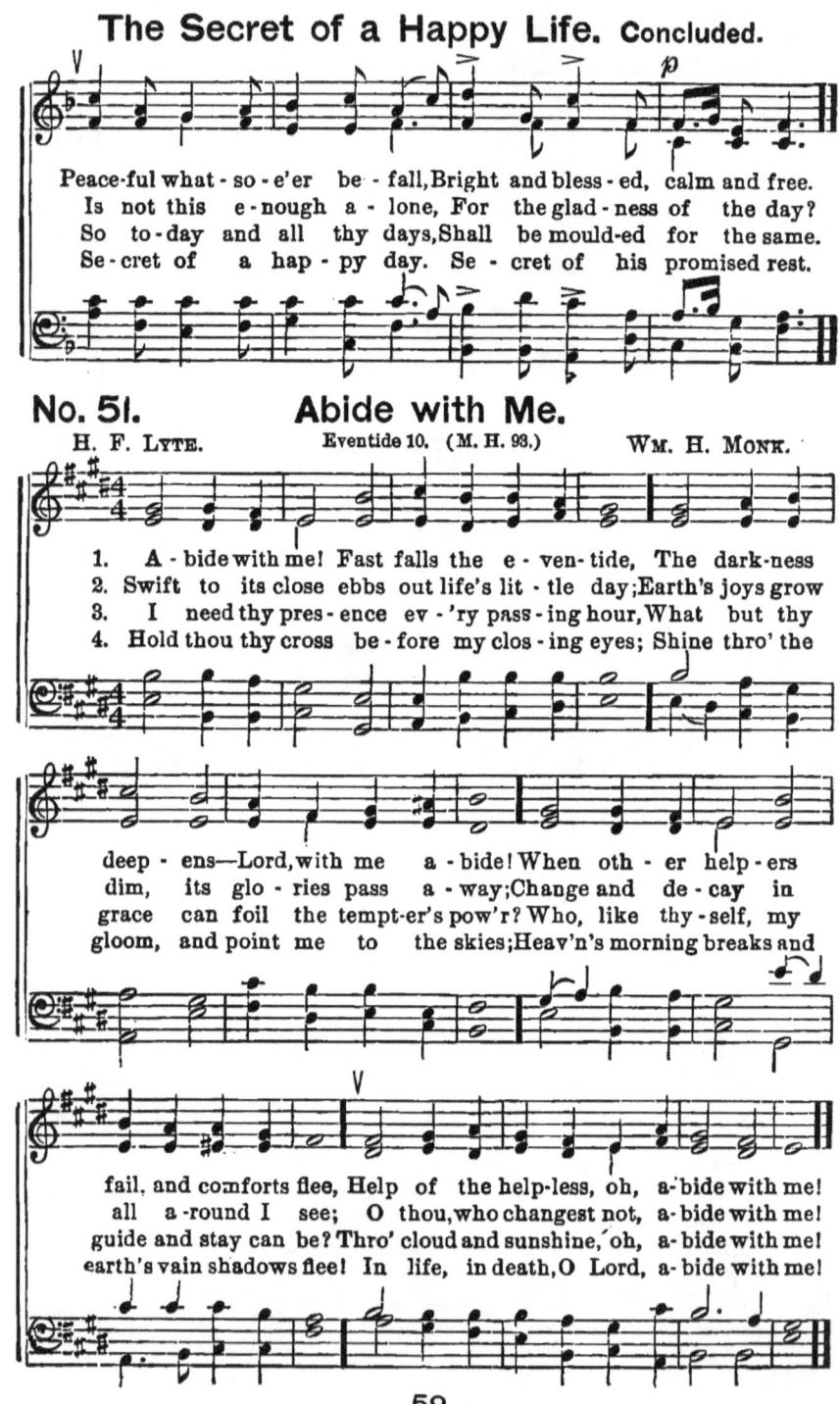

## 'Twas Rum that Spoiled my Boy. Concluded.

heart-sore, Turn - ing toward her home a - gain; And I've
wan-d'ring In some strange and dis - tant land, And I've
cru - el, Waves that drowned my sweet-est joy, I am
heav - en, All your moth - er - love em - ploy, That your

en - vied her her sad-ness, There was much to soothe her pain.
tho't, oh blest the watch-er! Hop - ing yet to clasp his hand.
sit - ting and la - ment-ing, Oh, 'twas rum that spoiled my boy!
lips may nev - er fal - ter, Oh, 'twas rum that spoiled my boy!

CHORUS.

Oh, 'twas rum that spoil'd my darling, Rum, enthron'd but to destroy:

Drive the monster from the nation, Then you'll shout, "We've sav'd the boy!"

61

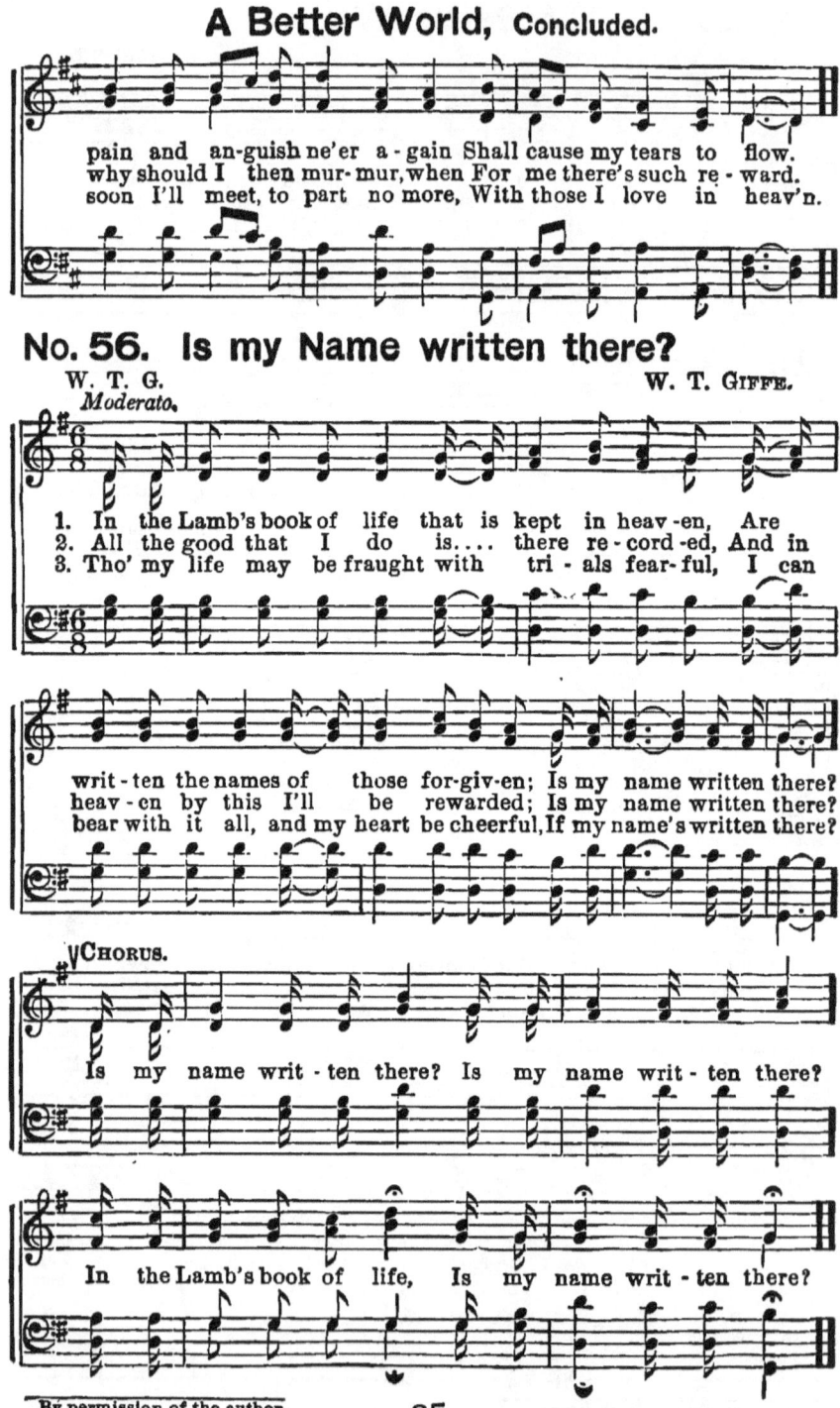

## Arise, He Calleth Thee. Concluded.

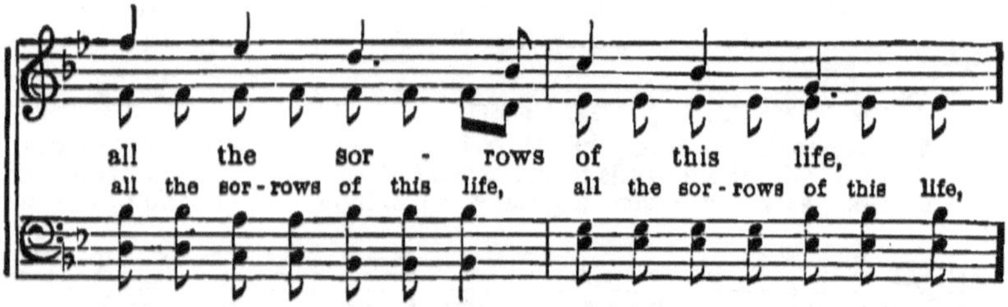

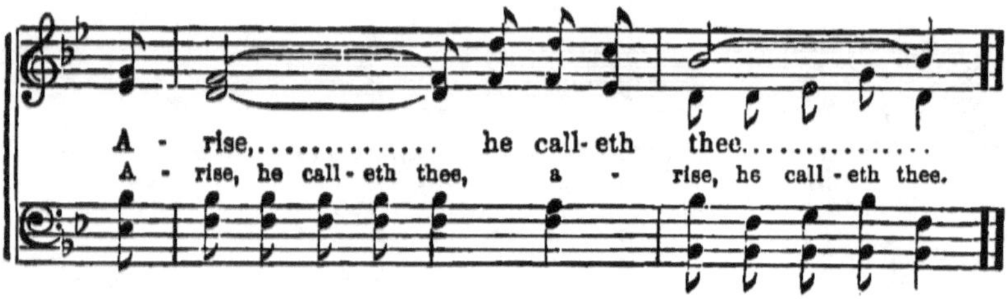

all the sor-rows of this life,
all the sor-rows of this life, all the sor-rows of this life,

A-rise,............ he call-eth thee.............
A-rise, he call-eth thee, a-rise, he call-eth thee.

### No. 58.  All for Jesus.

MARY D. JAMES. Arranged.

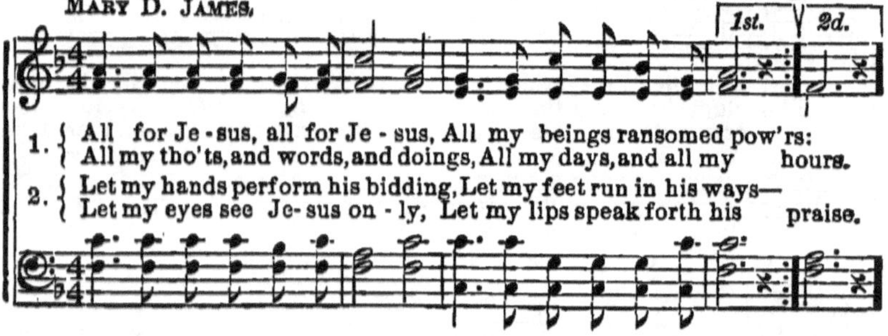

1. All for Je-sus, all for Je-sus, All my beings ransomed pow'rs:
   All my tho'ts, and words, and doings, All my days, and all my hours.
2. Let my hands perform his bidding, Let my feet run in his ways—
   Let my eyes see Je-sus on-ly, Let my lips speak forth his praise.

All for Je-sus, all for Je-sus, All my days, and all my hours; hours.
All for Je-sus, all for Je-sus, Let my lips speak forth his praise; praise.

3 Since my eyes were fixed on Jesus,
I've lost sight of all besides;
So enchained my spirit's vision,
Looking at the Crucified.
|: All for Jesus, all for Jesus,
Looking at the Crucified. :|

4 Oh, what wonder! how amazing!
Jesus, glorious King of kings—
Deigns to call me his beloved,
Lets me rest beneath his wings.
|: All for Jesus, all for Jesus,
Resting now beneath his wings. :|

# No. 59. Pardon is Waiting for Thee.

E. A. H.            Rev. ELISHA A. HOFFMAN.

Copyright, 1892, by E. O. Excell.

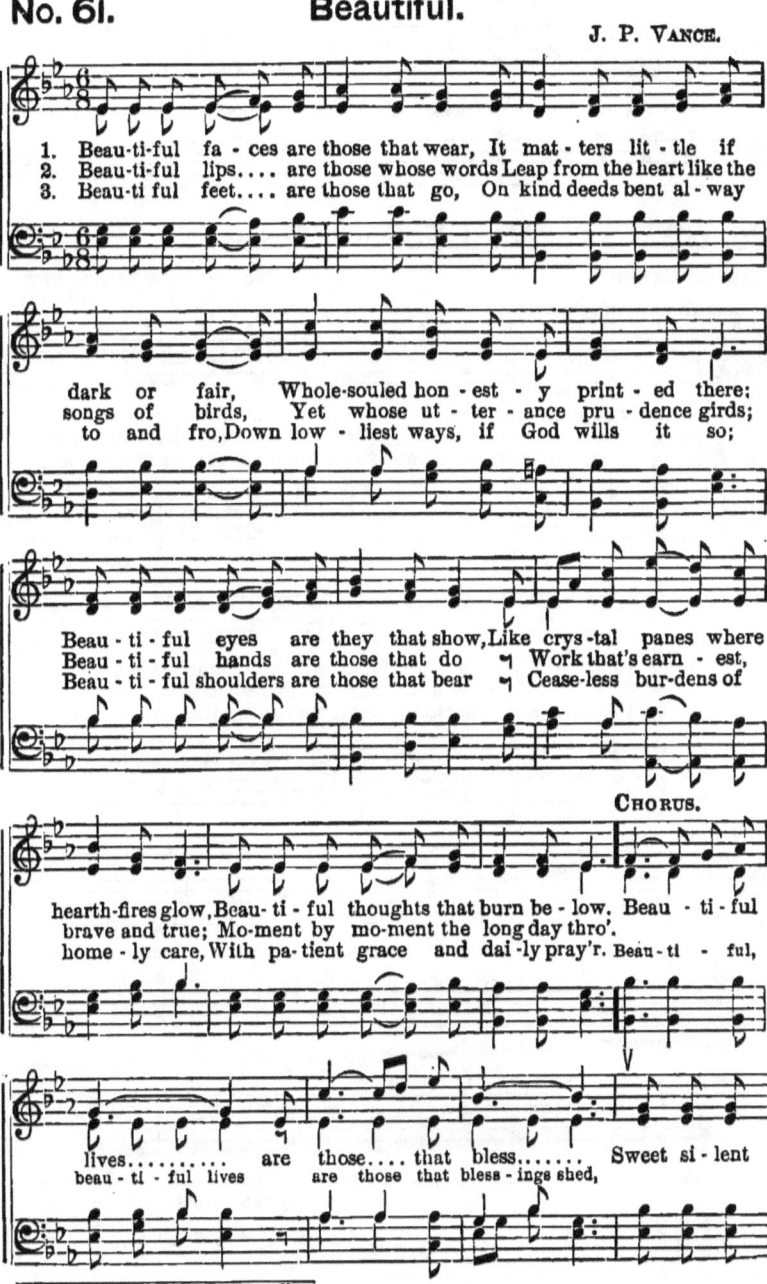

## Why Stand Ye Here Idle? Concluded.

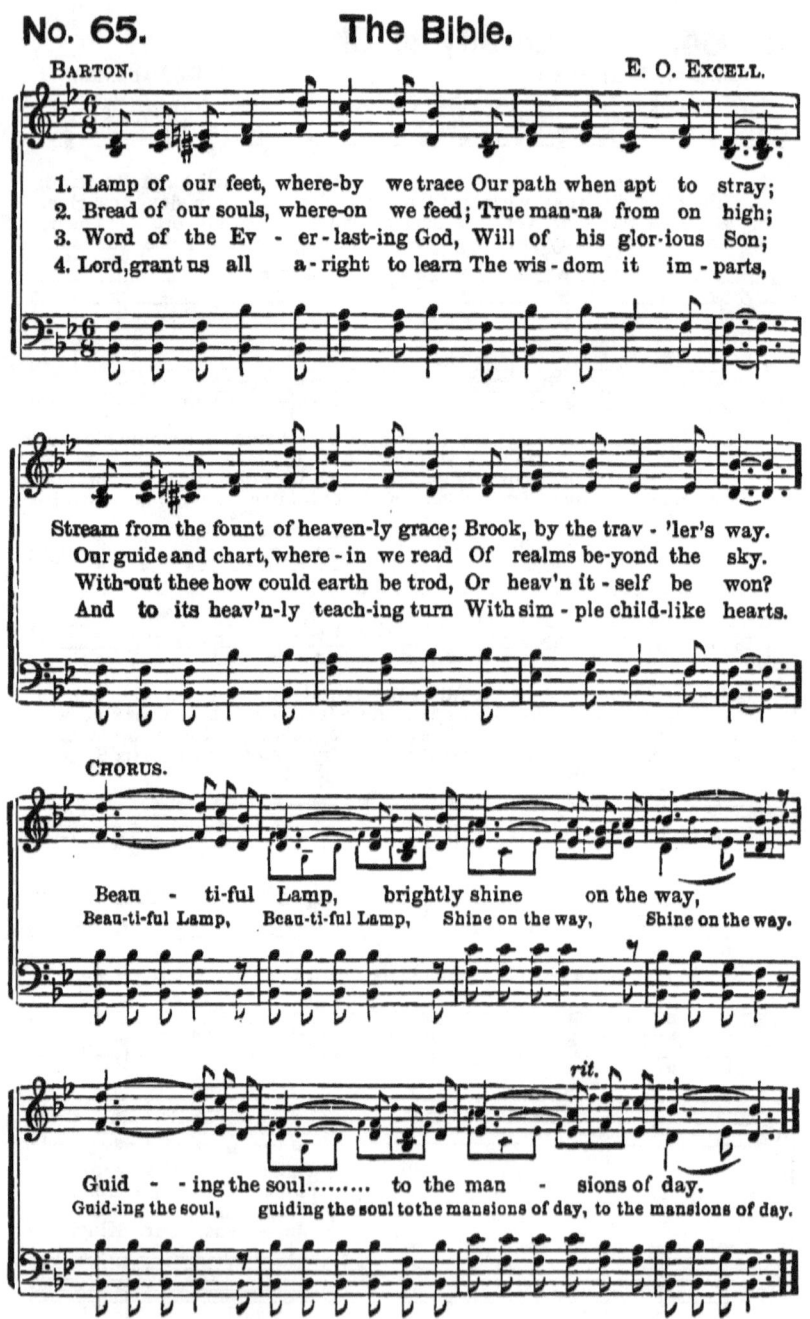

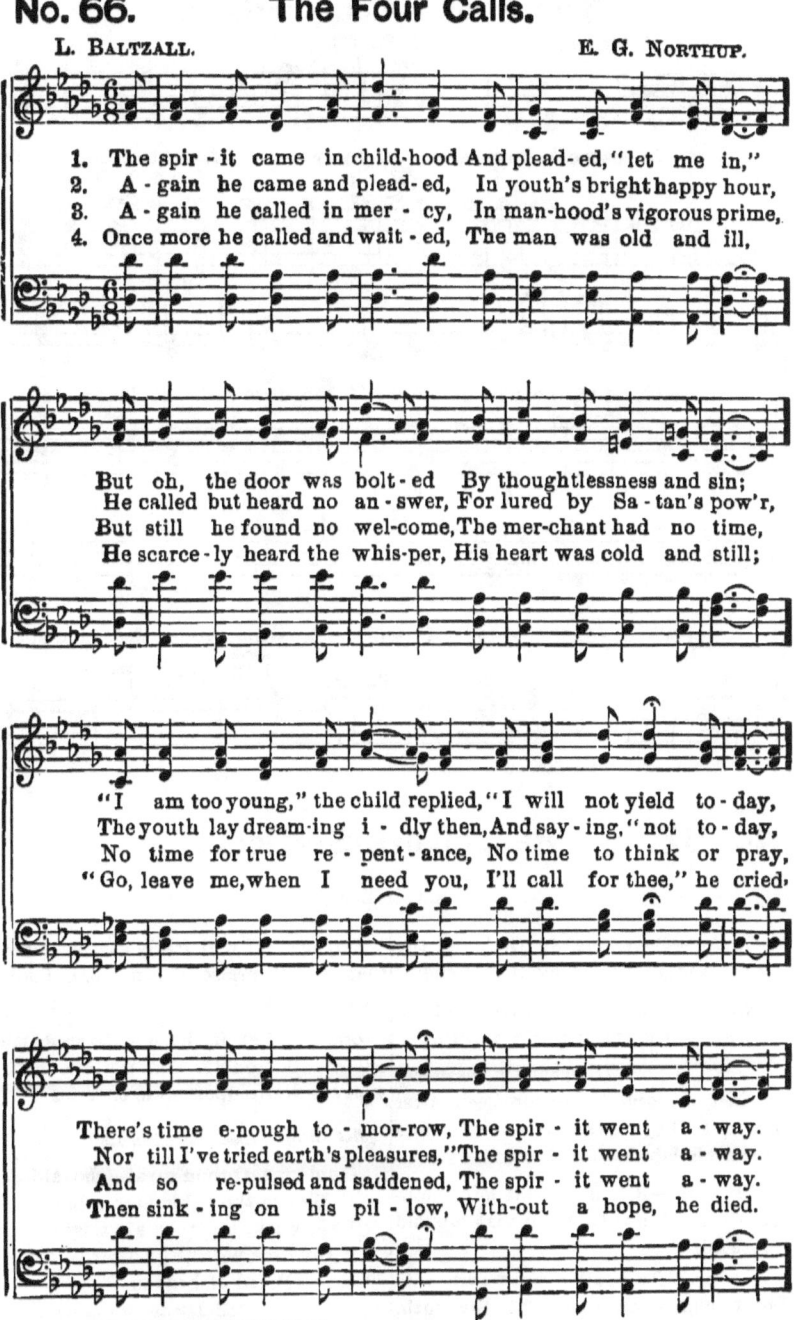

## The Four Calls, Concluded.

CODA. *After last verse. Prov. 1: 24-26.*

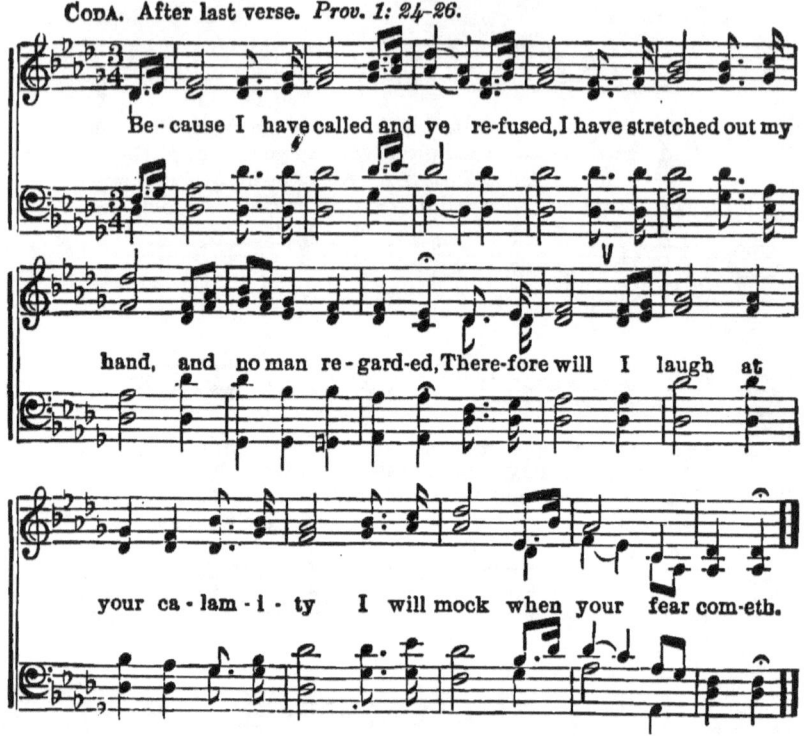

Be-cause I have called and ye re-fused, I have stretched out my hand, and no man re-gard-ed, There-fore will I laugh at your ca-lam-i-ty I will mock when your fear com-eth.

## No. 67.    Responsive Service.

### PSALM LIV.

*Leader.*—Save me, O God, by thy name, and judge me by thy strength.

*Response.*—Hear my prayer, O God; give ear to the words of my mouth.

*Leader.*—For strangers are risen up against me, and oppressors seek after my soul: they have not set God before them. Selah.

*Response.*—Behold; God is mine helper: the Lord is with them that uphold my soul.

*Leader.*—He shall reward evil unto mine enemies: cut them off in thy truth.

*Response.*—I will freely sacrifice unto thee: I will praise thy name, O Lord; for it is good.

*Leader.*—For he hath delivered me out of all trouble: and my eye hath seen his desire upon mine enemies.

*All Sing.*   (See music No. 428.)

Guide me, O thou great Jehovah,
   Pilgrim thro' this barren land;
I am weak, but thou art mighty,
   Hold me with thy powerful hand:
   ‖: Bread of heaven,
   Feed me till I want no more. :‖

## No. 68. The Gospel Net.

T. M. T.      T. MARTIN TOWNE.

1. Let down your net to-night, oh brother, Let down with hope and with pray'r; Deep in the wa-ters of sin, oh brother, Souls are yet per-ish-ing there.
2. Let down your net to-night, oh neighbor; Toil on with love and with tears; Like the dis-ci-ples, o-bey the or-der, Souls shall be saved from their fears.
3. Let down your net to-night, oh christian, Yield not to doubt nor de-spair; In-to deep wa-ters, launch out, oh christian, All in this great work may share.
4. Sa-tan is trailing his net, oh sin-ner, Art-ful-ly trail-ing for thee; Halt! or its mesh-es will surely ensnare you, Turn, and for-ev-er be free.

CHORUS.

Let down your net to-night, in faith, Fish-ers of men, are ye; Christ is on board, hath spok-en the word, Might-y to save is he.

Copyright, 1892, by E. O. Excell.

## No. 70. In Thy Love.

(The words, "Jesus, Lover of my Soul," may be used to this tune.)

Neal A. McAulay.  
E. O. Excell.

SOLO.

1. Fa-ther I am weak and sin-ful, Ev-er prone to go a-stray; Like a way-ward child of er-ror, I so oft-en lose my way.
2. In the bil-lows of temp-ta-tion, When its waves are run-ning high, Bear me o'er life's sea of troub-le, Leave me not to sink and die.
3. Fa-ther, when the shades are fall-ing, And the night of death is near; Guide me thro' the gloom-y val-ley, With thy light my jour-ney cheer.
4. O-pen, then, the pearl-y por-tals, That un-wor-thy though I be, I may join the ransomed le-gions, There to dwell e-ter-nal-ly.

Copyright, 1889, by E. O. Excell.

## In Thy Love. Concluded.

### No. 71. Come Let Us Join.

I. Watts.  Amizon. C. M. (M. H. 2.)  C. G. Glaser.

1. Come, let us join our cheerful songs With an-gels round the throne;
2. "Wor-thy the Lamb that died." they cry, "To be ex-alt-ed thus!"
3. Je-sus is wor-thy to re-ceive Hon-or and pow'r di-vine;
4. Let all that dwell a-bove the sky, And air, and earth, and seas,
5. The whole cre-a-tion join in one, To bless the sa-cred name

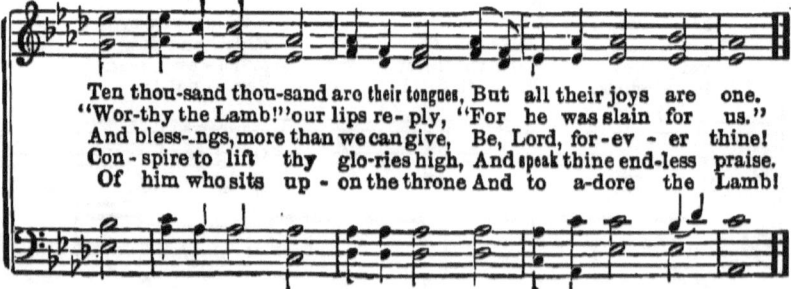

Ten thou-sand thou-sand are their tongues, But all their joys are one.
"Wor-thy the Lamb!" our lips re-ply, "For he was slain for us."
And bless-ings, more than we can give, Be, Lord, for-ev-er thine!
Con-spire to lift thy glo-ries high, And speak thine end-less praise.
Of him who sits up-on the throne And to a-dore the Lamb!

### No. 72. Jesus Knows.

PHŒBE ROWE.          CAREY BOGGESS.

Copyright, 1892, by E. O. Excell.

## Jesus Knows. Concluded.

3 I leave it all with Jesus,
  For he knows
  What to make me
  When to take me,
  At life's close;
  Jesus knows,
  Yes, he knows.

I leave it all with Jesus,
  For he knows,
  There I'll leave me,
  He'll receive me,
  For he knows;
  Jesus knows,
  Yes, he knows.

## No. 73. Lord, We Come Before Thee.

(Pleyel's Hymn, 7s. M. H. 21.)

WILLIAM HAMMOND.                    IGNACE PLEYEL.

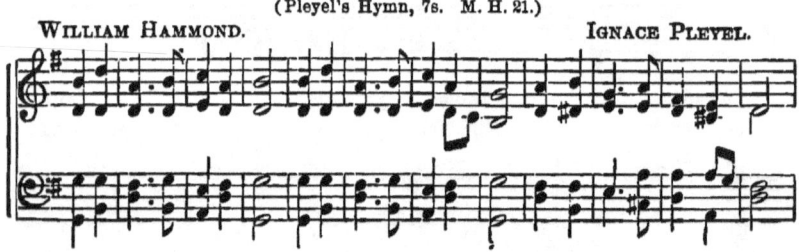

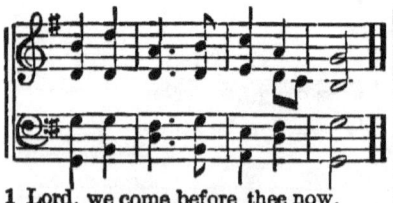

1 Lord, we come before thee now,
  At thy feet we humbly bow;
  O do not our suit disdain;
  Shall we seek thee, Lord, in vain?

2 Lord, on thee our souls depend;
  In compassion now descend;
  Fill our hearts with thy rich grace,
  Tune our lips to sing thy praise.

3 In thine own appointed way,
  Now we seek thee, here we stay;
  Lord, we know not how to go,
  Till a blessing thou bestow.

4 Send some message from thy word,
  That may joy and peace afford;
  Let thy Spirit now impart
  Full salvation to each heart.

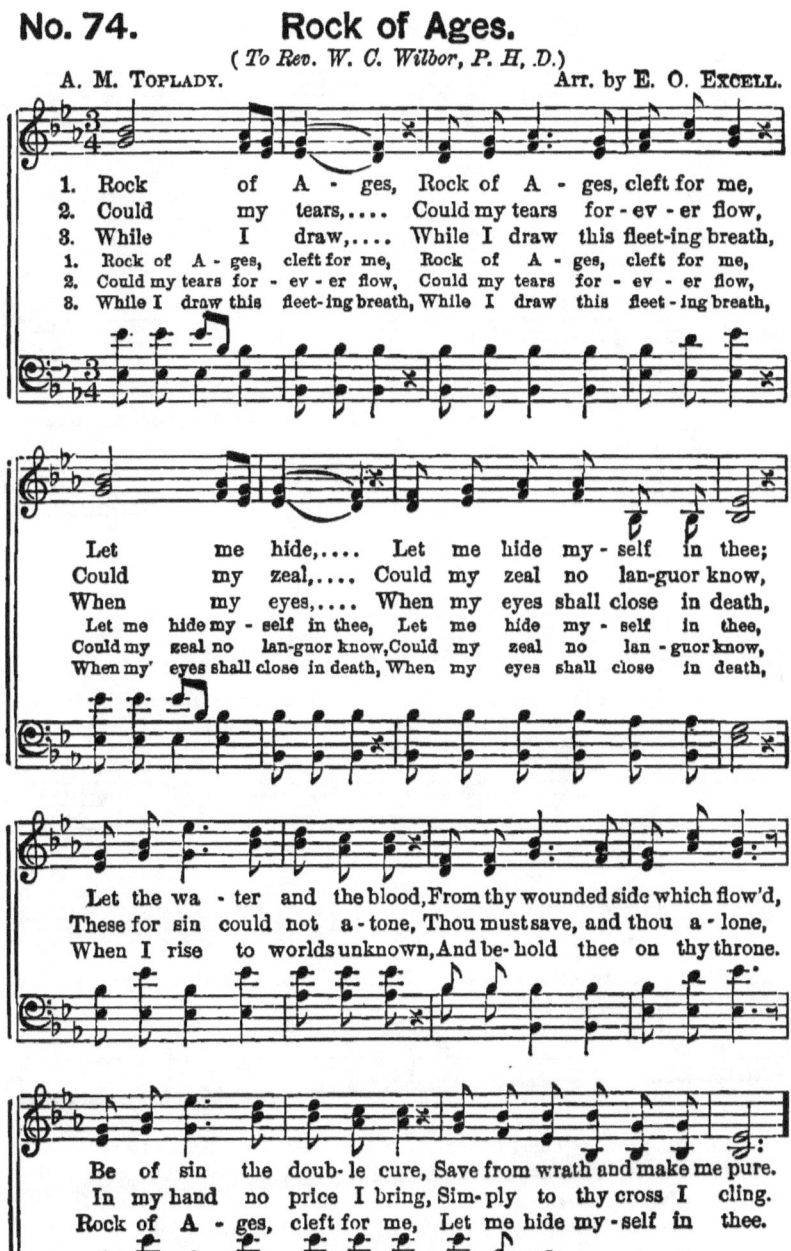

# Rock of Ages. Concluded.

Rock of Ages, Rock of Ages, cleft for me,
Rock of Ages, Let me hide in thee.
Let me hide my-self in thee.

## No. 75.  There is a Fountain.

COWPER.  UNKNOWN.

1, { There is a fountain fill'd with blood Drawn from Immanuel's veins,
    { And sin-ners plung'd beneath that flood   (*Omit.*) }
D, S,  *And sin-ners plung'd beneath that flood*   (*Omit.*)

Lose all their guilty stains, Lose all their guilty stains, Lose all their guilty stains,
*Lose all their guilty stains.*

2 The dying thief rejoiced to see
　That fountain in his day;
And there have I, as vile as he,
　Wash'd all my sins away.

3 Dear dying Lamb, Thy precious blood
　Shall never lose its power,
Till all the ransom'd Church of God
　Be saved, to sin no more.

4 E'er since by faith I saw the stream
　Thy flowing wounds supply,
Redeeming love has been my theme,
　And shall be till I die.

5 Then in a nobler, sweeter song,
　I'll sing Thy power to save, [tongue
When this poor lisping stammering
　Lies silent in the grave.

## Just Over There. Concluded.

## No. 79.  Responsive Service.

### PSALM XCVI.

*Leader.*—God be merciful unto us, and bless us; and cause his face to shine upon us; Selah.

*Response.*—That thy way may be known upon earth, thy saving health among all nations.

*Leader.*—Let the people praise thee, O God; let all the people praise thee.

*Response.*—O let the nations be glad and sing for joy: for thou shalt judge the people righteously, and govern the nations upon earth. Selah.

*Leader.*—Let the people praise thee, O God; let all the people praise thee.

*Response.*—Then shall the earth yield her increase; and God, even our own God, shall bless us.

*Leader.*—God shall bless us; and all the ends of the earth shall fear him.

*All Sing.*  (See music No. 190.)

Depth of mercy! can there be
Mercy still reserved for me?
Can my God his wrath forbear?
Me, the chief of sinners spare?
CHO.—God is love! I know, I feel;
Jesus lives and loves me still;
Jesus lives,
He lives and loves me still.

### No. 82. He Wept in Blood for Me.

LOUISA E. LITZSINGER.  WM. A. MAY.

1. When sorrow's cup pours out its woe,
And bitter tears unbidden flow,
My hiding place shall ever be,
In him who wept in blood for me.

2. When trials hard and cares oppress,
To sink my soul in deep distress,
My resting place, my strength is he,
Who bore the greater cross for me.

3. His pity brought him to the tree,
Whereon he shed his blood for me,
Thro' him I claim the promise giv'n,
Thro' him alone I enter heav'n.

Copyright, 1892, by E. O. Excell.

## He Wept in Blood for Me. Concluded.

93

## No. 88. Healing.

A. S. M. Arr.         WM. A. MAY.

1. Upon my heart I find a stain I cannot wash away,
   And if it were not for thy blood, It (*Omit*)............
   must forever stay.

2. Upon my heart I find a scar, I cannot, Lord, efface;
   But thou canst heal the deepest wound, Oh, (*Omit*)............
   heal it by thy grace.

REFRAIN.
It must forever stay, (ever stay,) It must forever stay; And if it were not for thy blood, (for thy blood,) It must forever stay. (ever stay.)
Oh, heal it by thy grace, (by thy grace,) Oh, heal it by thy grace; For thou canst heal the deepest wound, (deepest wound,) Oh heal it by thy grace. (by thy grace.)

3 Upon my heart I find a blot,
   I cannot, Lord, remove;
Oh, wash and heal and cleanse me now,
   And hide me in thy love.
     REFRAIN.
Oh, hide me in thy love,
Oh, hide me in thy love,
Oh, wash and heal and cleanse me now,
And hide me in thy love.

4 All this I know that thou canst do,
   For such thy promise is:
And from this time I'll live for thee,
   And trust thee more than this.
     REFRAIN.
And trust thee more than this,
And trust thee more than this,
And from this time I'll live for thee,
And trust thee more than this

Copyright, 1892, by E. O. Excell.

## The World, the Flesh, Concluded.

### The Angelic Warning.

## No. 92. Leave it all to Jesus.

W. H. GARDNER.  E. H. PACKARD.

*Marching time.*

1. Tho' the clouds are round about you, And the night is dark and drear;
2. Should a flood of doubts perplex you, And no rest come to your heart;
3. Oh, when earthly friends forsake you, And no help-ing hand stands by;
4. If you on-ly trust the Mas-ter, Sweet will be your journey here;

If you leave it all to Je-sus, He will help you, nev-er fear.
If you leave it all to Je-sus, They will ev-'ry one de-part.
If you leave it all to Je-sus, To your aid he'll quickly fly.
Yes, oh, leave it all to Je-sus, And the clouds will dis-ap-pear.

**REFRAIN.**

Leave it all to Je-sus, He will find a way; Leave it all to Je-sus, He will find a way; If we trust his lov-ing arm, He will keep us from all harm;

Leave it all to Je-sus, Leave it all to Je-sus,

Copyright, 1892, by E. O. Excell.

## Leave it all to Jesus. Concluded.

Leave it all to Je - sus, He will find a way.
Leave it all to Je - sus,

## No. 93. Where will you Spend Eternity?

Rev. E. A. HOFFMAN.      J. H. TENNEY

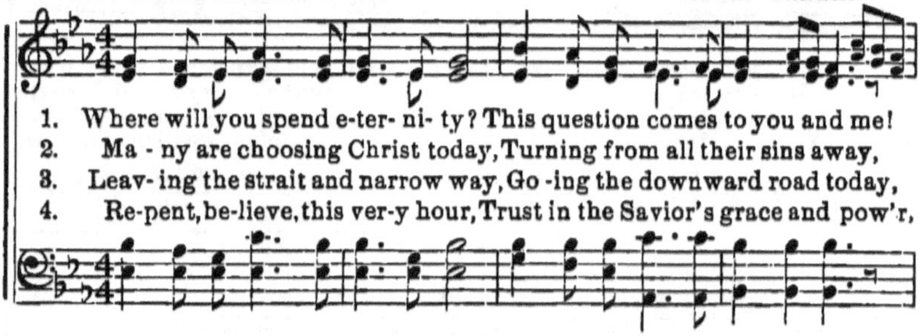

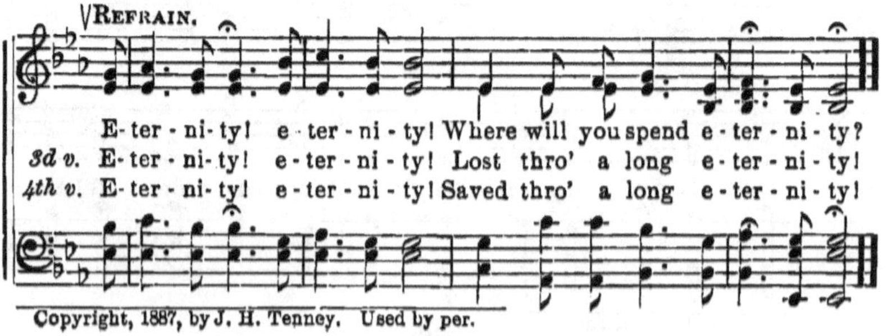

1. Where will you spend e-ter- ni- ty? This question comes to you and me!
2. Ma - ny are choosing Christ today, Turning from all their sins away,
3. Leav- ing the strait and narrow way, Go -ing the downward road today,
4. Re-pent, be-lieve, this ver-y hour, Trust in the Savior's grace and pow'r,

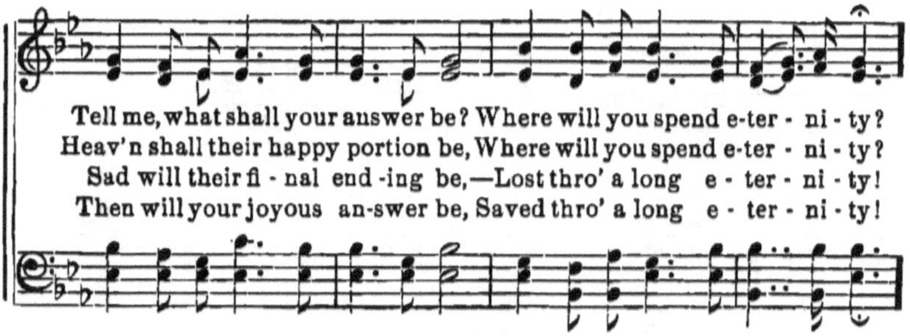

Tell me, what shall your answer be? Where will you spend e-ter - ni - ty?
Heav'n shall their happy portion be, Where will you spend e-ter - ni - ty?
Sad will their fi - nal end-ing be,—Lost thro' a long e - ter - ni - ty!
Then will your joyous an-swer be, Saved thro' a long e - ter - ni - ty!

REFRAIN.

E - ter - ni - ty! e - ter - ni - ty! Where will you spend e - ter - ni - ty?
*3d v.* E - ter - ni - ty! e - ter - ni - ty! Lost thro' a long e - ter - ni - ty!
*4th v.* E - ter - ni - ty! e - ter - ni - ty! Saved thro' a long e - ter - ni - ty!

Copyright, 1887, by J. H. Tenney. Used by per.

## No. 95. Responsive Service.

**PSALM CIII.**

*Leader.*—Bless the Lord, O my soul: and all that is within me, bless his holy name.

*Response.*—Bless the Lord, O my soul, and forget not all his benefits.

*Leader.*—Who forgiveth all thine iniquities: who healeth all thy diseases;

*Response.*—Who redeemeth thy life from destruction; who crowneth thee with loving kindness and tender mercies:

*Leader.*—Who satisfieth thy mouth with good things; so that thy youth is renewed like the eagle's.

*Response*--The Lord executeth righteousness and judgment for all that are oppressed.

*Leader.*—He hath made known his ways unto Moses, his acts unto the children of Israel.

*All Sing.* (See music No. 262.)

 Down at the cross where my Savior died,
 Down where for cleansing from sin I cried,
 There to my heart was the blood applied,
  Glory to his name;
 CHO.—Glory to his name, etc.

## No. 98. Say, are You Ready?

A. S. KIEFFER.  T. C. O'KANE.

1. Should the Death an-gel knock at thy chamber In the still watch of to-night, Say, will your spir-it pass in-to tor-ment, Or to the land of de-light?
2. Ma-ny sad spir-its now are de-part-ing In-to the world of de-spair; Ev-'ry brief mo-ment brings your doom nearer; Sin-ner, O sin-ner, be-ware!
3. Ma-ny re-deemed ones now are as-cend-ing In-to the man-sions of light; Je-sus is plead-ing, pa-tient-ly plead-ing, Oh, let him save you to-night.

CHORUS.

Say, are you read-y? Oh, are you read-y? If the Death an-gel should call? (should call!) Say, are you read-y? Oh, are you read-y? Mer-cy stands wait-ing for all.

By permission of the author.

# Come, Thou Fount. Concluded.

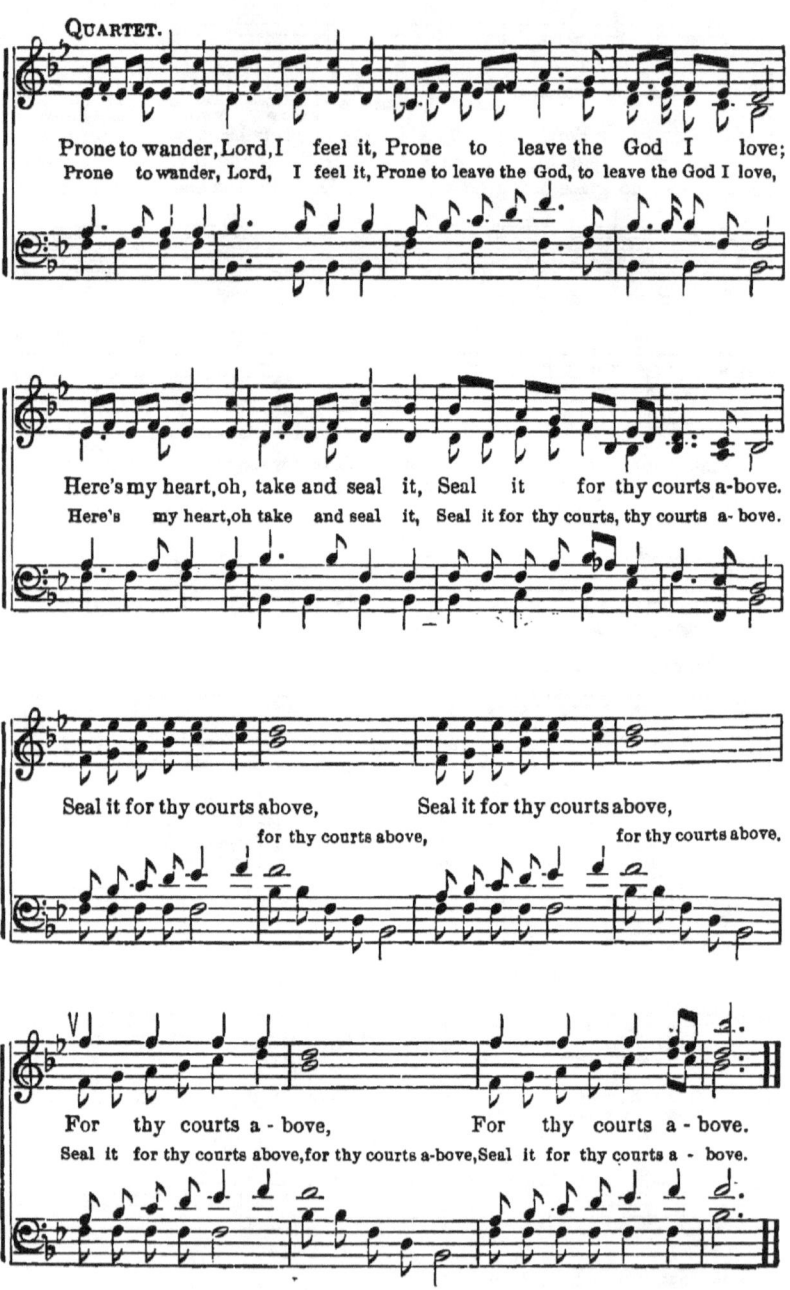

113

## Nearer Thee. Concluded.

### No. 102. "Old Time Religion."
Arr. CHARLIE TILLMAN.

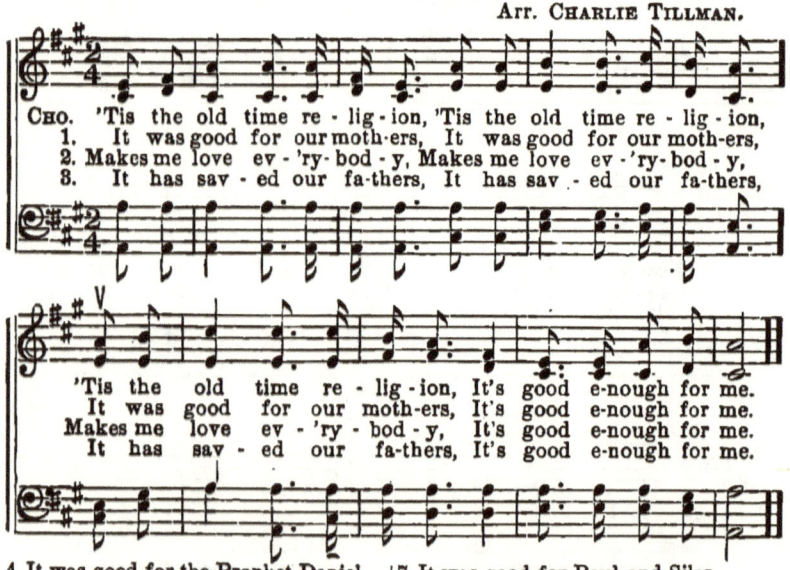

4 It was good for the Prophet Daniel,
  It's good enough for me.
5 It was good for the Hebrew Children,
  It's good enough for me.
6 It was tried in the fiery furnace,
  It's good enough for me.

7 It was good for Paul and Silas,
  It's good enough for me.
8 It will do when I am dying,
  It's good enough for me.
9 It will take us all to heaven,
  It's good enough for me.

Copyright, 1891, by Charlie D. Tillman. By per.

## Blessed Stranger. Concluded.

Kind-ness he will e'er ex-tend, Want or fear I ne'er shall know.

### No. 104. Under the Cross.
(*To my Choir, Sam Jones' meetings, Durham, N. C.*)

WM. MCDONALD.      E. O. EXCELL.

1. I am com-ing to the cross; I am poor, and weak, and blind;
2. Long my heart has sighed for thee, Long has evil reigned within;
3. Here I give my all to thee, Friends, and time, and earthly store;

I am counting all but dross, I shall full sal-va-tion find.......
Je-sus sweetly speaks to me, "I will cleanse you from all sin."...
Soul and bod-y thine to be, Whol-ly thine for ev-er - more......
Hal - le - lu - jah!

**CHORUS.**

Un-der the cross I lay my sins, Un-der the cross they lie;

Un-der the cross I lay my sins, Un-der the cross I'll die.

Copyright, 1889, by E. O. Excell.

## Jesus is Born. Concluded.

Heav'n and earth re-joic-es, Je-sus Christ is born;
Join your mer-ry voi-ces, On this Christmas morn.

## No. 108. I am on my Way to Zion.

W. G. TOMER.

1. I am on my pil-grim journey; Ere I reach the nar-row sea,
2. I was lost, but Je-sus found me, Taught my heart to seek his face;
3. Now my soul with rap-ture glowing, Sings a-loud with pard'ning love;
4. I shall yet be-hold my Sav-ior, When the day of life is o'er.

I would tell the wondrous sto-ry, What the Lord has done for me.
From a wild and lone-ly des-ert, Bro't me to his fold of grace.
Looks be-yond a world of sor-row, To the pilgrim's home a-bove.
I shall cast my crown be-fore him, And shall praise him ev-er-more.

CHORUS. *With fervor.*

Glo-ry, glo-ry, hal-le-lu-jah! Tho' a stran-ger here I roam;
I am on my way to Zi-on, I'm a pil-grim go-ing home.

Copyright, 1892, by E. O. Excell.

## The Answered Prayer. Concluded.

4 Gray crept the dawn behind the hill,
　The dreary night went shivering by,
And o'er the watchers spent and chill,
　The sun looked down with pitying eye;
But no song rose amid the gloom
　That hung athwart that darken'd room,
But no song rose amid the gloom
　That hung athwart that darken'd room.

5 For God had heard the prayer she sang,
　That happy mother bending low,
And answered it at break of day,
　While yet the cot swung to and fro,
"From sin and sorrow," in his love,
　God called the little one above;
"From sin and sorrow," in his love,
　God called the little one above.

### No. 110. As We Go.

F. H. C.            Flora Hamilton Cassel.

1. We will give our hearts to Jesus, As we go, as we go;
2. We will seek to lead to Jesus, As we go, as we go;
3. We will ev-er work for Jesus, As we go, as we go;

For he loves the little children Here below.
Many friends who ought to love him Here below.
Helping to enlarge his kingdom Here below.

REFRAIN.
Loving Jesus ev-'ry day,
Working as we sing and pray; Help us, Savior, on our way,
As we go, as we go; Help us ev-er on our way, As we go.

By permission.

## Going Down to the Grave. Concluded.

God Who dwelleth on high, Come trusting his word, And thou shalt not die.

### No. 114.  By and By.

C. H. MANN.  J. H. TENNEY.

Andante.

1. We shall be at home with Jesus, By and by, by and by;
2. We shall know in whom we've trusted, By and by, by and by;
3. When fulfilled our expectation, By and by, by and by;

He'll from sin and pain release us, By and by, by and by;
Ev - 'ry wrong shall be adjusted, By and by, by and by;
We shall fill some humble station, By and by, by and by;

When in us his work's perfected, Which by sin we once rejected, We shall be by him accepted, By and by, by and by.
Sweet will be the day of resting, Happy day! so full of blessing, To the grace of God attesting, By and by, by and by.
Thro' the Savior's intercession, After full and free confession, We shall gain a rich possession, By and by, by and by.

Copyright, 1892, by E. O. Excell.

## No. 116. *The Children's King.

Dr. E. T. Cassel.     Flora H. Cassel.

1. Do you hear those voi-ces sound? List the tem-ple courts re-sound,
2. See them march the courts athrong, Vain-ly priests for-bid their song,
3. Sa-cred walls re-peat the strain, Loud ho-san-nas glad re-frain;
4. Let the cho-rus still pro-long, Je-sus Christ ap-proves the song;

Hark! a thou-sand chil-dren sing, "Da-vid's Son, the children's King."
Hail, all hail! they shout and sing, "Da-vid's Son, the children's King."
Je-sus hears no sweet-er thing, "Da-vid's Son, the children's King."
Per-fect praise the chil-dren bring, "Da-vid's Son, the children's King."

CHORUS.

Ho-san-nas sing,............ Ho-san-nas sing,......
To Christ our King,     To
............ To Da-vid's Son, the chil-dren's King.
Christ our King,

## No. 117. Oh, how Happy, how Happy.

(M. H. 442.) For music see No. 115.

1 Oh, how happy are they,
  Who the Savior obey,
And have laid up their treasures above!
  Tongue can never express
  The sweet comfort and peace
Of a soul in its earliest love.

2 That sweet comfort was mine,
  When the favor divine
I received thro' the blood of the Lamb;
  When my heart first believed,
  What a joy I received—
What a heaven in Jesus' name!

3 'Twas a heaven below
  My Redeemer to know,
And the angels could do nothing more
  Than to fall at his feet,
  And the story repeat,
And the Lover of sinners adore.

4 Jesus, all the day long,
  Was my joy and my song;
Oh, that all his salvation might see!
  He hath loved me, I cried,
  He hath suffered and died,
To redeem even rebels like me.

*Copyright, 1892, by E. O. Excell.

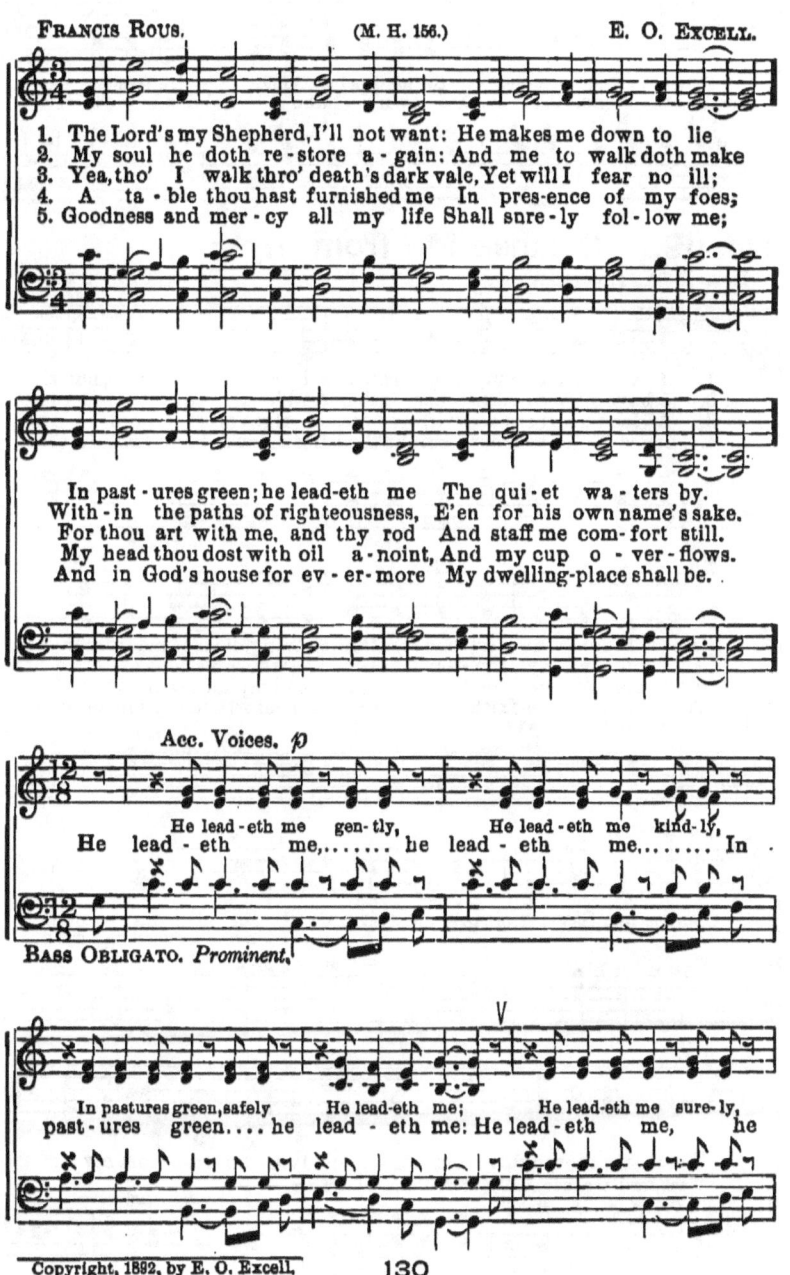

## No. 121. Saved to the Uttermost.

W. J. K.            Wm. J. Kirkpatrick.

1. Saved to the ut-ter-most: I am the Lord's, Je-sus, my Sav-ior, sal-vation af-fords, Gives me his spir-it a wit-ness with-in, Whisp'ring of par-don, and sav-ing from sin.
2. Saved to the ut-ter-most: Je-sus is near, Keep-ing me safe-ly, he cast-eth out fear, Trust-ing his prom-is-es, how I am blest Lean-ing up-on him, how sweet is my rest.
3. Saved to the ut-ter-most: this I can say, "Once all was darkness, but now it is day," Beau-ti-ful vis-ions of glo-ry I see, Je-sus in bright-ness re-vealed un-to me.
4. Saved to the ut-ter-most: cheerfully sing Loud hal-le-lu-jahs to Je-sus, my King, Ran-som'd and par-don'd, redeem'd by his blood, Cleans'd from un-right-eous-ness, glo-ry to God.

REFRAIN.

Saved, saved, saved to the ut-ter-most: Saved, saved, by pow-er divine; Saved, saved, saved to the ut-ter-most, Je-sus, the Sav-ior, is mine.

Used by permission.

## No. 124. Savior, Wash Me in the Blood.

COWPER.     COPYRIGHT, 1887, BY E. O. EXCELL.     E. O. EXCELL.

1. There is a fountain fill'd with blood, Drawn from Immanuel's veins;
And sin-ners plung'd beneath that flood, Lose all their guil-ty stains.
2. The dy-ing thief re-joiced to see That fount-ain in His day,
And there may I tho' vile as he, Wash all my sins a-way.

CHORUS.

Sav-ior, wash ..... me in the blood, Sav-ior,
Sav-ior, wash me in the blood, In the blood, the blood of the Lamb, Sav-ior,
wash ..... me in the blood, Oh, wash ....
wash me in the blood, In the blood, the blood of the Lamb, Oh, wash me in the
... me in the blood, And I shall be whiter than the snow.
blood, in the blood, the blood of the Lamb,

3 Thou dying Lamb, Thy precious blood
Shall never lose its power,
Till all the ransomed church of God
Are saved, to sin no more.

4 E'er since by faith I saw the stream,
Thy flowing wounds supply,
Redeeming love has been my theme,
And shall be till I die.

## No. 128. By and By, Yes, By and By.

WM. ALFRED GAY.     WM. A. MAY.

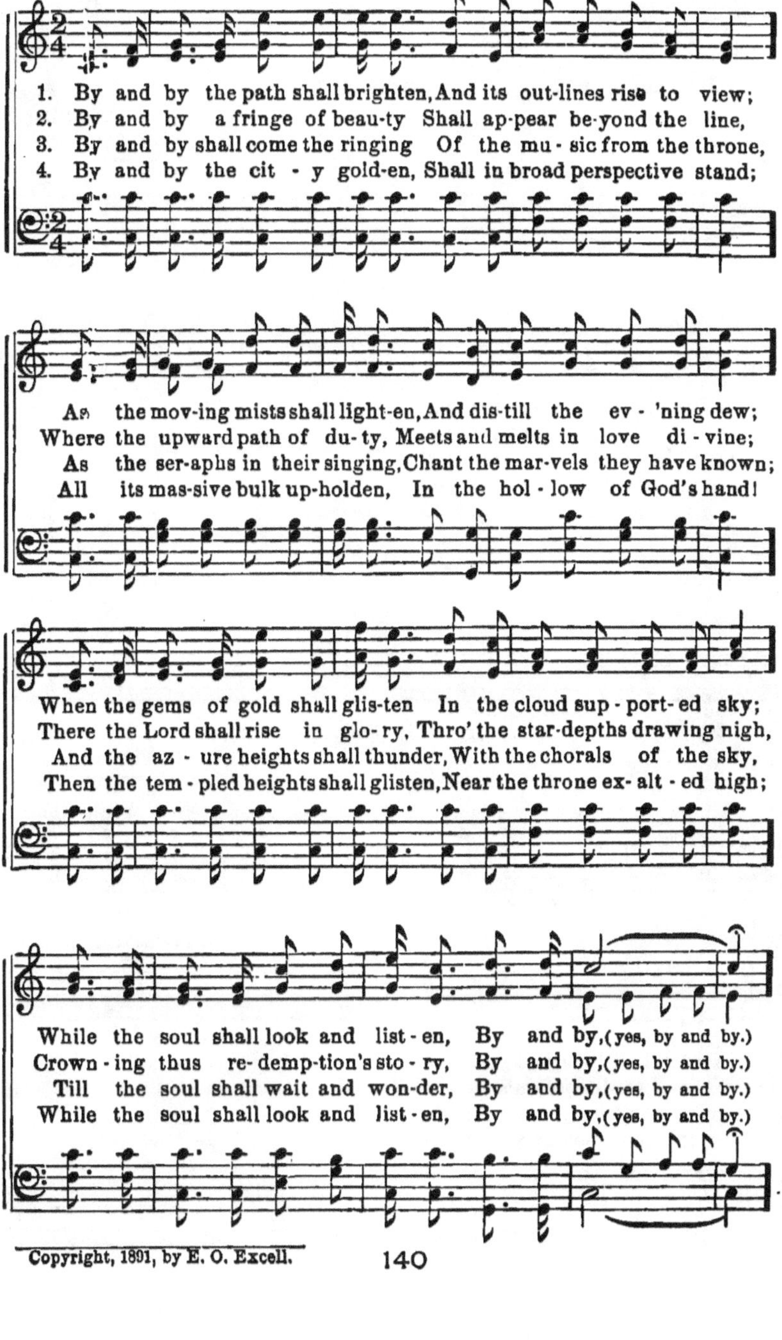

1. By and by the path shall brighten, And its out-lines rise to view;
2. By and by a fringe of beau-ty Shall ap-pear be-yond the line,
3. By and by shall come the ringing Of the mu-sic from the throne,
4. By and by the cit-y gold-en, Shall in broad perspective stand;

As the mov-ing mists shall light-en, And dis-till the ev-'ning dew;
Where the upward path of du-ty, Meets and melts in love di-vine;
As the ser-aphs in their singing, Chant the mar-vels they have known;
All its mas-sive bulk up-holden, In the hol-low of God's hand!

When the gems of gold shall glis-ten In the cloud sup-port-ed sky;
There the Lord shall rise in glo-ry, Thro' the star-depths drawing nigh,
And the az-ure heights shall thunder, With the chorals of the sky,
Then the tem-pled heights shall glisten, Near the throne ex-alt-ed high;

While the soul shall look and list-en, By and by,(yes, by and by.)
Crown-ing thus re-demp-tion's sto-ry, By and by,(yes, by and by.)
Till the soul shall wait and won-der, By and by,(yes, by and by.)
While the soul shall look and list-en, By and by,(yes, by and by.)

Copyright, 1891, by E. O. Excell.

## By and By, Yes, By and By. Concluded.

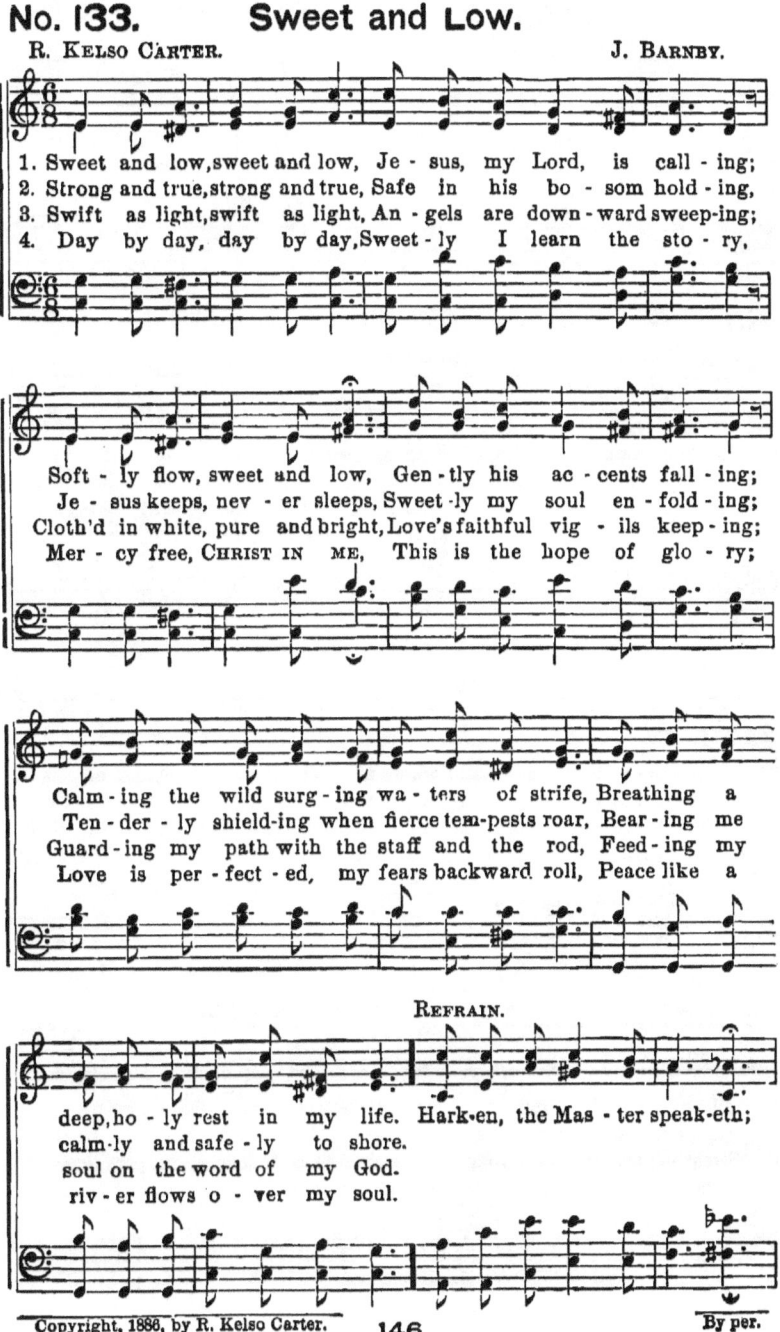

## Sweet and Low. Concluded.

"Storms o-bey my will, Love thy heart shall fill; Peace, be still!"
Peace, peace,

## No. 134.  America.
L. F. SMITH.    National Hymn.

1. My coun-try, 'tis of thee, Sweet land of lib-er-ty,
2. My na-tive coun-try, thee, Land of the no-ble free,
3. Let mu-sic swell the breeze, And ring from all the trees
4. Our fa-thers' God, to thee, Au-thor of lib-er-ty,

Of thee I sing; Land where my fa-thers died, Land of the
Thy name I love; I love thy rocks and rills, Thy woods and
Sweet freedom's song; Let mor-tal tongues a-wake, Let all that
To thee we sing; Long may our land be bright, With free-dom's

*cres.*

Pil-grims' pride, From ev - 'ry mount-ain side, Let free-dom ring.
templed hills, My heart with rapture thrills, Like that a - bove.
breathe partake, Let rocks their si-lence break, The sound pro-long.
ho - ly light, Pro - tect us with thy might, Great God, our King!

## My Mother's Hands. Concluded.

My mother's dear hands, her beautiful hands, Which guided me safe o'er life's sands, I bless God's name for the mem'ry Of mother's own beautiful hands.

5 Oh, those beautiful, beautiful hands!
I stood by her coffin one day,
And I kissed those hands so cold and white,
As quiet and peaceful she lay.

6 Oh, those beautiful, beautiful hands
I shall clasp them again once more,
As my feet touch the bank of the heav'nly land;
We shall meet on that shining shore.

### No. 136. The Lord's Prayer.

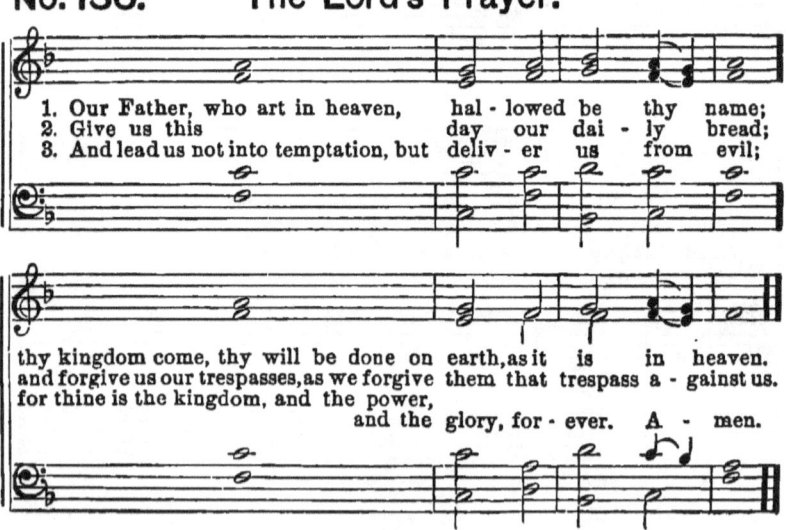

1. Our Father, who art in heaven, hallowed be thy name; thy kingdom come, thy will be done on earth, as it is in heaven.
2. Give us this day our daily bread; and forgive us our trespasses, as we forgive them that trespass against us.
3. And lead us not into temptation, but deliver us from evil; for thine is the kingdom, and the power, and the glory, forever. A-men.

### No. 137. To the Highways.

E. A. H.                      Rev. ELISHA A. HOFFMAN.

1. Brother, you have known the Master, Lo! these ma-ny, ma-ny years;
He has pardon'd your transgressions, Hush'd your sorrows, stayed your tears;
2. Brother, think how much he loved you, How he bore your sin and shame;
Bit-ter pain and bit-ter an-guish, You, a sin-ner, to re-claim.

In re-turn for his com-pas-sion, For his love un-bought, unpriced,
An-gels are not thus ex-alt-ed, Cher-u-bim nor ser-a-phim;

For his good-ness and his mer-cy, Have you bro't one soul to Christ?
In re-turn for such af-fec-tion, Have you bro't one soul to him?

CHORUS.

To the high - ways, To the hedg - es, Find the
To the highways, O my brother! To the hedg-es, O my broth-er!

souls that are a-stray; To the high - ways, To the
To the highways, O my broth-er! To the

Copyright, 1892, by E. O. Excell.

## To the Highways. Concluded.

hedg - es, Bring a soul to Christ to-day.
hedg - es, O my broth-er!

3 Brother, by the love he bears you,
  Pure and tender, rich and free;
Finding its most true expression
  In the cross of Calvary.
Consecrate yourself in service,
  To the Lord who made you whole;
Bring some wand'rer to the Savior,
  Rescue an immortal soul.

4 Has he not redeemed and saved you,
  Cleansed your soul from guilt and sin?
Rescued you from condemnation,
  Brought the Holy Spirit in?
Why not, in responsive feeling,
  Filled with gratitude and love;
Save one soul, to add one jewel
  To his glorious crown above?

## No. 138. Come, Ye Disconsolate.

THOS. MOORE. (M. H. 683.) SAMUEL WEBBE.

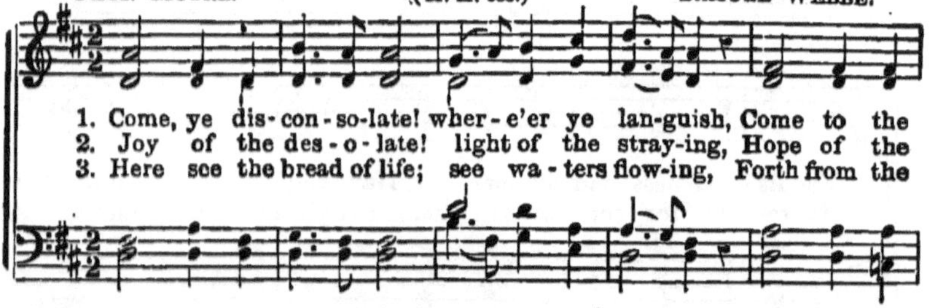

1. Come, ye dis-con-so-late! wher-e'er ye lan-guish, Come to the
2. Joy of the des-o-late! light of the stray-ing, Hope of the
3. Here see the bread of life; see wa-ters flow-ing, Forth from the

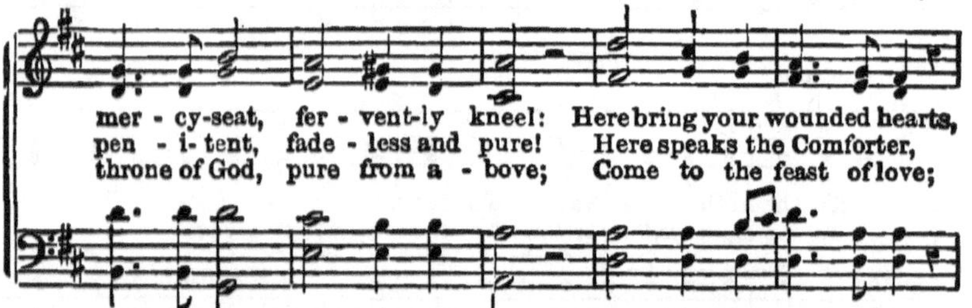

mer - cy-seat, fer-vent-ly kneel: Here bring your wounded hearts,
pen - i-tent, fade-less and pure! Here speaks the Comforter,
throne of God, pure from a-bove; Come to the feast of love;

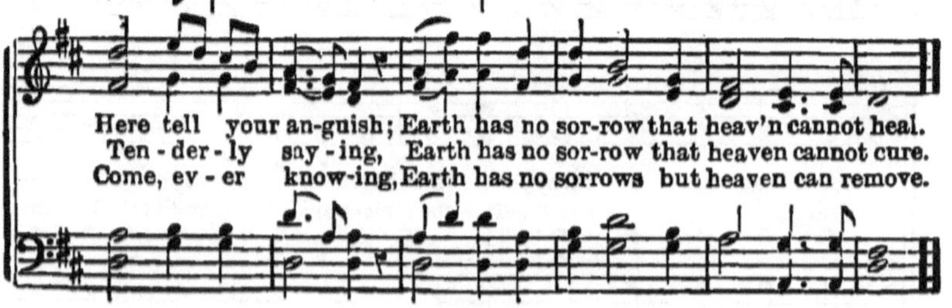

Here tell your an-guish; Earth has no sor-row that heav'n cannot heal.
Ten-der-ly say-ing, Earth has no sor-row that heaven cannot cure.
Come, ev-er know-ing, Earth has no sorrows but heaven can remove.

3. Once while resting on a pillow
   In the vessel, fast asleep,
   There arose a mighty tempest
   On the wild and raging deep;
   "Peace, be still," the Lord comanded,
   Every angry wave did stay;
   I am glad to tell you, sinners,
   He is just the same to-day.

4. Surely you have heard how Jesus
   Prayed down in Gethsemane,
   How he shed his precious life-blood
   On the rugged, shameful tree,
   Cruel thorns his forehead piercing,
   As his spirit passed away;
   Sinner, won't you come and love him?
   He is just the same to-day.

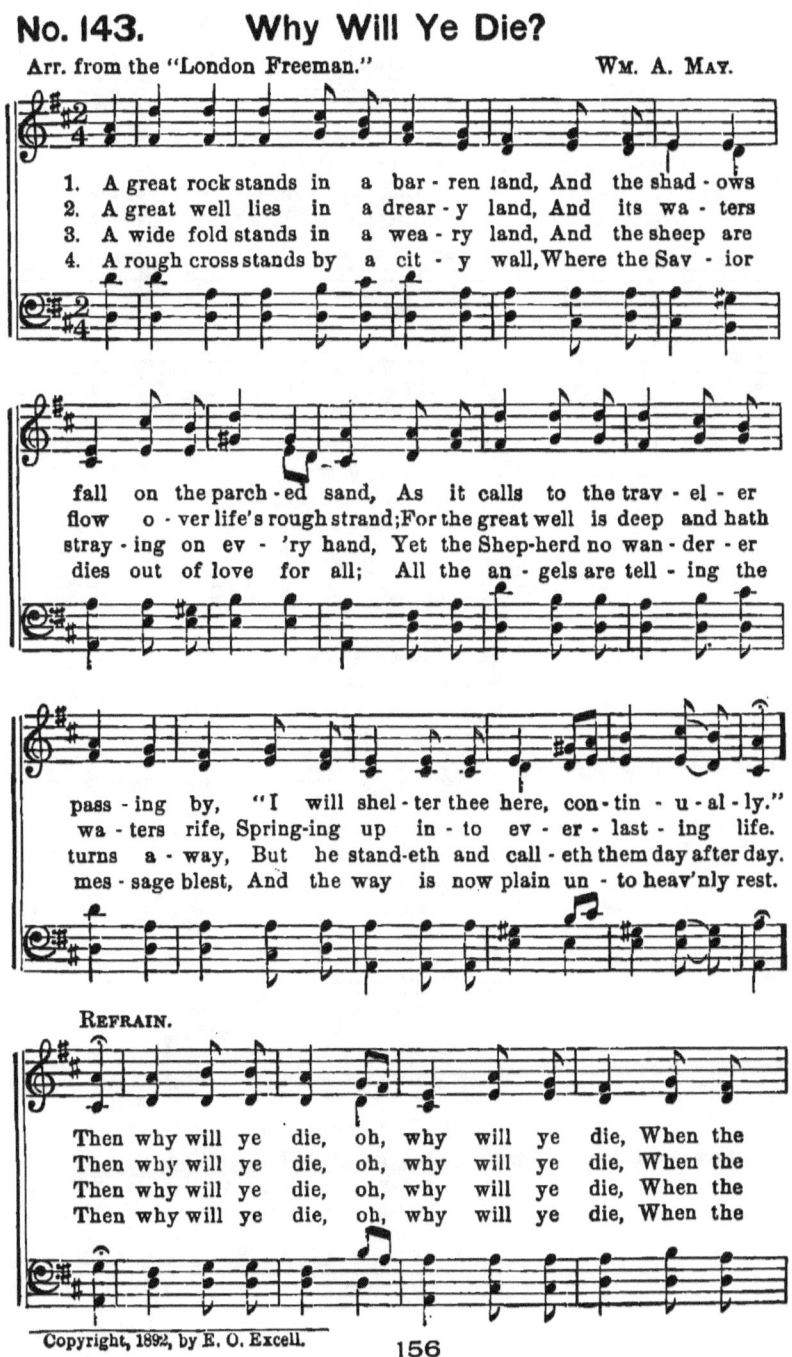

## Why Will Ye Die? Concluded.

shel-ter-ing rock is stand-ing nigh? Oh, why will ye die, oh,
great flow-ing well is ly-ing nigh? Oh, why will ye die, oh,
wel-com-ing fold is stand-ing by? Oh, why will ye die, oh,
blood-stainéd cross is stand-ing nigh? Oh, why will ye die, oh,

why will ye die, When the shel-ter-ing rock is stand-ing nigh?
why will ye die, When the great flow-ing well is ly-ing nigh?
why will ye die, When the wel-com-ing fold is stand-ing by?
why will ye die, When the blood-stain-ed cross is stand-ing nigh?

## No. 144. There's a Wideness in God's Mercy.

Wellesley. 8. 7. (M. H. 149.)

FREDERICK W. FABER.  LIZZIE S. TOURJEE.

1. There's a wide-ness in God's mercy, Like the wide-ness of the sea,
2. There is wel-come for the sin-ner, And more grac-es for the good;
3. For the love of God is broad-er Than the meas-ure of man's mind;
4. If our love were but more simple, We should take him at his word;

There's a kind-ness in his jus-tice, Which is more than lib-er-ty.
There is mer-cy with the Sav-ior; There is heal-ing in his blood.
And the heart of the e-ter-nal, Is most won-der-ful-ly kind.
And our lives would be all sun-shine In the sweet-ness of our Lord.

# No. 145. Beautiful Bethlehem.

E. R. Latta.     Chas. Edw. Prior.

1. Beau-ti-ful Beth-le-hem, In Ju-de-a's clime!
2. Beau-ti-ful Beth-le-hem, In Ju-de-a's land!
3. Beau-ti-ful Beth-le-hem, Glad my feet would stray

Oh! what a fa-vored spot, In the old-en time.
Where the glad Ma-gi once Saw the bright star stand.
Un-to the sa-cred spot, Where the dear babe lay.

Thine was the an-gel-song In the star-ry night,
Thine were the gifts so rare By the wise men made,
Oh! that the an-gel-song, It were mine to hear!

Thine was the shep-herd's joy, Thine a won-drous sight.
Thine was their wor-ship true To Mes-si-ah paid.
Oh! that the guid-ing star, Might to me ap-pear!

By permission.

## Beautiful Bethlehem. Concluded.

CHORUS.

Beau-ti-ful Beth-le-hem, How I love the word!

Beau-ti-ful Beth-le-hem, Birth-place of the Lord.

## No. 146. Rise, My Soul.

ROBERT SEAGRAVE. Amsterdam. 7s. 6s. Pec. (M. H. 1069.) JAMES NARES.

1. Rise, my soul, and stretch thy wings; Thy bet-ter portion trace;
Rise from tran-si-to-ry things Toward heav'n, thy native place;
Sun and moon and stars de-cay; Time shall soon this earth re-move;
Rise, my soul, and haste a-way To seats pre-pared a-bove.

2 Rivers to the ocean run,
  Nor stay in all their course;
Fire, ascending, seeks the sun;
  Both speed them to their source:
So a soul that's born of God,
  Pants to view his glorious face,
Upward tends to his abode,
  To rest in his embrace.

3 Cease, ye pilgrims, cease to mourn;
  Press onward to the prize;
Soon our Savior will return,
  Triumphant in the skies;
Yet a season, and you know
  Happy entrance will be given;
All our sorrows left below,
  And earth exchanged for heaven,

## Workers for the King. Concluded.

And are loy - al ev - 'ry one;
There a-waits a robe and crown,
For us when the day is done.

## No. 148. Holy, Holy, Holy Lord.

CHARLES WESLEY.     Hendon, 7s.     C. H. A. MALAN.

1. Ho-ly, ho-ly, ho-ly Lord, God the Father, and the Word, God the Comforter, receive Blessings more than we can give, Blessings more than we can give.

2 One, inexplicably three,
One, in simplest unity;
God, incline thy gracious ear,
Us thy lisping creatures hear.

3 Thee, while man, the earth-born, sings,
Angels shrink within their wings;

Prostrate Seraphim above
Breathe unutterable love.

4 Happy they who ever rest,
With thy heavenly presence blest!
They the heights of glory see,
Sound the depths of Deity.

161

## I have Looked and I Live. Concluded.

love, (in his love,) Not a care do I know, I am trusting as I go;

"Look and live," "look and live" is the message from above.

### No. 150. Come, Holy Spirit. C. M.
I. WATTS.     St. Martin's. (M. H. 277.)     WM. TANSUR.

1. Come, Holy Spirit, Heav'nly Dove, With all thy quick'ning pow'rs;
2. Look, how we grov-el here below, Fond of these earth-ly toys;
3. In vain we tune our for-mal songs, In vain we strive to rise;

Kindle a flame of sa-cred love In these cold hearts of ours.
Our souls, how heav-i-ly they go, To reach e-ter-nal joys.
Ho-san-nas lan-guish on our tongues, And our de-vo-tion dies.

4 Father, and shall we ever live
   At this poor dying rate,
   Our love so faint, so cold to thee,
   And thine to us so great?

5 Come, Holy Spirit, Heavenly Dove,
   With all thy quick'ning pow'rs;
   Come, shed abroad a Savior's love,
   And that shall kindle ours.

# Wait a Little, You May See. Concluded.

## No. 152. 'Mid Scenes of Confusion.

Home, 11. (M. H. 1054.)     Sir H. R. BISHOP.

1 'Mid scenes of confusion and creature complaints, [with saints!
How sweet to the soul is communion
To find at the banquet of mercy there's room, [home.
And feel in the presence of Jesus at Home! home! sweet, sweet home!
Prepare me, dear Savior, for glory, my home. [dren of peace!
2 Sweet bonds that unite all the chil-

And, thrice precious Jesus, whose love cannot cease, [I roam,
Tho' oft from thy presence in sadness
I long to behold thee in glory, at home.
3 I sigh from this body of sin to be free, [with thee.
Which hinders my joy and communion
Tho' now my temptation like billows may foam, [thee at home.
All, all will be peace, when I'm with

## Won't You Trust Him? Concluded.

help you, He will save you,
Yes, he will help you, Yes, he will save you,
He will guide you on From day to day................
He will guide you on from day, from day to day.

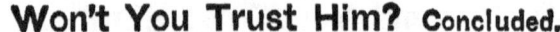

## No. 154. Jesus Bids Us Shine.

E. O. EXCELL.

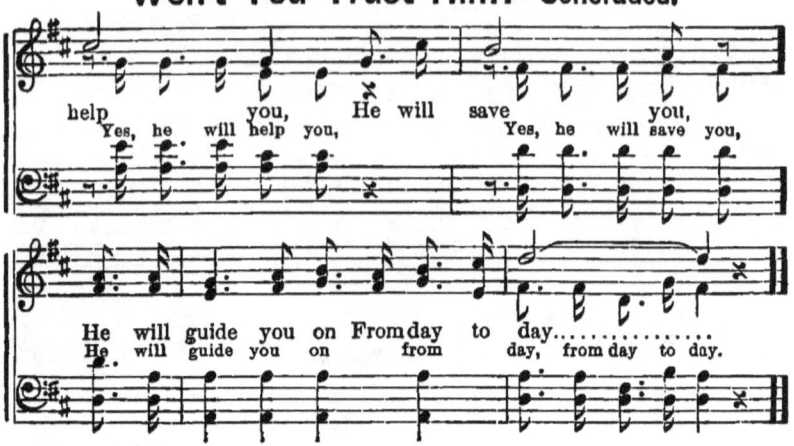

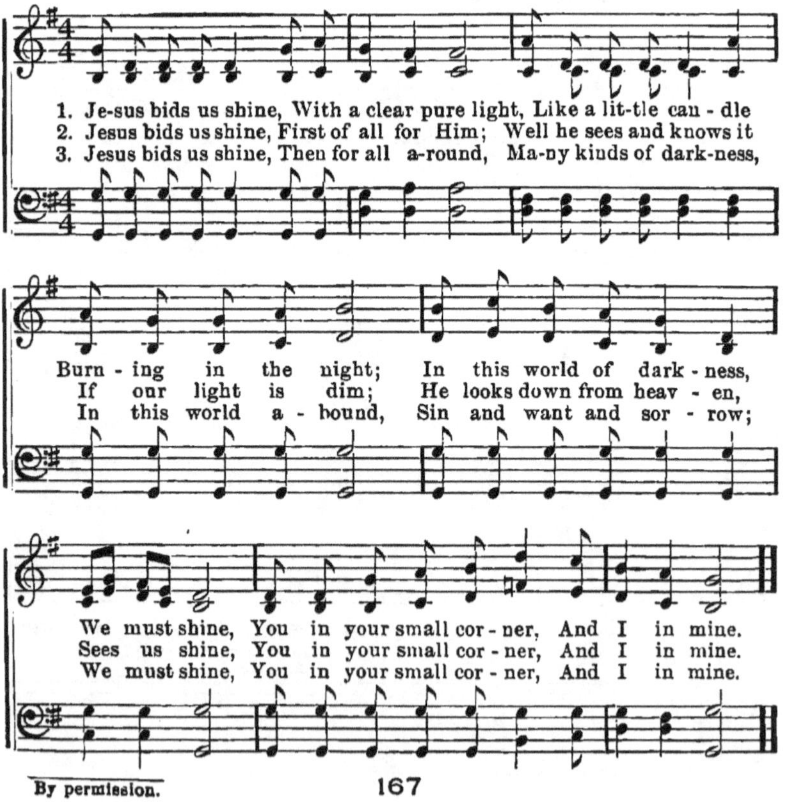
1. Je-sus bids us shine, With a clear pure light, Like a lit-tle can - dle
2. Jesus bids us shine, First of all for Him; Well he sees and knows it
3. Jesus bids us shine, Then for all a-round, Ma-ny kinds of dark-ness,
Burn - ing in the night; In this world of dark - ness,
If our light is dim; He looks down from heav - en,
In this world a - bound, Sin and want and sor - row;
We must shine, You in your small cor - ner, And I in mine.
Sees us shine, You in your small cor - ner, And I in mine.
We must shine, You in your small cor - ner, And I in mine.

By permission.

## Heralds of Jesus. Concluded.

### No. 156. Shall we Meet?

H. L. Hastings.  Elihu S. Rice.

1. Shall we meet be-yond the riv-er, Where the surg-es cease to roll?
2. Shall we meet be-yond the riv-er, When our storm-y voyage is o'er?

Where in all the bright for-ev-er, Sor-row ne'er shall press the soul?
Shall we meet and cast the anchor By the bright ce-les-tial shore?

D.S. *Shall we meet be-yond the riv-er, Where the surg-es cease to roll?*

CHORUS.

Shall we meet, shall we meet, Shall we meet be-yond the riv-er?

3 Shall we meet in yonder city,
  Where the towers of crystal shine?
  Where the walls are all of jasper,
  Built by workmanship divine.
4 Where the music of the ransomed
  Rolls its harmony around,
  And creation swells the chorus
  With its sweet melodious sound.

5 Shall we meet there many a loved one
  That was torn from our embrace?
  Shall we listen to their voices,
  And behold them face to face?
6 Shall we meet with Christ our Savior,
  When he comes to claim his own?
  Shall we know his blessed favor,
  And sit down upon his throne?

Used by permission.

## Linger With me. Concluded.

hold in thine my hand; Linger with me, yes, still
Closely hold in thine my hand; Linger with me

linger, Till within............ Immanuel's land.
Till within

### No. 158. Sun of My Soul.

JOHN KEPLER.   Hursley, L. M. (M. H. 103.)   HENRY MONK.

1. Sun of my soul, thou Savior dear. It is not night if
2. When the soft dews of kindly sleep My wearied eyelids
3. Abide with me from morn till eve, For without thee I

thou be near; O may no earth-born cloud arise To hide thee
gently steep, Be my last thought, how sweet to rest Forever
cannot live; Abide with me when night is nigh, For without

from thy servant's eyes.
on my Savior's breast.
thee I dare not die.

4 If some poor wandering child of thine
Hath spurned today the voice divine,
Now, Lord, the gracious work begin,;
Let him no more lie down to sin.

5 Watch by the sick; enrich the poor
With blessings from thy boundless store
Be every mourner's sleep to-night,
Like infant's slumbers, pure and light.

6 Come near and bless us when we wake,
Ere thro' the world our way we take,
Till in the ocean of thy love,
We lose ourselves in heaven above,

## Sailing. Concluded.

CHORUS.   D.S.

Sail-ing on...... to the Port of the blest, Sailing on to the harbor of rest.
Sail-ing on,                              Sailing on,

## No. 160.   On the Evergreen Shore.

ISAAC WATTS.   JOHN B. SHAW.

1. There is a land of pure de-light, Where saints immor-tal reign;
2. There ev-er-last-ing spring a-bides, And nev-er with'ring flow'rs;
3. Sweet fields, be-yond the swell-ing flood, Stand dressed in liv-ing green;
4. Oh, could we make our doubts remove, The gloom-y doubts that rise,

In - fi - nite day excludes the night, And pleas-ures ban - ish pain.
Death, like a nar-row sea, di-vides This heav'n-ly land from ours.
So to the Jews old Ca-naan stood, While Jor-dan rolled be-tween.
And see the Ca-naan that we love, With un - be - cloud - ed eyes.

CHORUS.

On the ev - er-green shore, On the ev - er-green shore, We will

meet o - ver there, by and by; meet o - ver there, by and by.

Copyright, 1892, by E. O. Excell.

## No. 161. Are you Doing all the Good you can?

CHAS. H. GABRIEL.  T. MARTIN TOWNE.

1. All a-round on ev-'ry side there's work to do, Lift your eyes, the field of har-vest scan;
   Je-sus calls, but lo! the faith-ful ones are few, Are you doing all the good *(Omit.)* you can?

CHORUS.
Do-ing good, do-ing good, Walk-ing in the gos-pel's blessed way;.......... Do-ing good, do-ing good, Work-ing for the Mas-ter as you may.

Are you do-ing, do-ing good, Ev-er do-ing, do-ing good, Walk-ing in the gos-pel's bless-ed way; Are you do-ing, do-ing good, Ev-er do-ing, do-ing good, Work-ing for the Mas-ter as you may.

Copyright, 1892, by E. O. Excell.

## Are you Doing all the Good? Concluded.

2 There are precious souls that must be gathered in,
  Gathered by the dear Redeemer's plan;
  See them dying out upon the wastes of sin!
  Are you doing all the good you can?
3 Let no one be idle, for the days go by;
  Strike asunder Satan's galling ban,
  Answer quickly—"Jesus, Master, here am I!"
  And be doing all the good you can.

### No. 162.   What Then?

Anon.                                       E. C. Avis.

1. Af-ter the joys of earth, Af-ter its songs of mirth,
2. Af-ter an emp-ty name, Af-ter a wea-ry frame,
3. Af-ter this sad fare-well, To a world loved too well,

Af-ter its hours of light, Af-ter its dreams so bright,
Af-ter this con-scious smart, Af-ter an ach-ing heart,
Af-ter this si-lent bed, With the for-got-ten dead,

*p With Expression.*

What then? On-ly an emp-ty name, On-ly a wea-ry frame,
What then? On-ly a sad fare-well To a world lov'd too well,
What then? Oh! then the judgment throne, Oh! then the last hope gone,

On-ly a con-scious smart. On-ly an ach-ing heart.
On-ly a si-lent bed, With the for-got-ten dead.
Then all the woes that dwell In an e-ter-nal hell!

Copyright, 1886, by E. C. Avis, by per.

# No. 163. Look and Live.

W. A. O.     COPYRIGHT, 1887, BY E. O. EXCELL.     W. A. OGDEN.

1. I've a mes-sage from the Lord, Hal - le - lu - jah! The mes-sage un-to you I'll give, 'Tis re-cord-ed in His word, Hal - le - lu - jah! It is on - ly that you "look and live."
2. I've a mes-sage full of love, Hal - le - lu - jah! A mes-sage, oh! my friend for you, 'Tis a mes-sage from a-bove, Hal - le - lu - jah! Je - sus said it; and I know 'tis true.
3. Life is of - fered un - to thee, Hal - le - lu - jah! E-ter - nal life thy soul shall have, If you'll on - ly look to Him, Hal - le - lu - jah! Look to Je - sus, who a - lone can save.
4. I will tell you how I came; Hal - le - lu - jah! To Je - sus, when He made me whole; 'Twas be - liev-ing on His name, Hal - le - lu - jah! I trust - ed and He saved my soul.

D. S. *'Tis re - cord - ed in His word,*
*Fine.*

*Hal - le - lu - jah! It is on - ly that you "look and live."*

CHORUS.     D. S.

"Look and live," my brother, live, Look to Je-sus now and live,
"Look and live," "my brother, live," "Look and live."

## Mercy is Boundless and Free. Concluded.

D. C. Refrain.

last-ing thy soul may re-ceive, Mer-cy is boundless and free.
wait-ing, he'll save you to-night, Mer-cy is boundless and free.
long-er, but come as thou art, Mer-cy is boundless and free.
mer-cy be-lieve on his name, Mer-cy is boundless and free.

### No. 166. Christmas. C. M.

N. Tate. (M. H. 192.) G. F. Handel.

1. While shep-herds watched their flocks by night, All seat-ed on the ground, The an-gel of the Lord came down. And glo-ry shone a-round, And glo-ry shone a-round.
2. "Fear not" said he, for might-y dread Had seized their troub-led mind, "Glad ti-dings of great joy I bring, To you and all man-kind, To you and all man-kind.
3. "To you, in Da-vid's town, this day, Is born of Da-vid's line, The Sav-ior, who is Christ, the Lord, And this shall be the sign; And this shall be the sign.
4. "The heav'n-ly babe you there shall find To hu-man view dis-played, All mean-ly wrapp'd in swath-ing bands, And in a man-ger laid, And in a man-ger laid.

5 Thus spake the seraph, and forthwith
  Appeared a shining throng
Of angels, praising God, who thus
  Addressed their joyful song.

6 "All glory be to God on high,
  And to the earth be peace:
Good-will henceforth from heav'n to men
  Begin, and never cease!"

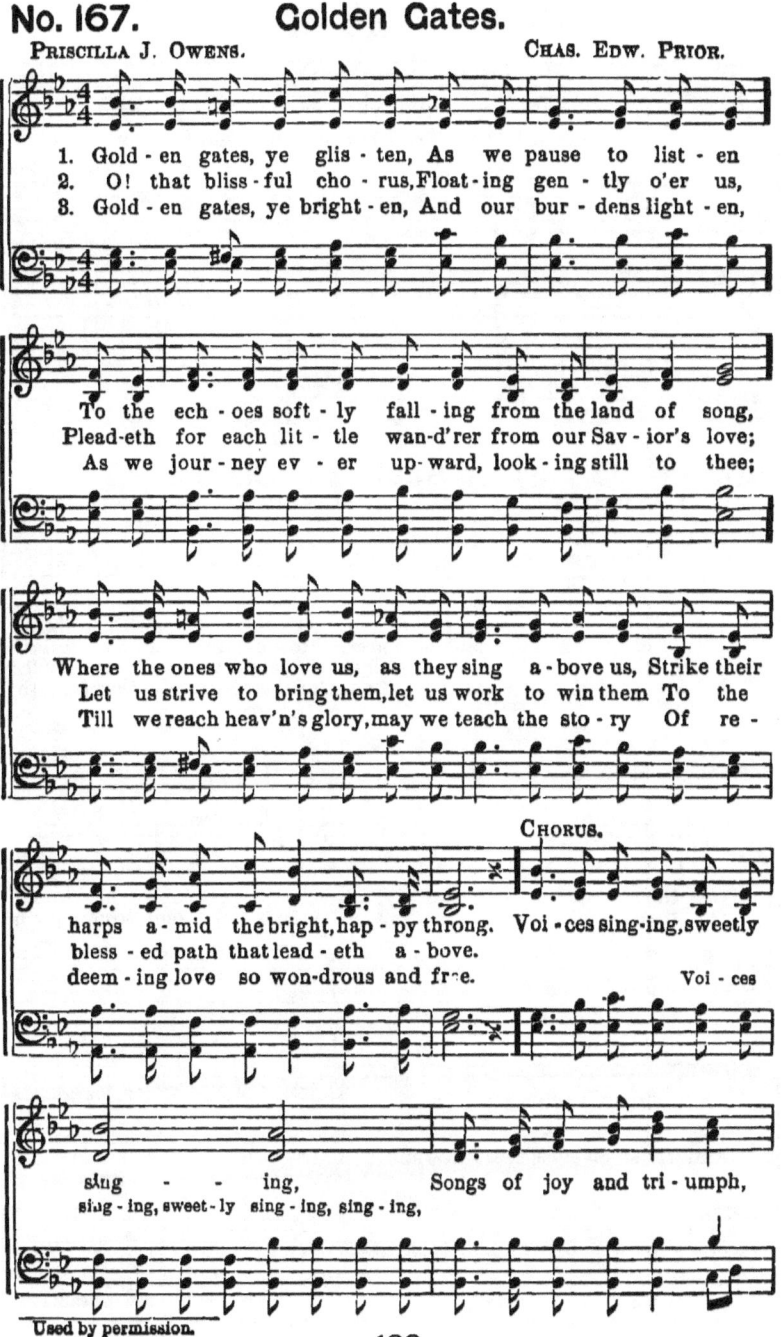

## Golden Gates. Concluded.

### No. 168. O Day of Rest and Gladness.

C. WORDSWORTH.   Mendebras, 7, 6. (M. H. 72.)   Arr. by LOWELL MASON.

1. { O day of rest and gladness, O day of joy and light;
     O balm of care and sadness, Most beautiful, most bright;
2. { On thee, at the creation The light first had its birth;
     On thee, for our salvation, Christ rose from depths of earth;

On thee the high and lowly, Thro' ages joined in tune,
On thee, our Lord, victorious, The Spirit sent from heav'n;

Sing "holy, holy, holy," To the great God Triune.
And thus on thee, most glorious, A triple light was giv'n.

3 To-day on weary nations
   The heav'nly manna falls;
  To holy convocations
   The silver trumpet calls,

Where gospel light is glowing
  With pure and radiant beams
And living water flowing
  With soul-refreshing streams.

### He is Able to Deliver. Concluded.

a - ble to de-liv-er thee; Tho' by sin op-prest, Go to
a-ble, he is a-ble,

him for rest; Our God is a-ble to de-liv-er thee.

### No. 170. Blest be the Tie.

JOHN FAWCETT.        GEO. NAEGELI

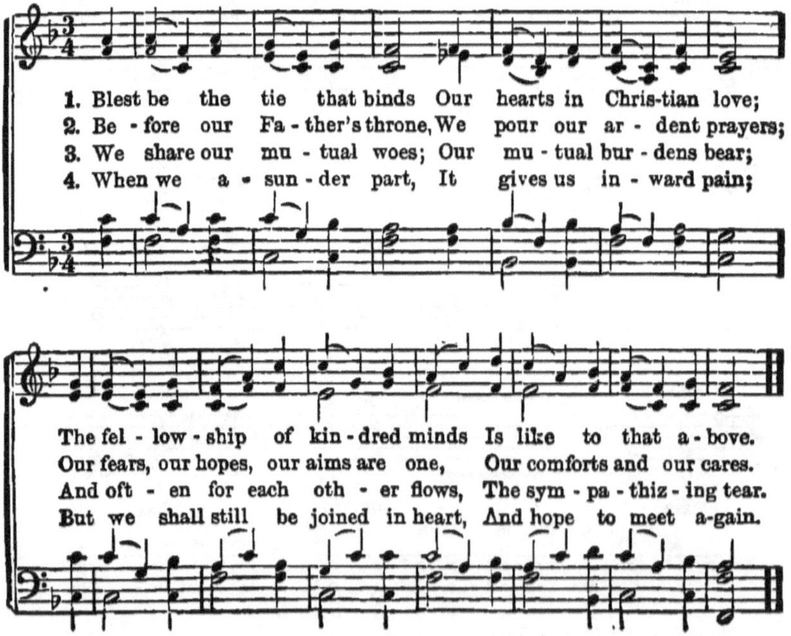

1. Blest be the tie that binds Our hearts in Chris-tian love;
2. Be - fore our Fa - ther's throne, We pour our ar - dent prayers;
3. We share our mu - tual woes; Our mu - tual bur - dens bear;
4. When we a - sun - der part, It gives us in - ward pain;

The fel - low - ship of kin - dred minds Is like to that a - bove.
Our fears, our hopes, our aims are one, Our comforts and our cares.
And oft - en for each oth - er flows, The sym - pa - thiz - ing tear.
But we shall still be joined in heart, And hope to meet a-gain.

# No. 171. In Sight of the Crystal Sea.

J. E. RANKIN, D. D.  
J. W. BISCHOFF.

*Rather slow.*

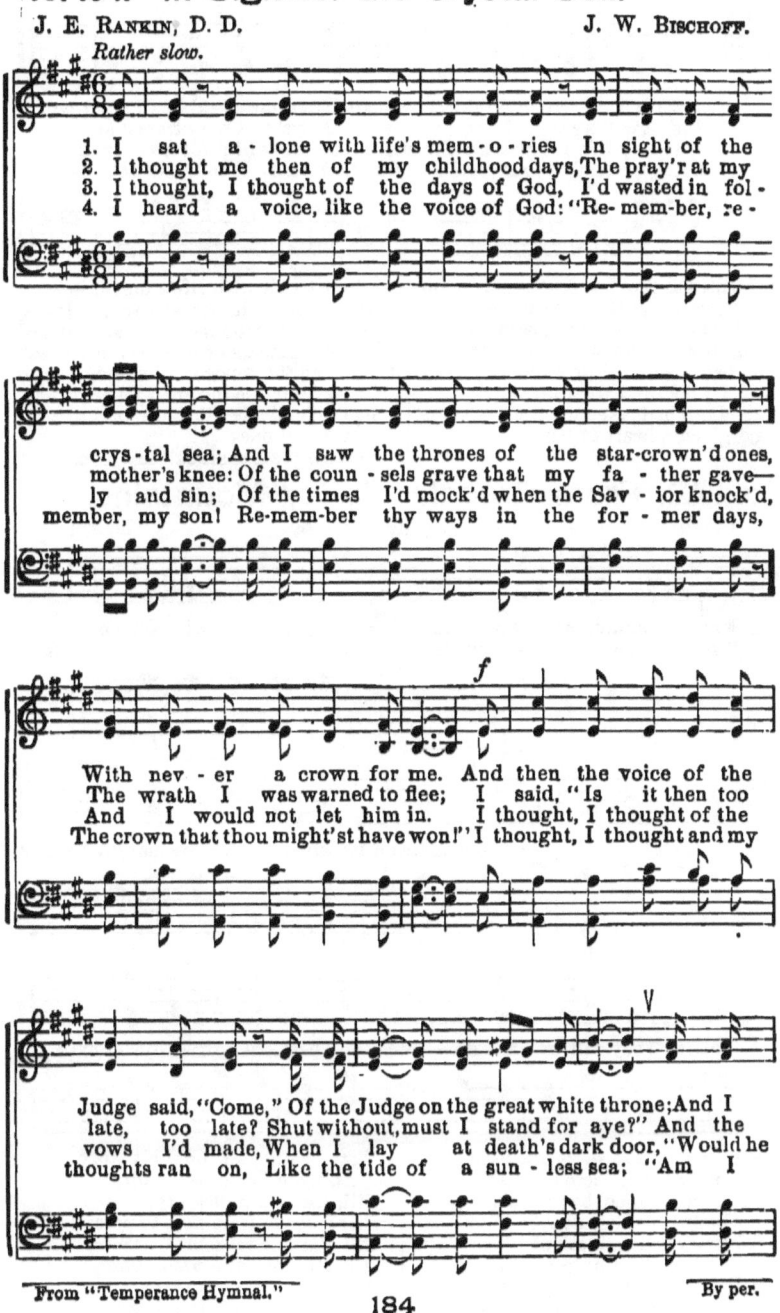

1. I sat a-lone with life's mem-o-ries In sight of the crys-tal sea; And I saw the thrones of the star-crown'd ones, With nev-er a crown for me. And then the voice of the Judge said, "Come," Of the Judge on the great white throne;
2. I thought me then of my childhood days, The pray'r at my mother's knee: Of the coun-sels grave that my fa-ther gave— The wrath I was warned to flee; I said, "Is it then too late, too late? Shut without, must I stand for aye?" And the
3. I thought, I thought of the days of God, I'd wasted in fol-ly and sin; Of the times I'd mock'd when the Sav-ior knock'd, And I would not let him in. I thought, I thought of the vows I'd made, When I lay at death's dark door, "Would he
4. I heard a voice, like the voice of God: "Re-mem-ber, re-member, my son! Re-mem-ber thy ways in the for-mer days, The crown that thou might'st have won!" I thought, I thought and my thoughts ran on, Like the tide of a sun-less sea; "Am I

From "Temperance Hymnal." By per.

## In Sight of the Crystal Sea. Concluded.

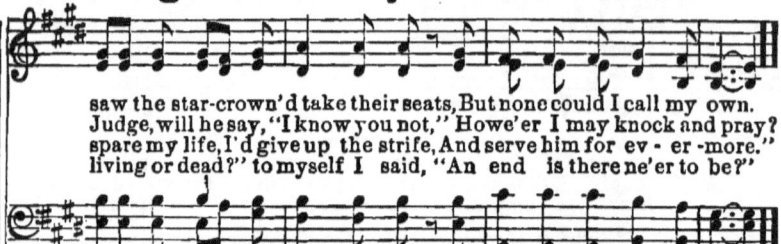

saw the star-crown'd take their seats, But none could I call my own.
Judge, will he say, "I know you not," Howe'er I may knock and pray?
spare my life, I'd give up the strife, And serve him for ev - er -more."
living or dead?" to myself I said, "An end is there ne'er to be?"

5 It seemed as tho' I woke from a dream,
How sweet was the light of day!
Melodious sounded the Sabbath bells
From towers that were far away.
I then became as a little child,
And I wept, and wept afresh;
For the Lord had taken my heart of stone,
And given a heart of flesh.

6 Still oft I sit with life's memories,
And think of the crystal sea;
And I see the thrones of the star-crowned ones
I know there's a crown for me. ["Come,"
And when the voice of the Judge says,
Of the Judge on the great white throne,
I know 'mid the thrones of the star-crowned ones
There's one I shall call my own.

## No. 172. From Greenland's Icy Mountains.

HEBER.     Missionary Hymn. 7s. 6s.     MASON.

1. From Greenland's i - cy mountains, From In - dia's cor - al strand;
Where Af-ric's sun-ny foun-tains, (Omit) Roll
down their gold-en sand; From many an ancient riv - er, From many a palm-y
plain, They call us to de - liv - er, Their land from er-ror's chain.

2 Shall we, whose souls are lighted,
With wisdom from on high,
Shall we, to men benighted,
The lamp of life deny?
Salvation! oh, salvation!
The joyful sound proclaim,
Till earth's remotest nation
Has learned Messiah's name.

3 Waft, waft, ye winds, his story,
And you, ye waters, roll,
Till, like a sea of glory,
It spreads from pole to pole;
Till o'er our ransomed nature,
The Lamb for sinners slain,
Redeemer, King, Creator,
In bliss returns to reign.

## No. 173. Work for Little Servants.

Miss ALICE ARMSTRONG.     Motion Song.     WM. A. MAY.

1. 1 In the ser-vice of the Sav-ior, There is much that 2 *we* can do,
2. 10 If we pray each morn at waking, 11 "Lord, what shall I do to-day?"
3. 18 When at night we lit-tle chil-dren 19 Count what God has helped us do,

For we 3 read "a child shall lead them," In the 4 Bi-ble; old and true.
12 God will help each lit-tle ser-vant, 13 Will-ing-ly to go his way.
20 All will thank him for his good-ness, 21 And will ask his help a-new.

CHORUS.

5 Eyes and 6 ears are faith-ful help-ers 7 Ev-'ry child has at command,
14 Eyes will see where help is need-ed, 15 Hands will lend their ready aid;
22 Eyes to see and ears to list-en; Heed-ful of di-vine command;

*poco rit.*

8 They will work, at slight-est bid-ding, 9 Or, will i-dly wait-ing stand.
16 Feet will run to do love's errand, 17 Lips will leave harsh words unsaid.
23 Lips and hands and feet make an-swer, 24 Un-to per-fect love's de-mand.

1. Hands extended, palms upward, with slight sweeping motion to No. 2. Inquiring expression on face.
2. Left hand at side. Right hand touches breast at "we."
3. At "read," bring right hand slanting upward, before the face as if reading from a book.
4. At "Bible," turn palm outward as if displaying an open book to the audience.
5 & 6. Point to the eyes and ears successively with index fingers *of both hands* when words are sung.
7. Sweeping movement of right hand outward and upward.

Copyright, 1892, by E. O. Excell.

## Work for Little Servants. Concluded.

8. Both hands extended in front, level with hips, palms up.
9. Hands at side, idly hanging.
10. Hands at breast folded in attitude of prayer. Keep in position to No. 12. This verse should be sung a little softer than 1st. verse to chorus, when tone may be increased.
11. Face and eyes turned inquiringly upward.
12. Left hand at side. Right hand pointing upward.
13. Sweeping movement of right hand.
14. Left hand to eye.
15. Both hands, palms up, extended.
16. Left foot slightly forward.
17. Index finger, right hand, to lips.
18. Hands clasped in front, in easy attitude.
19. Rapidly touch opened fingers of left hand slightly extended, with forefinger of right hand.
20. Sweeping motion with both hands from center of body outward, maintain position through No. 21.
22. Looking upward as in supplication, hands extended; from last position of No. 20.
23. Indicate successively the lips, hands and feet.
24. Hands clasped even with breast, arms in position of folded, head turned a trifle to the left, in attitude of listeners, eyes slightly uplifted, lips just parting in a smile, left foot forward a little bit—eagerness to do or be doing.

## No. 174. Safely through Another Week.

JOHN NEWTON.   Sabbath Morn, 7, 61. (M. H. 88.)   ARR. by L. MASON.

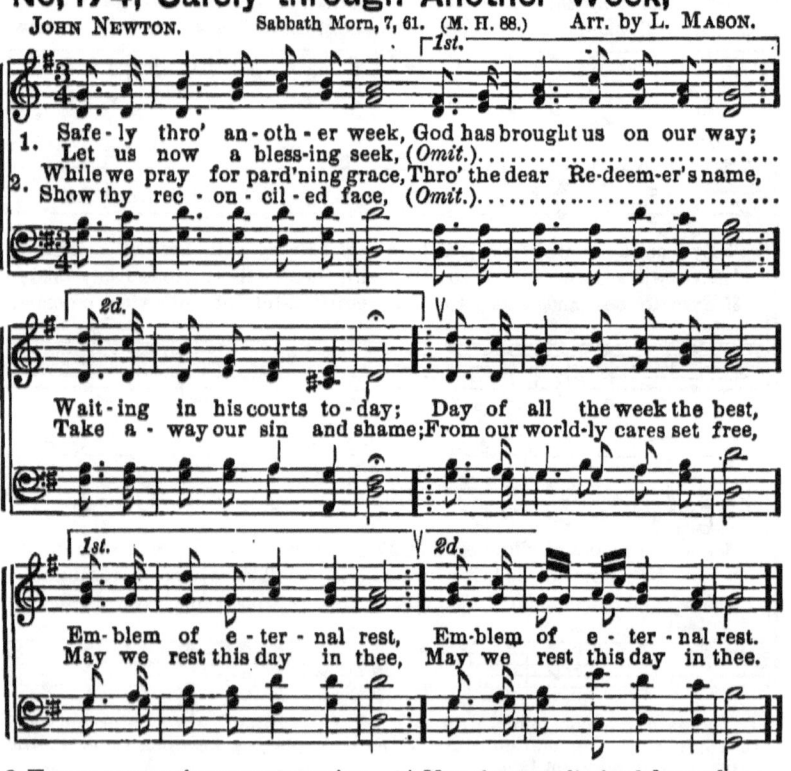

1. Safe-ly thro' an-oth-er week, God has brought us on our way;
Let us now a bless-ing seek, (Omit.)........
Wait-ing in his courts to-day; Day of all the week the best,
Em-blem of e-ter-nal rest, Em-blem of e-ter-nal rest.

2. While we pray for pard'ning grace, Thro' the dear Redeemer's name,
Show thy rec-on-cil-ed face, (Omit.)........
Take a-way our sin and shame; From our world-ly cares set free,
May we rest this day in thee, May we rest this day in thee.

3 Here we come thy name to praise;
  Let us feel thy presence near:
May thy glory meet our eyes,
  While we in thy house appear;
Here afford us, Lord, a taste
Of our everlasting feast.

4 May the gospel's joyful sound
  Conquer sinners, comfort saints;
Make the fruits of grace abound,
  Bring relief to all complaints:
Thus may all our Sabbaths prove,
Till we join the Church above.

# No. 175. Endeavor.

*(Written for the Society of Christian Endeavor.)*

F. H. C.  
Flora Hamilton Cassel.

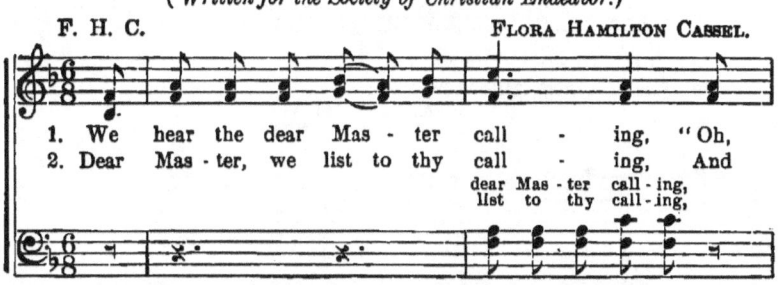
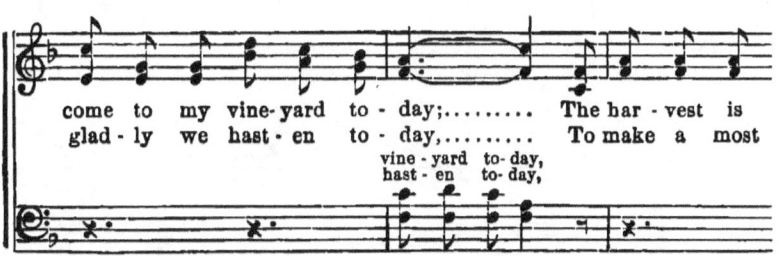
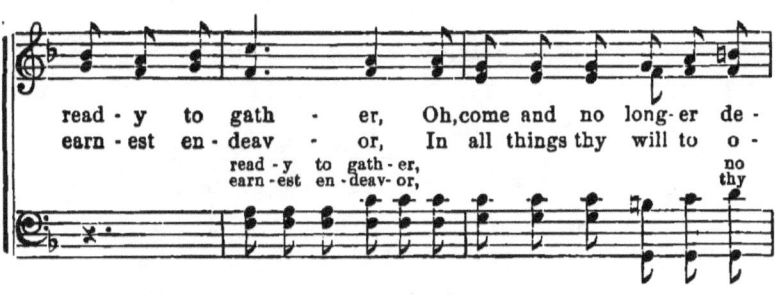
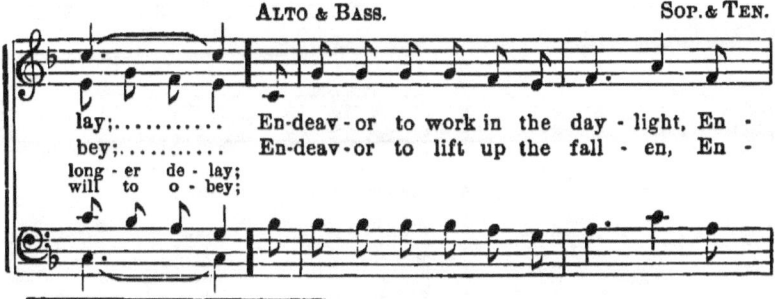

Copyright, 1892, by E. O. Excell.

# Endeavor. Concluded.

## Gracious Promises. Concluded.

## No. 179. Tell of His Love.

*(To C. E. Reese.)*

E. E. HEWITT.  COPYRIGHT, 1894, BY E. O. EXCELL.  E. O. EXCELL.

1. Je-sus came from heav'n for me, Tell of His love, won-der-ful love,
2. Scorn'd, reject-ed, cru-ci-fied, Tell of His love, won-der-ful love,
3. Ris'n from the ac-curs-ed grave, Tell of His love, won-der-ful love,
4. All your burdens He will bear, Tell of His love, won-der-ful love,
   His won-der-ful love,

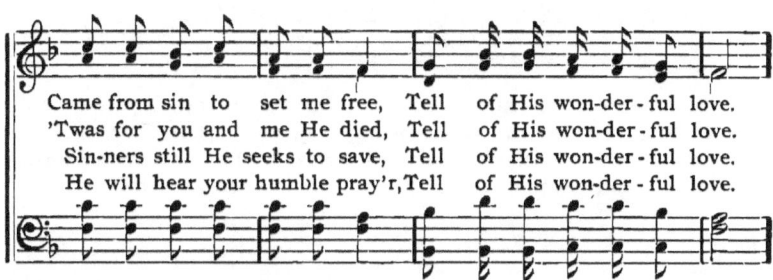

Came from sin to set me free, Tell of His won-der-ful love.
'Twas for you and me He died, Tell of His won-der-ful love.
Sin-ners still He seeks to save, Tell of His won-der-ful love.
He will hear your humble pray'r, Tell of His won-der-ful love.

CHORUS.

Love, love, .... Tell of His won-der-ful love, ....
Love, love, won-der-ful love,  won-der-ful love,

Love, love, ...... Tell of His won-der-ful love.
Love, love, won-der-ful love,

### No. 180. Lord, For-give!

E. A. H.     COPYRIGHT, 1894, BY E. O. EXCELL.     Rev. ELISHA A. HOFFMAN.

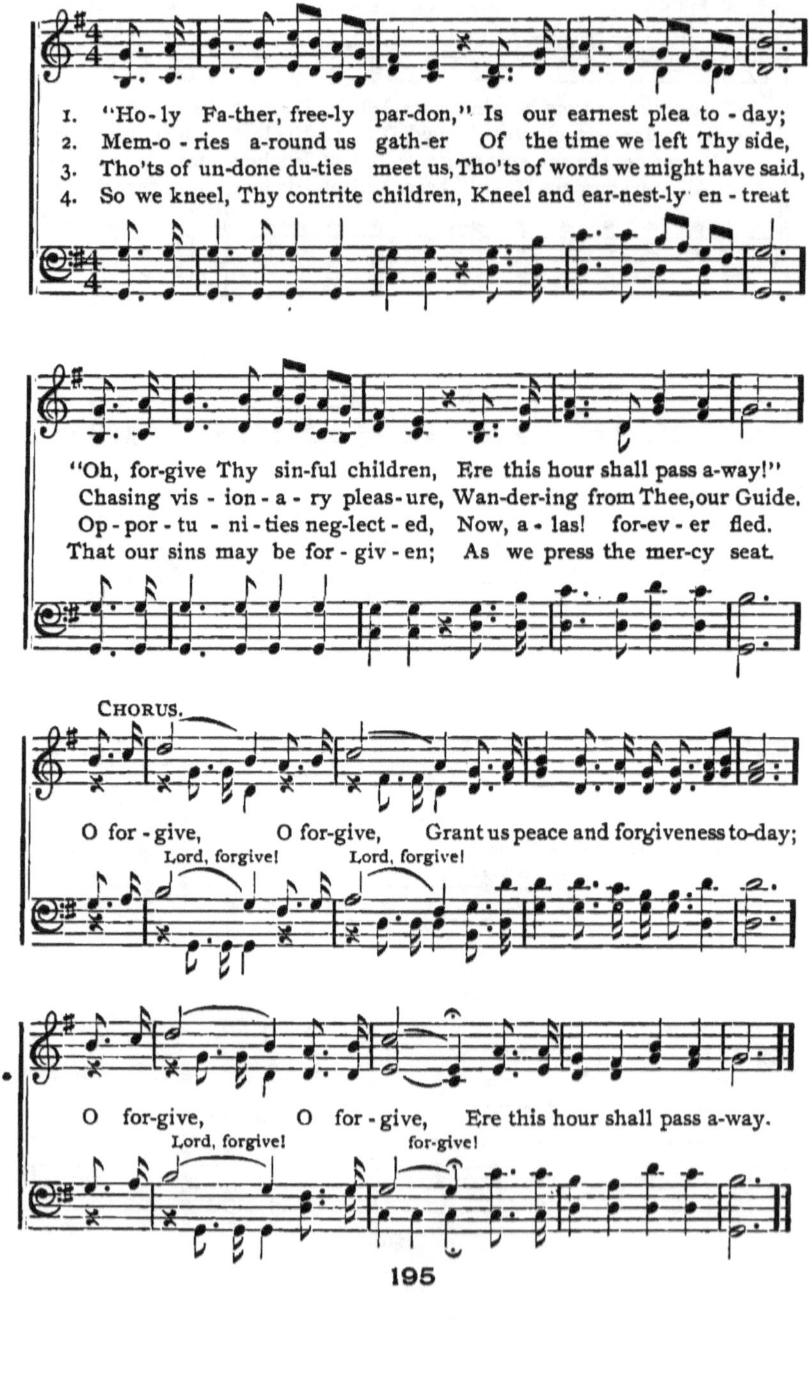

1. "Ho-ly Fa-ther, free-ly par-don," Is our earnest plea to-day;
2. Mem-o-ries a-round us gath-er Of the time we left Thy side,
3. Tho'ts of un-done du-ties meet us, Tho'ts of words we might have said,
4. So we kneel, Thy contrite children, Kneel and ear-nest-ly en-treat

"Oh, for-give Thy sin-ful children, Ere this hour shall pass a-way!"
Chasing vis-ion-a-ry pleas-ure, Wan-der-ing from Thee, our Guide.
Op-por-tu-ni-ties neg-lect-ed, Now, a-las! for-ev-er fled.
That our sins may be for-giv-en; As we press the mer-cy seat.

**CHORUS.**

O for-give, O for-give, Grant us peace and forgiveness to-day;
Lord, forgive! Lord, forgive!

O for-give, O for-give, Ere this hour shall pass a-way.
Lord, forgive! for-give!

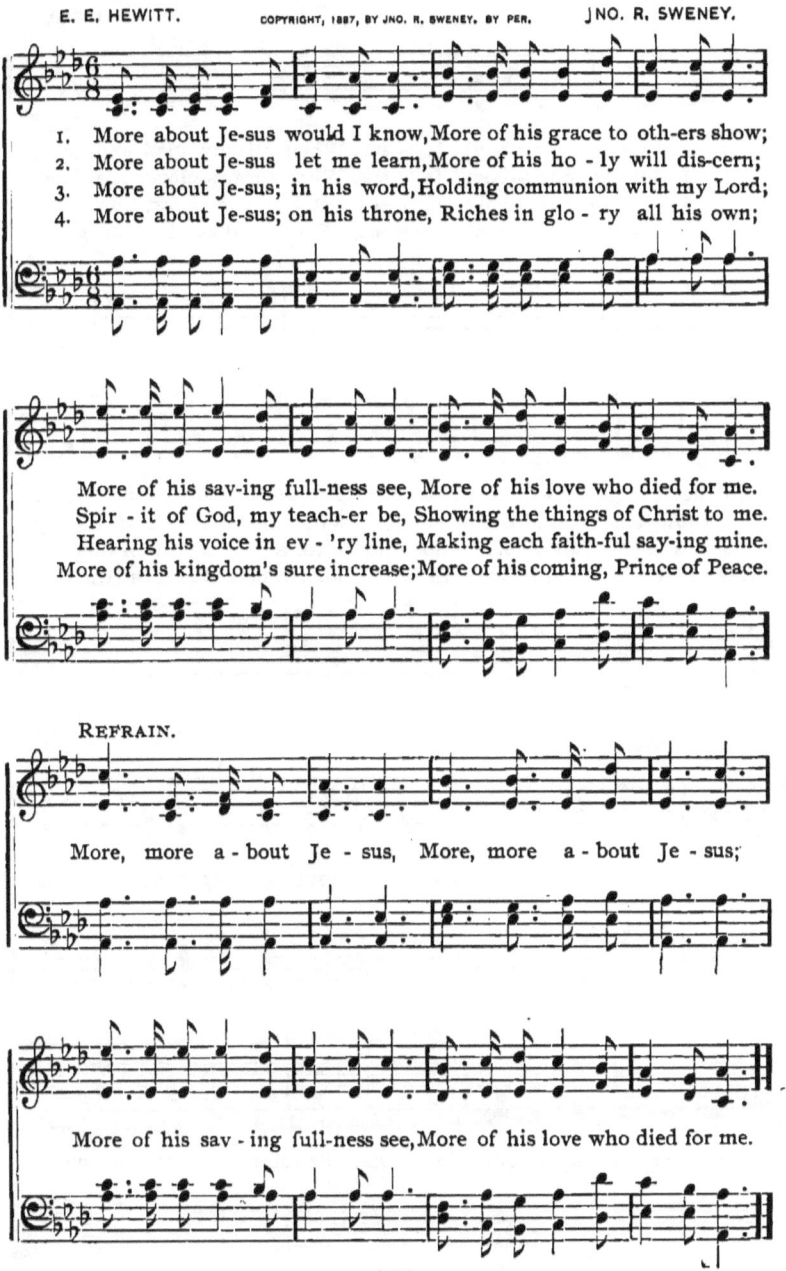

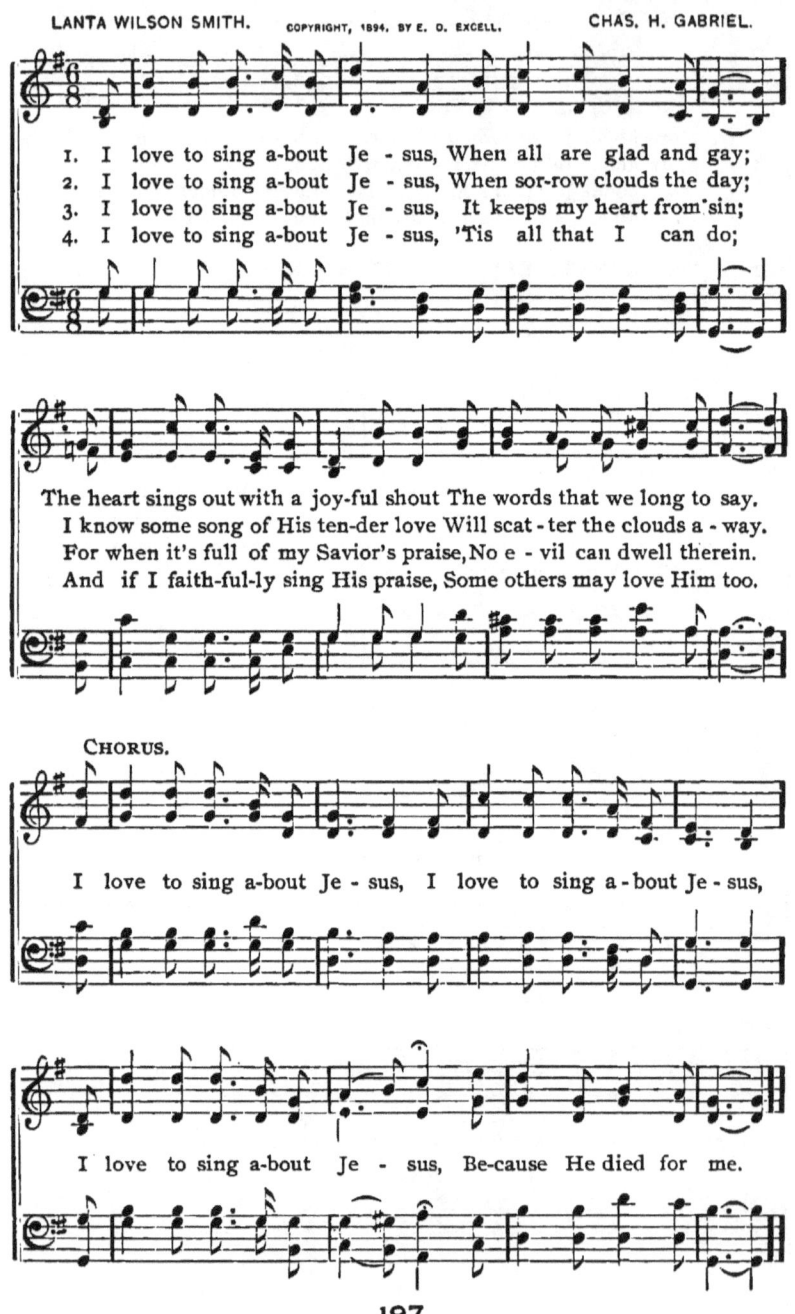

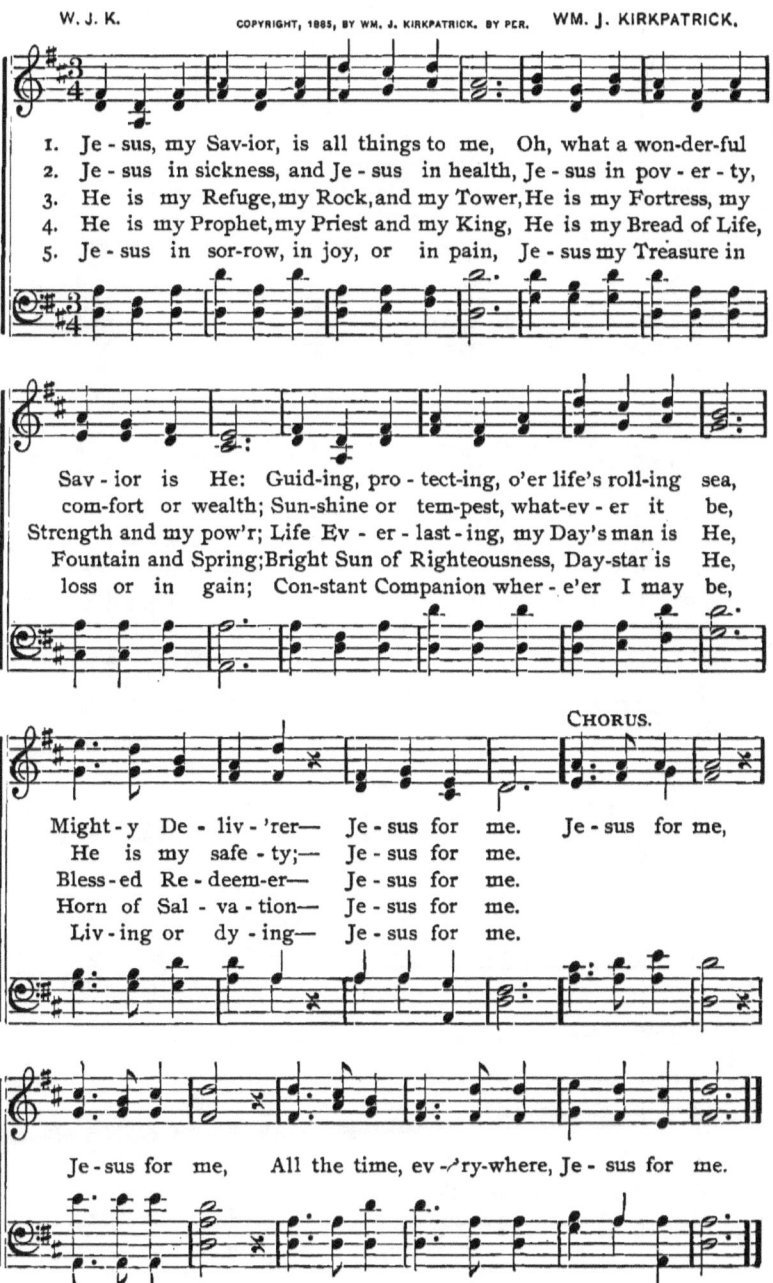

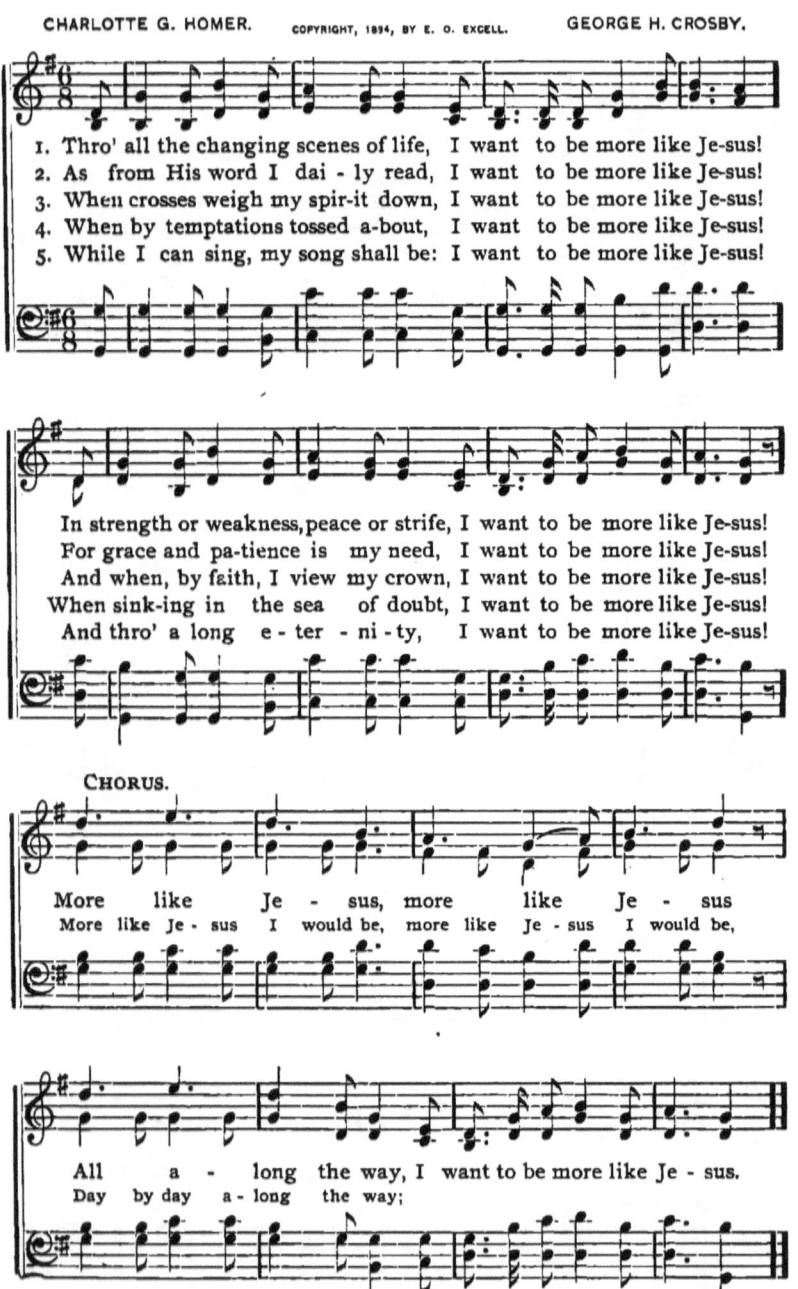

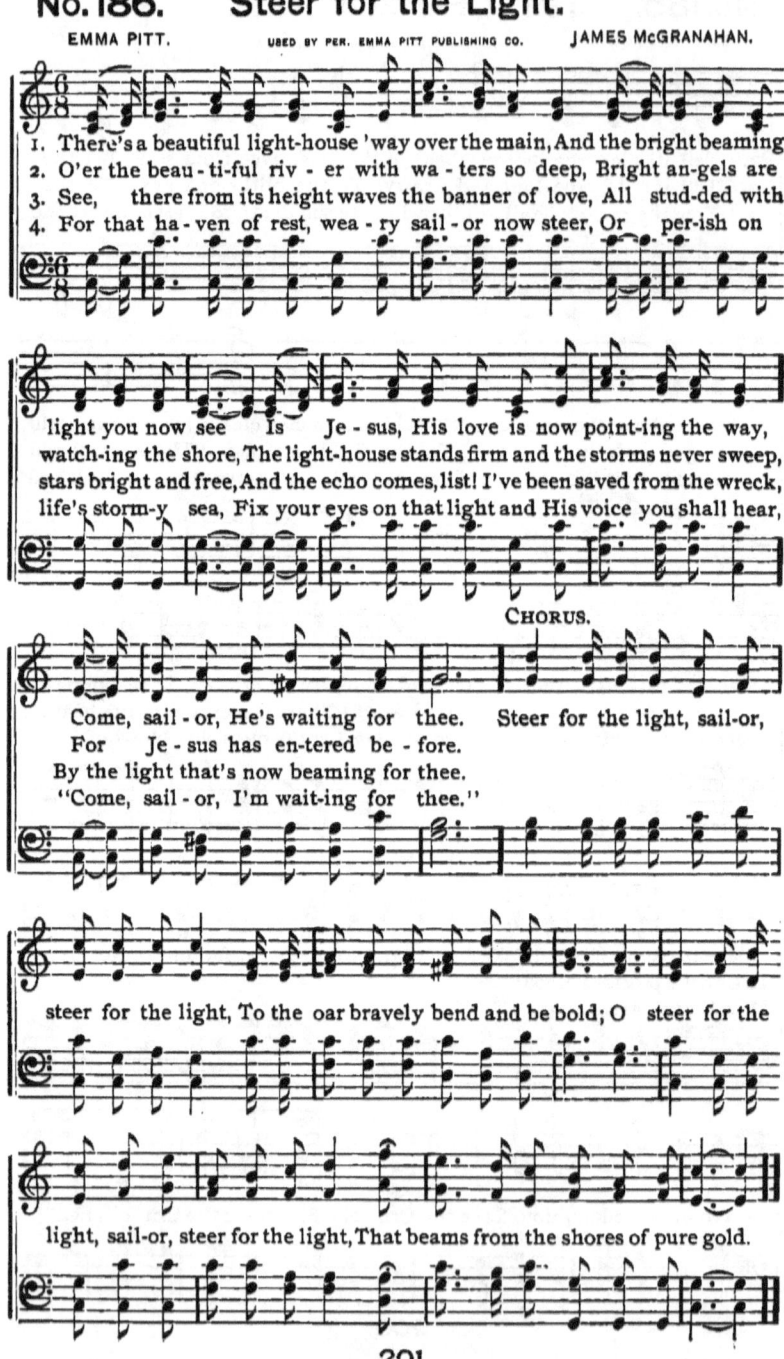

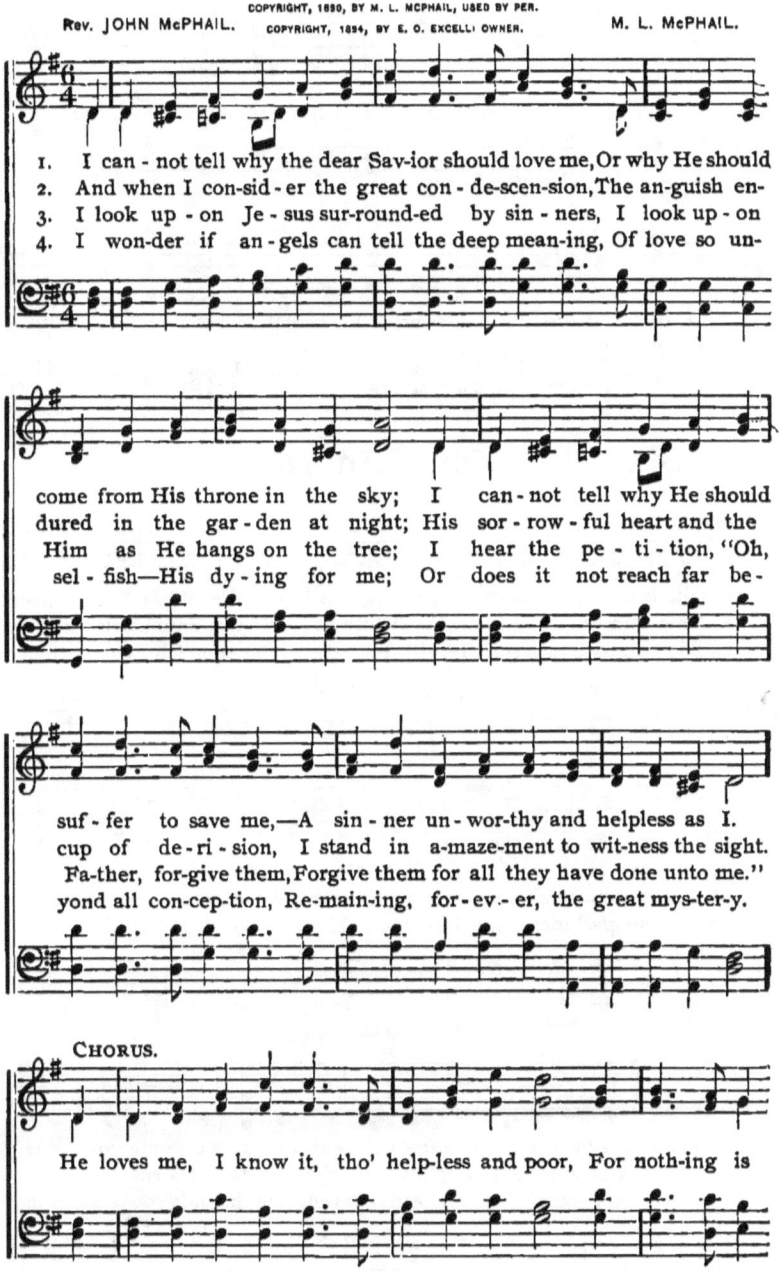

## I Cannot Tell Why. Concluded.

plain-er to me, I am sure; But why He should love me to suf-fer and die, I an-swer, I know not, I can-not tell why.

## No. 188. Oh, Turn Ye.

J. HOPKINS.

1. Oh, turn ye, oh, turn ye, for why will ye die, When God in great mer-cy is com-ing so nigh? Now Je-sus in-vites you, the Spir-it says "Come," And angels are wait-ing to wel-come you home.

2. How vain the de-lu-sion, that, while you de-lay, Your hearts may grow bet-ter, your chains melt a-way; Come guilt-y, come wretched, come just as you are, All help-less and dy-ing, to Je-sus re-pair.

3. The con-trite in heart he will free-ly re-ceive, Oh, why will you not the glad mes-sage be-lieve? If sin be your bur-den, why will you not come? 'Tis you he makes welcome; he bids you come home.

## Follow all the Way. Concluded.

pasture where He feedeth, I will follow, follow,
Pasture where He feedeth, pasture where He feedeth,

follow all the way, I will follow Jesus ev-'ry day.
fol-low, fol-low,

### No. 190. God is Love.

CHAS. WESLEY.      J. STEVENSON.

1. { Depth of mer-cy, can there be    Mer-cy still re-served for me? }
    { Can my God His wrath for-bear, Me, the chief of sinners spare? }
2. { I have long withstood His grace; Long provoked Him to His face; }
    { Would not hark-en to His calls; Griev'd Him by a thousand falls. }
3. { Now in-cline me to re-pent; Let me now my sin la-ment; }
    { Now my foul re-volt de-plore, Weep, be-lieve, and sin no more. }

REFRAIN. *Faster.*     *Smoothly.*     *Repeat pp.*

{ God is love, I know, I feel; } Jesus weeps, He weeps and loves me still.
{ Jesus weeps, and loves me still; }

4 Kindled His relentings are;
   Me He now delights to spare;
   Cries, "How shall I give thee up?"—
   Lets the lifted thunder drop.

5 There for me the Savior stands;
   Shows His wounds and spreads His
   God is love, I know, I feel; [hands;
   Jesus weeps and loves me still.

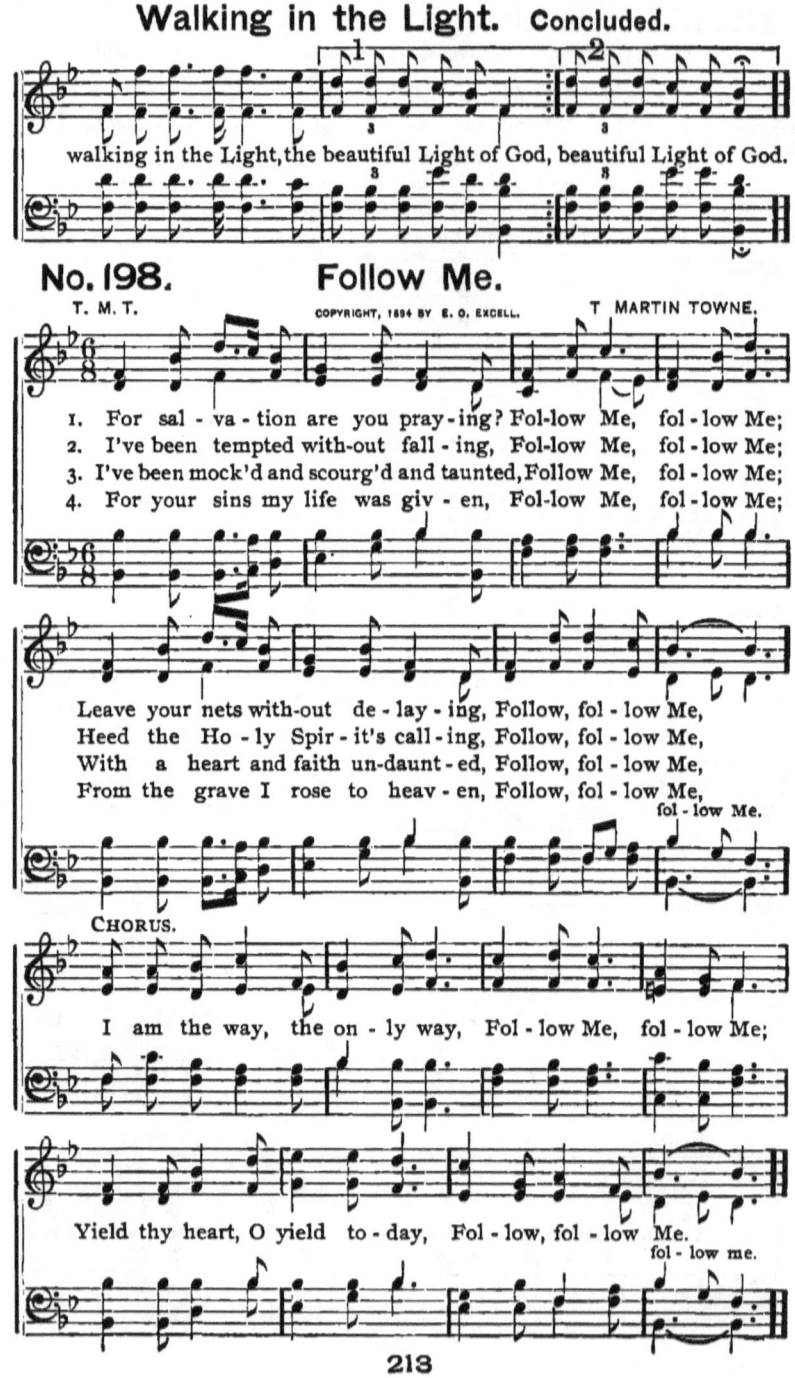

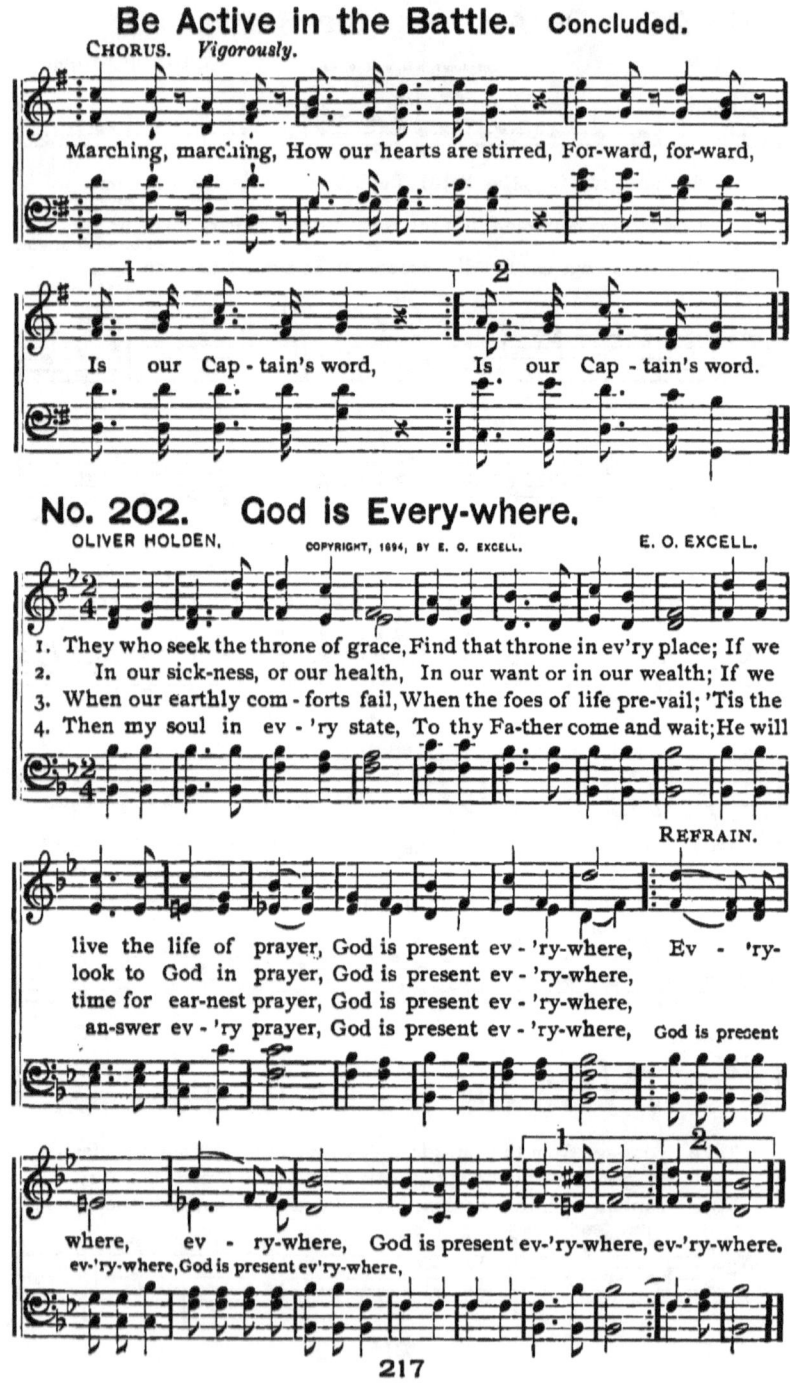

## No. 205. In Heavenly Love Abiding.

ANNA L. WARING.   COPYRIGHT, 1888, BY E. O. EXCELL.   E. O. EXCELL.

1. In heav'n-ly love a-bid-ing, No change my heart shall fear;
2. Wher-ev-er He may guide me, No want shall turn me back,
3. Green pastures are be-fore me, Which yet I have not seen;

And safe is such con-fid-ing, For noth-ing chan-ges here.
My Shepherd is be-side me, And noth-ing can I lack.
Bright skies will soon be o'er me, Where darkest clouds have been.

The storm may roar with-out me, My heart may low be laid,
His wis-dom ev-er wak-eth, His sight is nev-er dim,
My hope I can-not meas-ure, My path to life is free,

But God is 'round a-bout me, And can I be dis-mayed?
He knows the way He tak-eth, And I will walk with Him.
My Sav-ior has my treas-ure, And He will walk with me.

## Some Sweet Day, By and By, Concluded.

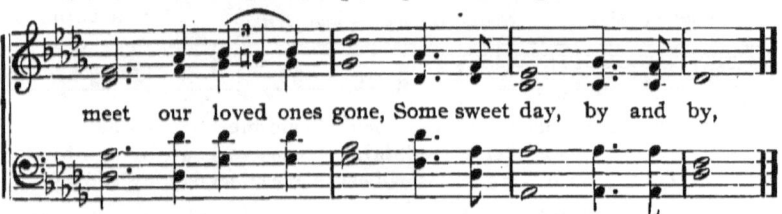

meet our loved ones gone, Some sweet day, by and by,

## No. 208. Weary the Waiting.

F. L. STANTON  COPYRIGHT, 1894, BY E. O. EXCELL.  J. M. DUNGAN.

1. { There's an end to all toil-ing, some day, sweet day, But it's wea-ry the
    There's a har-bor somewhere, it's a peace-ful bay, (*Omit.*)
2. { There's an end to the troub-les of souls oppressed, But it's wea-ry the
    At some-time in the fu-ture when God thinks best, (*Omit.*)
3. { There's an end to the world with its storm-y frown, But it's wea-ry the
    There's a light in that land that no dark can drown, (*Omit.*)

waiting, weary; } Where the sails will be furled and the ship will lay At
waiting, weary; } He will lay us so ten-der-ly down to rest, And
waiting, weary; } And where life's heavy burdens are all laid down,—A

an-chor some-where in the far a-way, But it's weary the waiting, weary.
roses will bloom where the thorns have prest, But it's weary the waiting, weary.
crown, O thank God for each cross, a crown; But it's weary the waiting, weary.

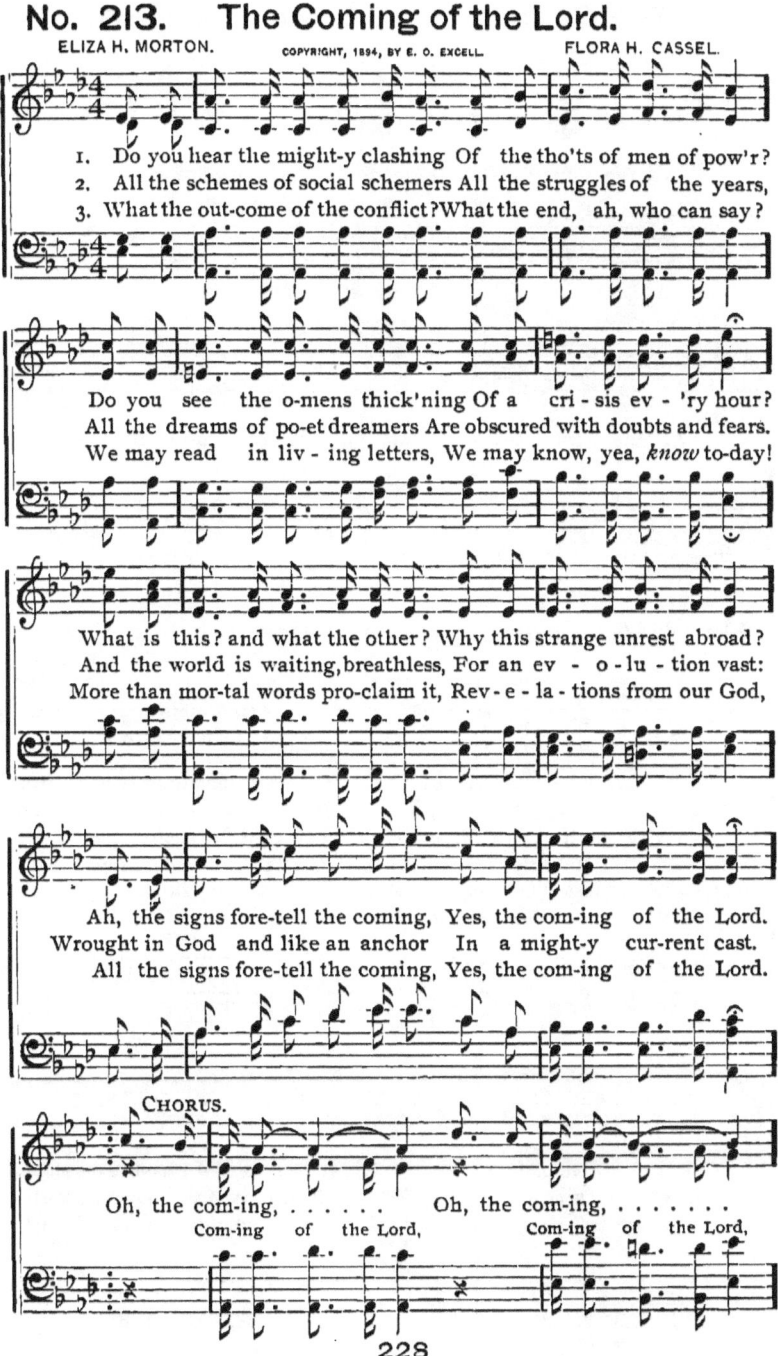

## The Coming of the Lord. Concluded.

*All the signs fore-tell the coming, Yes, the coming of the Lord,*

*All the signs foretell the com-ing, Yes, the com-ing of the Lord.*

## No. 214. Jesus, Savior, Pilot Me.

J. E. GOULD.

1. Je-sus, Sav-ior, pi-lot me, O-ver life's tempestuous sea;
D.C. *Chart and com-pass came from Thee; Je-sus, Sav-ior, pi-lot me.*
2. As a moth-er stills her child, Thou canst hush the ocean wild;
D.C. *Wondrous Sovereign of the sea, Je-sus, Sav-ior, pi-lot me.*
3. When at last I near the shore, And the fear-ful breakers roar,
D.C. *May I hear Thee say to me, "Fear not, I will pi-lot thee!"*

Unknown waves be-fore me roll, Hid-ing rocks and treacherous shoal;
Boisterous waves o-bey Thy will When Thou say'st to them, "Be still!"
'Twixt me and the peaceful rest, Then, while lean-ing on Thy breast,

## No. 215.  A Burden Bearer.

EBEN E. REXFORD.  COPYRIGHT, 1894, BY E. O. EXCELL.  FRANK M. DAVIS.

1. One of Christ's bur-den bear-ers, I fol-low where He leads,
2. I know His love will guide me A-long this earth-ly vale,
3. One of Christ's bur-den bear-ers, In His I sink my will,

Con-tent to trust Him whol-ly Who know-eth all my needs;
For nev-er one who trust-ed Has known a prom-ise fail;
And when His cross seems heav-y, Christ is my com-fort still;

The way may seem most drear-y, And lead thro' des-ert land,
In dark and storm-y weath-er, A-bove the tem-pest wild,
My heart grows strong-er, brav-er, At thought of what He bore,

But God is al-ways near me, My wants to un-der-stand.
I hear Him say-ing soft-ly, "Have faith in me, my child."
Con-tent a bur-den bear-er To be for-ev-er-more.

CHORUS.

One of Christ's bur-den bear-ers, To Him for help I call.

## A Burden Bearer. Concluded.

And know-ing He will an-swer, I trust Him all in all.

### No. 216. Leaning on Thee.

WM. H. GARDNER.   COPYRIGHT, 1894, BY E. O. EXCELL.   EDWIN MOORE.

1. Of - ten do my foot-steps fal - ter, Shad-ows gath-er ov - er me,
2. Hu - man love is of - ten faith-less, Earth-ly rich-es from us flee,
3. When death's val-ley dark I en-ter, Tho' no light there comes to me,

But I find Thee, Lord, be-side me, And I trust-ing, lean on Thee.
Then we find our sweet-est com-fort, Lean-ing, bless-ed Lord, on Thee.
Yet no doubts my soul will tor-ture, Lean-ing there, dear Lord, on Thee.

**REFRAIN.**

Lean - ing, Lord, on Thee, Lean - ing, Lord, on Thee,

When the way the dark-est seem-eth, then, dear Lord, I lean on Thee,

### No. 222. I Always go to Jesus.

JOSEPHINE POLLARD.     COPYRIGHT, 1894, BY E. O. EXCELL.     M. L. McPHAIL.

1. I al-ways go to Je-sus, When troubled or dis-tress'd;
2. When full of dread fore-bod-ings, And flow-ing o'er with tears,
3. When those are cold and faith-less Who once were fond and true,
4. I al-ways go to Je-sus, No mat-ter when or where

I al-ways find a ref-uge When I with Him can rest.
He calms a-way my sor-rows, And hush-es all my fears.
With care-less hearts for-sak-ing The old friends for the new.
I seek His gra-cious presence, I'm sure to find Him there.

I tell Him all my tri-als, I tell Him all my grief;
He com-pre-hends my weak-ness, The per-il I am in,
I turn to Him whose friendship Knows neither change nor end;
In times of joy or sor-row, What-e'er my need may be,

And while my lips are speak-ing He gives my heart re-lief.
And He sup-plies the ar-mor I need to con-quer sin.
I al-ways find in Je-sus, An ev-er faith-ful friend.
I al-ways go to Je-sus, And Je-sus com-forts me.

## No. 223. Abundantly Able to Save.

USED BY ARR. WITH THE BIGLOW & MAIN CO., OWNERS OF COPYRIGHT.

Rev. E. A. HOFFMAN. P. P. BLISS.

1. Who-ev-er re-ceiv-eth the Cru-ci-fied One, Who-ev-er be-liev-eth on God's on-ly Son, A free and a per-fect sal-vation shall have, For He is a-bun-dant-ly a-ble to save.
2. Who-ev-er re-ceiv-eth the mes-sage of God, And trusts in the pow'r of the soul-cleansing blood, A full and e-ter-nal re-demption shall have, For He is both a-ble and willing to save.
3. Who-ev-er re-pents and for-sakes ev-'ry sin, And o-pens his heart for the Lord to come in, A pres-ent and per-fect sal-vation shall have, For Je-sus is read-y this moment to save.

CHORUS.

My brother, the Mas-ter is calling for thee; .. His grace and His mer-cy are wondrously free; .. His blood as a ran-som for
Brother, the Mas-ter is come and is call-ing for thee; Brother, His grace and His mercy are wondrously free, Brother, His blood as a

## Abundantly Able to Save. Concluded.

sinners He gave, . . And He is a-bun - dant-ly a-ble to save.
ran-som for sinners He gave, And He is a-bundantly a-ble to save.

## No. 224. Steal Away to Jesus.

FROM THE GOSPEL IN SONG, BY PER.

E. O. EXCELL.

1. Re - turn, O wan-d'rer, to thy home, Thy Fa-ther calls for thee;
2. Re - turn, O wan-d'rer, to thy home, 'Tis Je - sus calls for thee;
3. Re - turn, O wan-d'rer, to thy home, 'Tis madness to de - lay;

No long-er now an ex - ile roam In guilt and mis-er - y.
The Spir-it and the Bride say, Come, O now for ref-uge flee.
There are no par-dons in the tomb, And brief is mer-cy's day.

CHORUS. *pp*

Steal a - way, steal a - way, Steal a - way to Je - sus;

*rit.*

Steal a - way, steal a-way home, For Je - sus waits to save you.

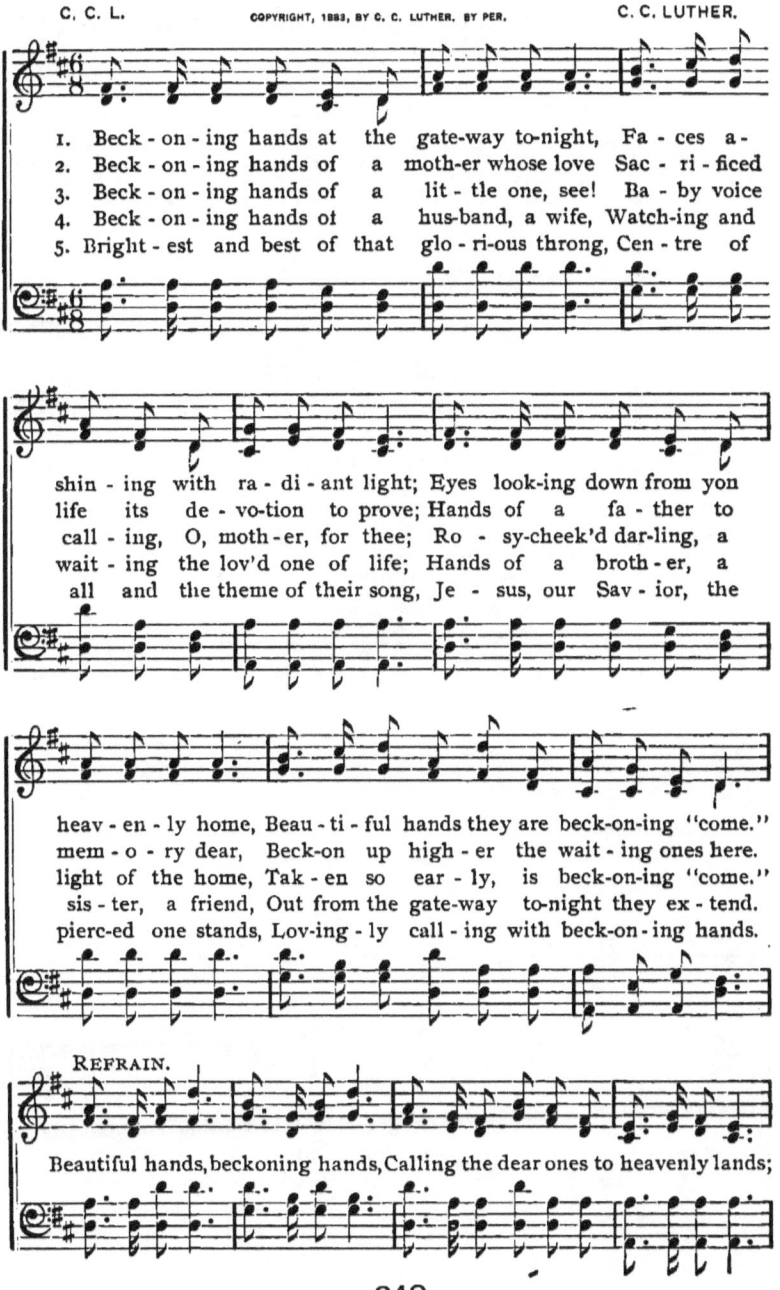

## Beautiful, Beckoning Hands. Concluded.

Beautiful hands, beckoning hands, Beautiful, beautiful, beckoning hands.

## No. 226. How They Sing in Glory.

HARRIET E. JONES.   COPYRIGHT, 1894, BY E. O. EXCELL.   FRANK M. DAVIS.

1. { When the burden'd heart relents, How they sing in glo - ry,
     { When the soul un-done re-pents, How they sing (*Omit.*) } in glo-ry;
2. { When they seek for Him who died, How they sing in glo - ry,
     { Come to Christ, the Cru-ci-fied, How they sing (*Omit.*) } in glo-ry;
3. { Would you help to swell the strain In the realms of glo - ry,
     { Come with all your woe and stain, To the King (*Omit.*) } of glo-ry;

When is heard the wea - ry sigh And the pen - i - ten - tial cry,
All the hosts of heav'n re-joice Prais - ing God with harp and voice,
Come, my broth - er, come to - day, Come to Je - sus while you may,

"Save me Je - sus, or I die," How they sing in glo - ry.
When He proves the sin - ners' choice, Christ, the King of glo - ry.
He will wash your sins a - way, Lead you home to glo - ry.

## Go Forward, Christian Soldiers. Concluded.

**CHORUS.**

Go for-ward Christian soldiers! Be-neath His banner true; ....
Go for-ward Chris-tian, Christian sol-diers, Be-neath His ban-ner, His ban-ner true;

The Lord Himself thy Lead-er, Shall all ... thy foes subdue.
The Lord Him-self, thy Lead-er, thy Leader, Shall all thy foes, thy foes sub-due.

### No. 228.   Just as I Am.

CHARLOTTE ELLIOT.                                      WM. BRADBURY.

1. Just as I am! with-out one plea, But that Thy blood was shed for me,
2. Just as I am! and wait-ing not To rid my-self of one dark blot,
3. Just as I am! tho' toss'd about, With many a conflict, many a doubt,

And that Thou bidd'st me come to Thee, O Lamb of God! I come! I come!
To Thee, whose blood can cleanse each spot, O Lamb of God! I come! I come!
Fight-ing and fears with-in, with-out, O Lamb of God! I come! I come!

4 Just as I am! poor, wretched, blind,
Sight, riches, healing of the mind,
Yea, all I need in Thee to find,
O Lamb of God! I come! I come!

5 Just as I am! Thou wilt receive,
Wilt welcome, pardon, cleanse, relieve;
Because Thy promise I believe:
O Lamb of God! I come! I come!

## Loyalty to Christ. Concluded.

land, Thro' loy-al-ty, loy-al-ty, Yes, loy-al-ty to Christ.

## No. 230. Jesus Is Passing By.

E. A. H.     COPYRIGHT, 1894, BY E. O. EXCELL.     Rev. E. A. HOFFMAN.

1. This is the sea-son of hope and grace, Je-sus is pass-ing by;
2. This is the hour for the soul's re-lease, Je-sus is pass-ing by;
3. This is the mo-ment to seek the Lord, While He is pass-ing by;
4. Trust in the Lord in this hour of need, While He is pass-ing by;

This, for sal-va-tion the time and place, Je-sus is pass-ing by.
Trust Him and thou shalt go forth in peace, Je-sus is pass-ing by.
This is the time to be-lieve His word, While He is pass-ing by.
And you will find Him a friend in-deed, Je-sus is pass-ing by.

CHORUS.

Je-sus is pass-ing by, Je-sus is pass-ing by;

Bring Him thy heart ere in grief He depart; Je-sus is pass-ing by

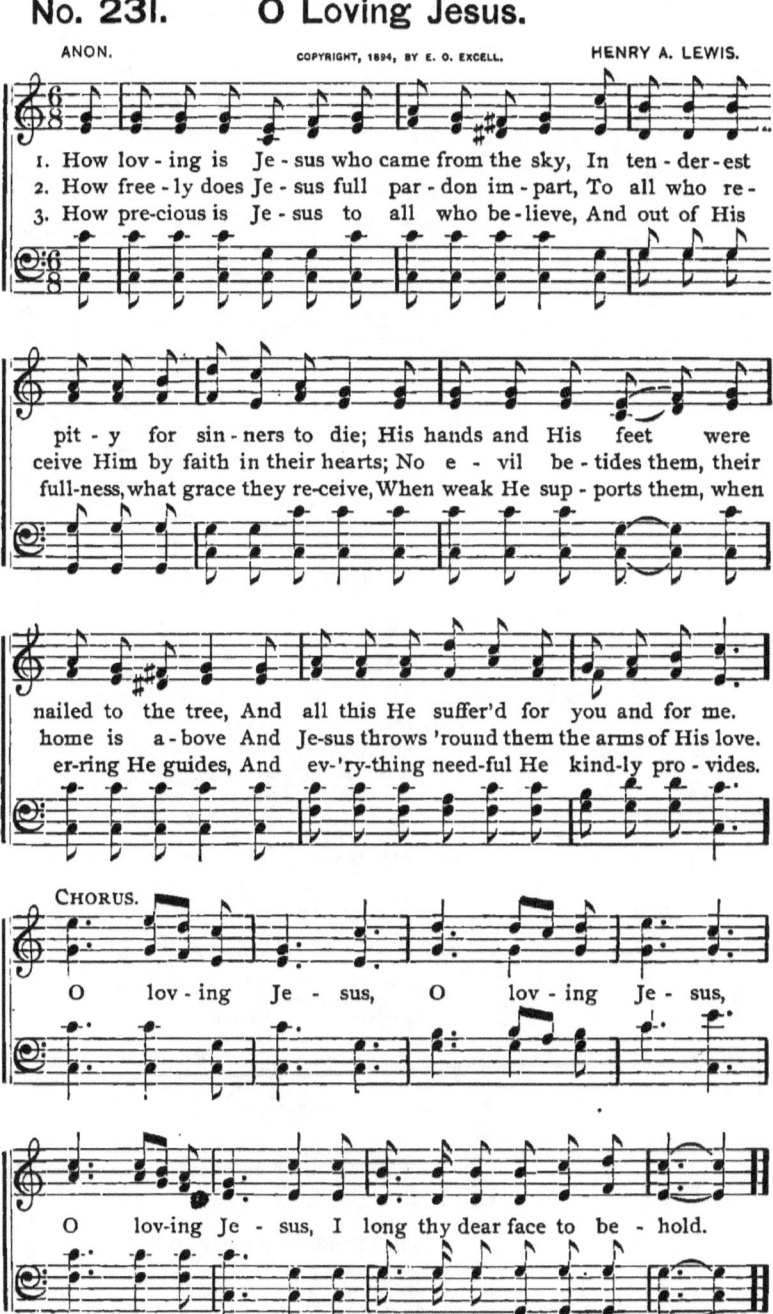

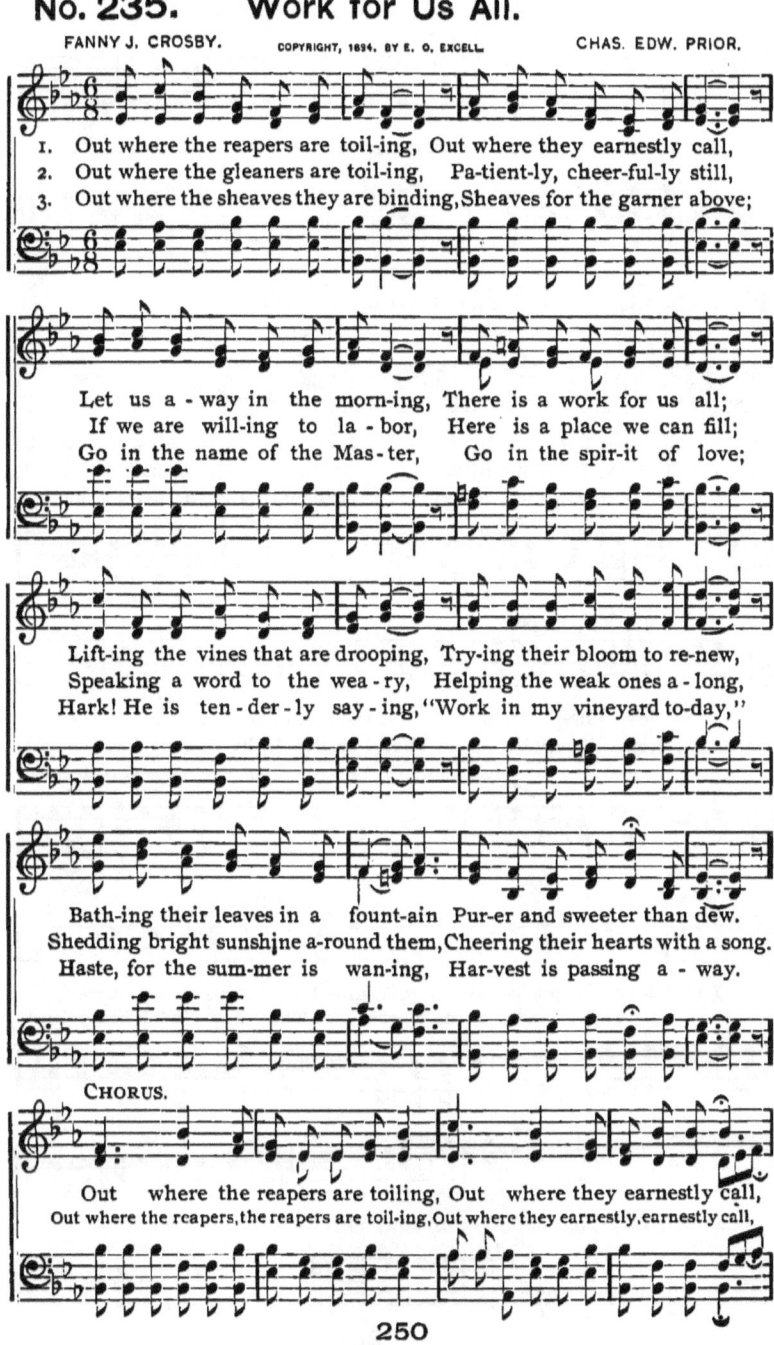

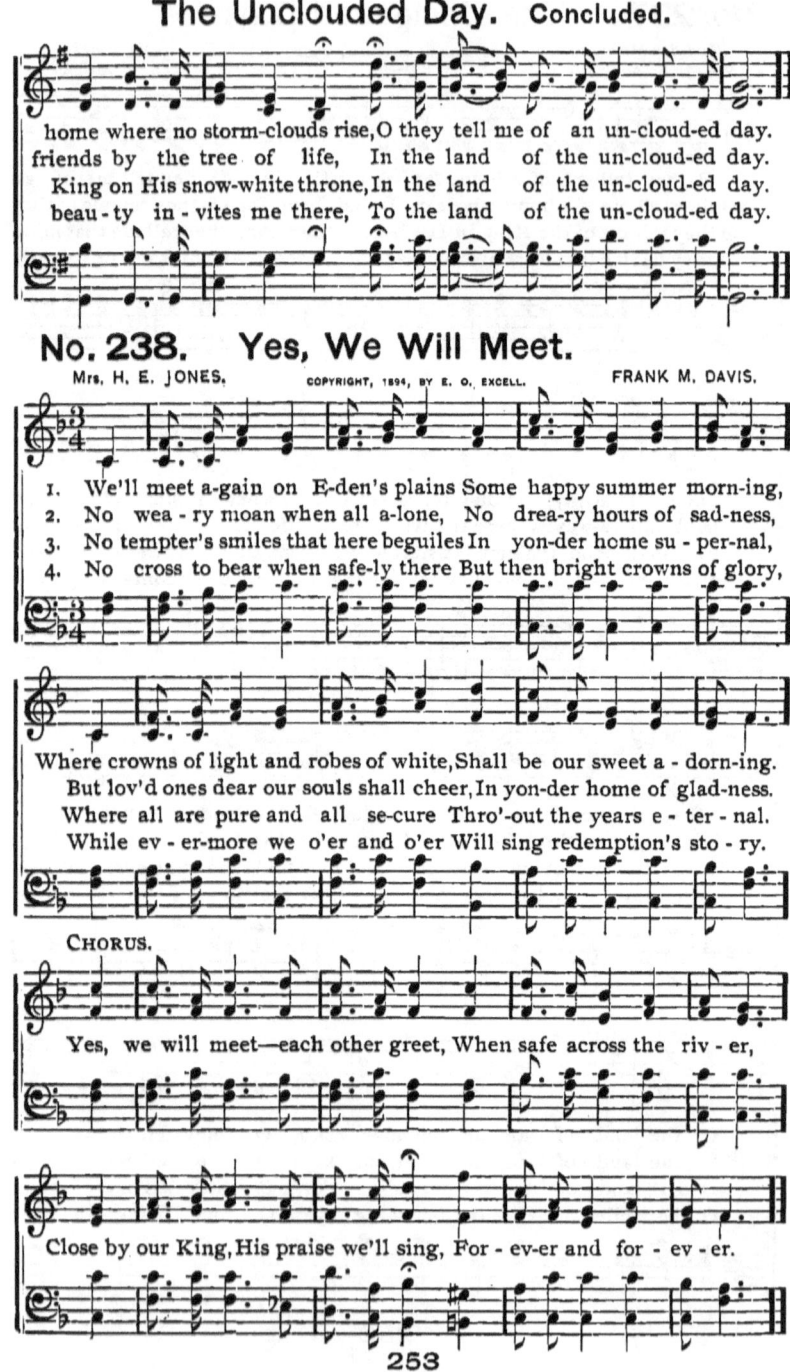

## No. 239. Some Blessed Day.

Rev. C. W. RAY, D. D.  COPYRIGHT, 1893, BY WM. J. KIRKPATRICK, BY PER.  WM. J. KIRKPATRICK.

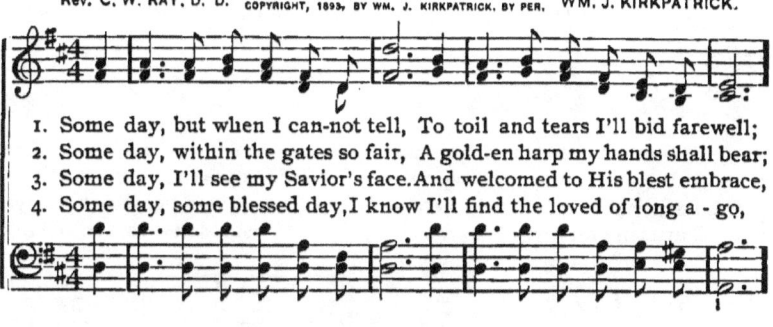

1. Some day, but when I can-not tell, To toil and tears I'll bid farewell;
2. Some day, within the gates so fair, A gold-en harp my hands shall bear;
3. Some day, I'll see my Savior's face. And welcomed to His blest embrace,
4. Some day, some blessed day, I know I'll find the loved of long a-go,

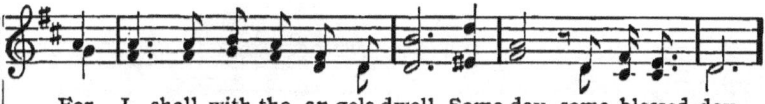

For I shall with the an-gels dwell, Some day, some blessed day.
And glist'ning robes of white I'll wear, Some day, some blessed day.
Shall with His peo-ple find a place, Some day, some blessed day.
And find how much to Christ I owe, Some day, some blessed day.

CHORUS.

Some day,........ Some day,........ I'll be at
Some bless-ed day,   some bless-ed day,

home with Christ to stay, Some day, some bless-ed day.

## No. 240. Coming To-day.

FANNY J. CROSBY.     COPYRIGHT, 1880, BY JNO. J. HOOD, BY PER.     JNO. R. SWENEY.

1. Out on the desert, looking, looking, Sinner, 'tis Je-sus looking for thee;
2. Still He is waiting, waiting, waiting, O, what compassion beams in His eye,
3. Lovingly pleading, pleading, pleading, Mercy, tho' slighted, bears with thee yet;
4. Spirits in glory, watching, watching, Long to behold thee safe in the fold;

Ten-der-ly calling, calling, calling, Hither, thou lost one, O, come unto me.
Hear Him repeating gently, gently, Come to thy Savior, O, why wilt thou die.
Thou canst be happy, happy, happy, Come, ere thy life-star forever shall set.
Angels are waiting, waiting, waiting, When shall thy story with rapture be told?

CHORUS.

Je-sus is looking, Jesus is calling, Why dost thou linger, why tarry away?

Run to Him quickly, say to Him gladly, Lord, I am coming, coming to-day.

## The Penitent's Plea. Concluded.

is my ev-'ry debt to pay, Blood to wash my ev-'ry sin a-way,
ev - 'ry debt to pay, Blood to wash my ev - 'ry sin a-way,

Power to keep me sin-less day by day, For me, for me!
Power to keep me sin - less day by day,

4. All the rivers of Thy grace I claim,
Over every promise write my name:
As I am I come believing,
As Thou art Thou dost, receiving,
Bid me rise a freed and pardoned slave;
Master o'er my sin, the world, the grave,
Charging me to preach Thy pow'r to save
To sin-bound souls.

## No. 242. From All that Dwell.

ISAAC WATTS.     DUKE STREET. L. M.     JOHN HATTON.

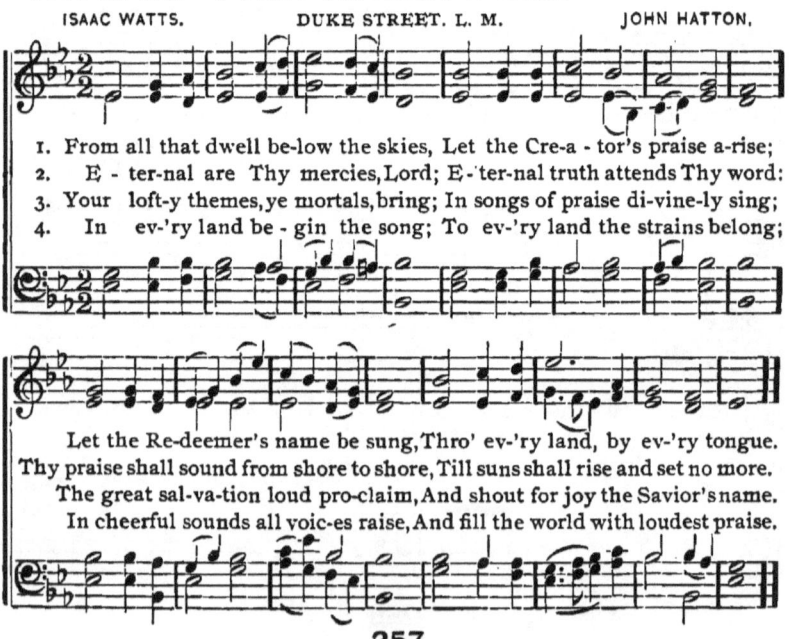

1. From all that dwell be-low the skies, Let the Cre-a - tor's praise a-rise;
2. E - ter-nal are Thy mercies, Lord; E - ter-nal truth attends Thy word:
3. Your loft-y themes, ye mortals, bring; In songs of praise di-vine-ly sing;
4. In ev-'ry land be - gin the song; To ev-'ry land the strains belong;

Let the Re-deemer's name be sung, Thro' ev-'ry land, by ev-'ry tongue.
Thy praise shall sound from shore to shore, Till suns shall rise and set no more.
The great sal-va-tion loud pro-claim, And shout for joy the Savior's name.
In cheerful sounds all voic-es raise, And fill the world with loudest praise.

## Call Them In! Concluded.

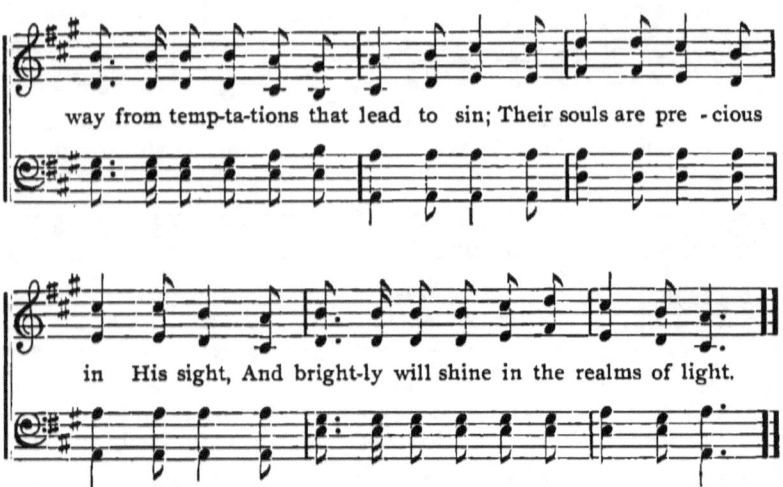

way from temp-ta-tions that lead to sin; Their souls are pre-cious
in His sight, And bright-ly will shine in the realms of light.

### No. 244. Where He Leads Me.

E. W. BLANDLY.     BY PERMISSION.     ARRANGED.

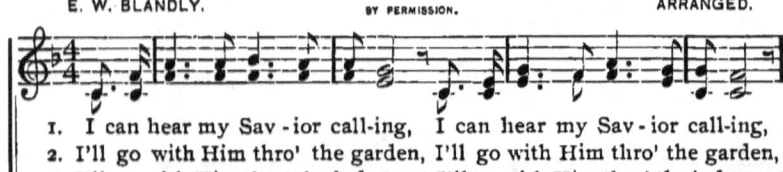

1. I can hear my Sav-ior call-ing, I can hear my Sav-ior call-ing,
2. I'll go with Him thro' the garden, I'll go with Him thro' the garden,
3. I'll go with Him thro' the judgment, I'll go with Him thro' the judgment
4. He will give me grace and glo-ry, He will give me grace and glo-ry,

CHO. *Where He leads me I will fol-low, Where He leads me I will fol-low,*

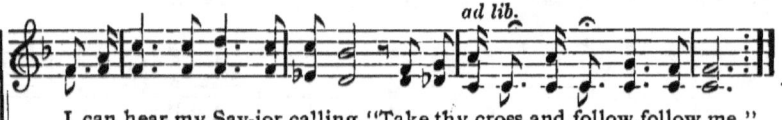

I can hear my Sav-ior calling, "Take thy cross, and follow, follow me."
I'll go with Him thro' the garden, I'll go with Him, with Him all the way.
I'll go with Him thro' the judgment, I'll go with Him, with Him all the way.
He will give me grace and glo-ry, And go with me, with me all the way.

*Where He leads me I will fol-low, I'll go with Him, with Him all the way.*

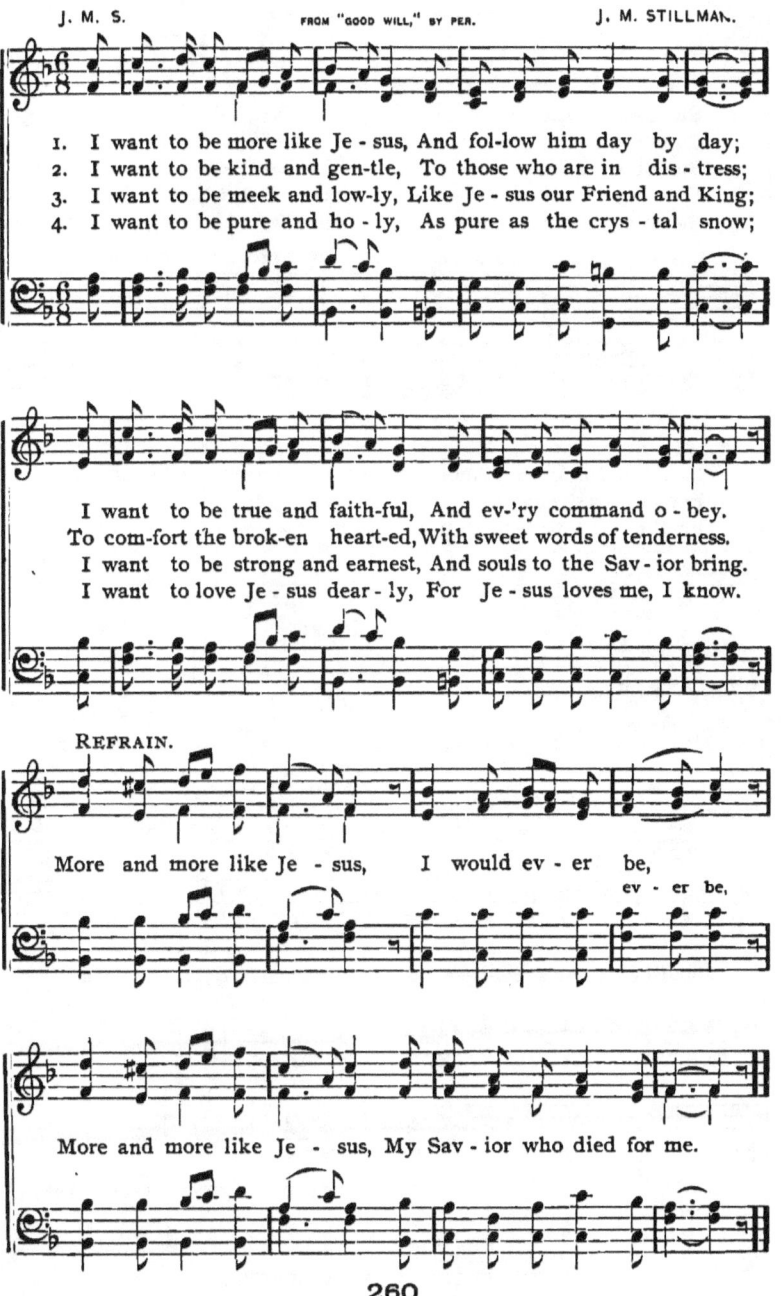

## No. 252. The Very Same Jesus.

L. H. EDMUNDS.  COPYRIGHT, 1891, BY WM. J. KIRKPATRICK. BY PER.  WM. J. KIRKPATRICK.

1. Come, sinners, to the Living One, He's just the same Jesus
2. Come, feast upon the "living bread," He's just the same Jesus
3. Come, tell him all your griefs and fears, He's just the same Jesus
4. Come, unto him for clearer light, He's just the same Jesus

As when he raised the widow's son, The very same Jesus.
As when the multitudes he fed, The very same Jesus.
As when he shed those loving tears, The very same Jesus.
As when he gave the blind their sight, The very same Jesus.

CHORUS.

The very same Jesus, The wonder working Jesus;

Oh, praise his name, he's just the same, The very same Jesus.

5. Calm 'midst the waves of trouble be,
He's just the same Jesus
As when he hush'd the raging sea,
The very same Jesus.

6. Some day our raptured eyes shall see
He's just the same Jesus;
Oh, blessed day for you and me!
The very same Jesus.

## Go Spread the Light. Concluded.

Go spread the light, ...... Go spread the light.
Go spread the light, ...... Go spread the light.

5. Go spread the light that man may see
   In Christ his immortality,
   And be in Him forever free;
   Go spread the light, Go spread the light.

6. Go spread the light on pinions fleet,
   Until this world and heaven meet
   In love and fellowship complete;
   Go spread the light, Go spread the light.

## No. 254. I Come to Thee.

ANNA MARLIM.  COPYRIGHT, 1897, BY E. O. EXCELL.  E. O. EXCELL.

1. { Thou art my strength and shield, My ref-uge and my grace;
     When earth-ly help-ers flee, Thou art my hid-ing place. }

2. { A home for wea-ry souls, A rock my trust to stay,
     My Shep-herd and my guide, Who on-ly knows the way. }

3. { My sins how man-i-fold, Yet, Thou canst cleanse them all;
     Oh, lead me to Thy home, And keep me lest I fall. }

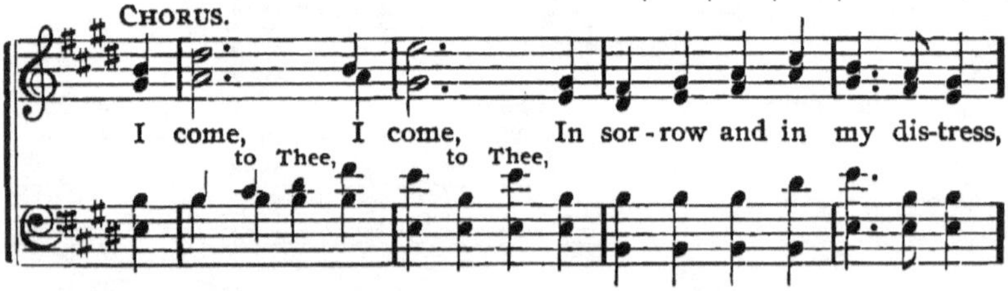

CHORUS.

I come, I come, In sor-row and in my dis-tress,
to Thee, to Thee,
I come, I come, To Thee for ho-li-ness.
to Thee, to Thee,

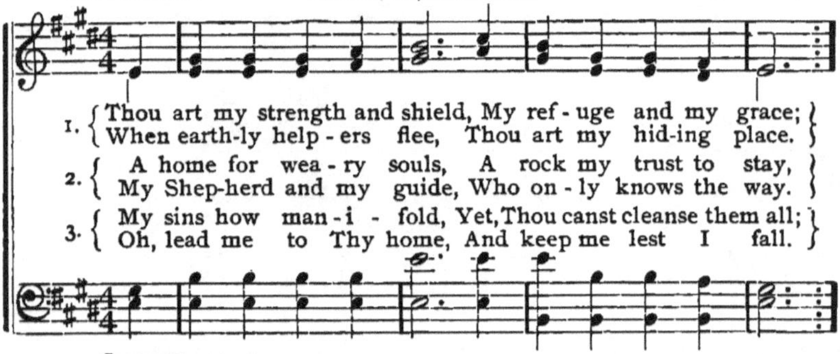

## Where is Your Trust? Concluded.

on-ly believe, And His pardon receive, You are safe for-ev-er-more.
pleasures will end, But, with Jesus your friend, You are safe for-ev-er-more.
tempest may beat, In this blessed retreat, You are safe for-ev-er-more.

## No. 256. Here Am I.

T, M. T.  COPYRIGHT, 1894, BY E. O. EXCELL.  T. MARTIN TOWNE.

1. Like Sam-u-el of old we wait; Thy still, small voice to hear,
2. As days and weeks and months roll by, And strong temptations come;
3. For-bid that we should be a-shamed When e'er Thy voice we hear,
4. And when the call of death shall come, And come it sure-ly will;

Once more at-tune our trembling hearts; O Ho-ly One, draw near.
Lord, may we nev-er miss Thy voice And in-to dark-ness roam.
To an-swer as did Sam-u-el, With-out a thought of fear.
May we be found in faith and love, These words re-peat-ing still.

CHORUS.

Here am I, here am I, Speak, for Thy ser-vant hear-eth;

Here am I, here am I, Speak, for Thy ser-vant hear-eth.

## Raise Me, Jesus, to Thy Bosom. Concluded.

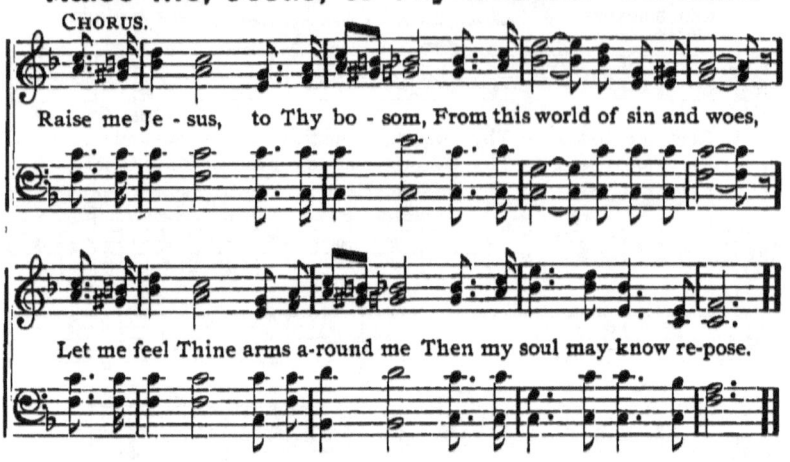

## No. 258. Hark! Ten Thousand.

THOMAS KELLY.     HARWELL. 8s & 7s.     LOWELL MASON.

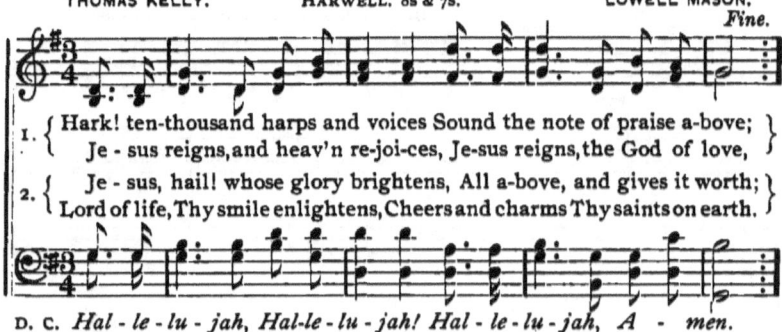

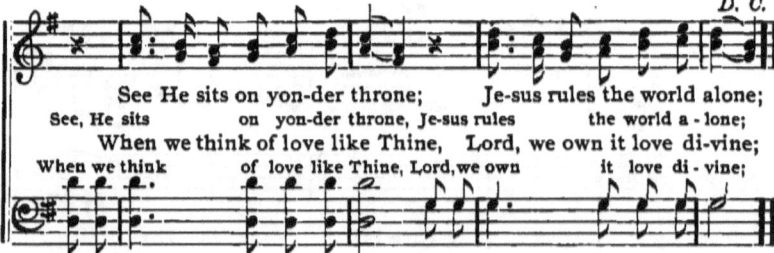

3 King of glory, reign forever;
   Thine an everlasting crown;
Nothing from Thy love shall sever
   Those whom Thou hast made Thine
Happy objects of Thy grace,
   Destined to behold Thy face.

4 Savior, hasten Thine appearing;
   Bring, oh, bring the glorious day,
When, the awful summons hearing,
   Heaven and earth shall pass away;
Then with golden harps we'll sing,
   "Glory, glory to our King."

## I Have Often Heard the Story. Concluded.

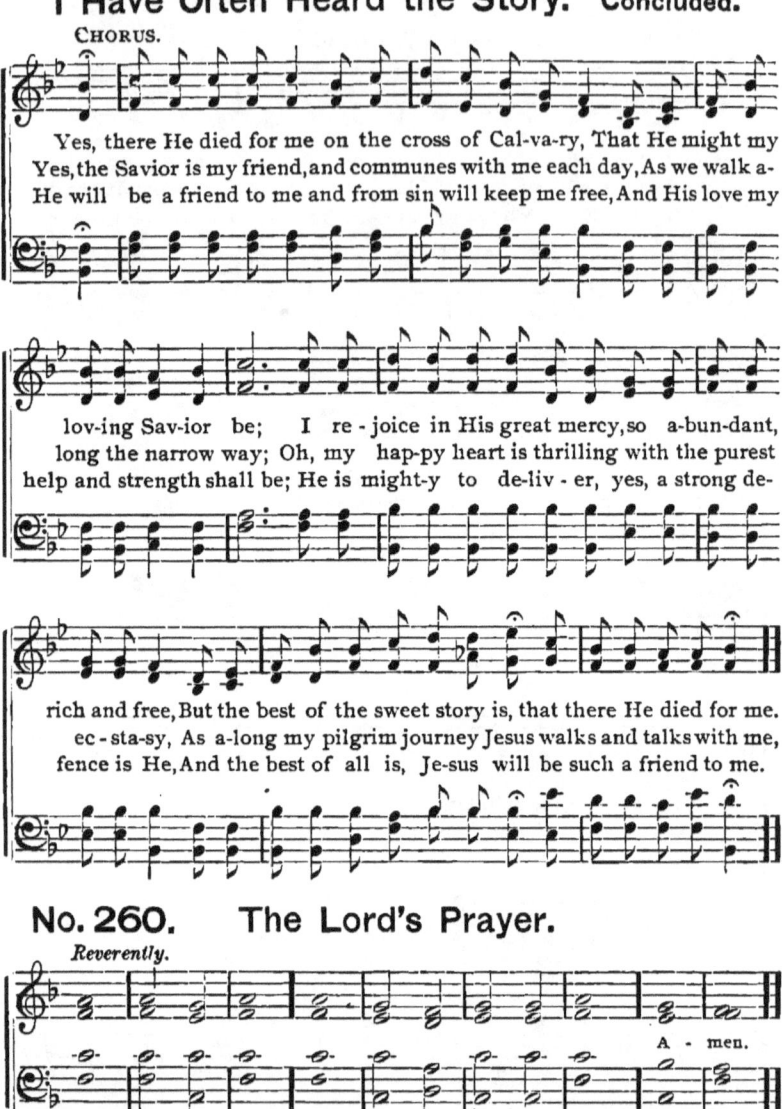

CHORUS.

Yes, there He died for me on the cross of Cal-va-ry, That He might my
Yes, the Savior is my friend, and communes with me each day, As we walk a-
He will be a friend to me and from sin will keep me free, And His love my

lov-ing Sav-ior be; I re-joice in His great mercy, so a-bun-dant,
long the narrow way; Oh, my hap-py heart is thrilling with the purest
help and strength shall be; He is might-y to de-liv-er, yes, a strong de-

rich and free, But the best of the sweet story is, that there He died for me.
ec-sta-sy, As a-long my pilgrim journey Jesus walks and talks with me,
fence is He, And the best of all is, Je-sus will be such a friend to me.

### No. 260. The Lord's Prayer.

*Reverently.*

A - men.

1. Our Father which art in heaven, hallowed | be thy name, ||Thy kingdom come, thy will be done in | earth, as-it | is in | heaven.

2. Give us this day our | daily | bread, || And forgive us our trespasses, as we forgive | them that | trespass a- | gainst us.

3. And lead us not into temptation, but deliver | us from | evil; ||For thine is the kingdom, and the power and the | glory for- | ever and | ever. ||A- | men.

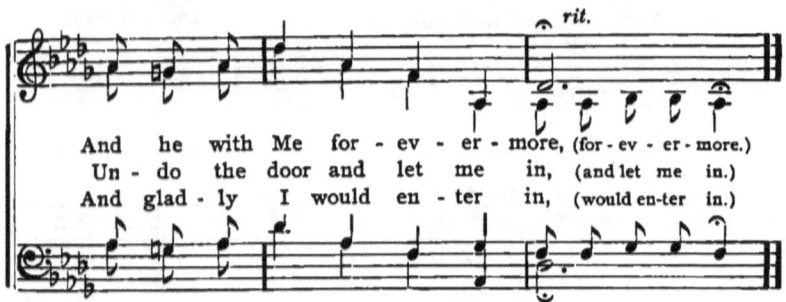# Behold, I Stand at the Door. Concluded.

And he with Me for-ev-er-more, (for-ev-er-more.)
Un-do the door and let me in, (and let me in.)
And glad-ly I would en-ter in, (would en-ter in.)

## No. 262. Glory to His Name.

Rev. E. A. HOFFMAN.    BY PERMISSION.    Rev. J. H. STOCKTON.

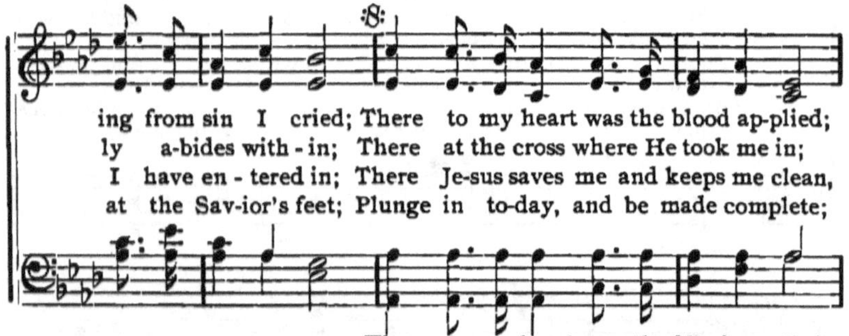

1. Down at the cross where my Sav-ior died, Down where for cleans-ing from sin I cried; There to my heart was the blood ap-plied;
2. I am so won-drous-ly sav'd from sin, Je-sus so sweet-ly a-bides with-in; There at the cross where He took me in;
3. Oh, pre-cious fount-ain, that saves from sin, I am so glad I have en-tered in; There Je-sus saves me and keeps me clean,
4. Come to this fount-ain, so rich and sweet; Cast thy poor soul at the Sav-ior's feet; Plunge in to-day, and be made complete;

D. C. *There to my heart was the blood ap-plied;*

*Fine.* CHORUS.    D. S.

Glo-ry to His name. Glory to His name, Glo-ry to His name,

*Glo-ry to His name!*

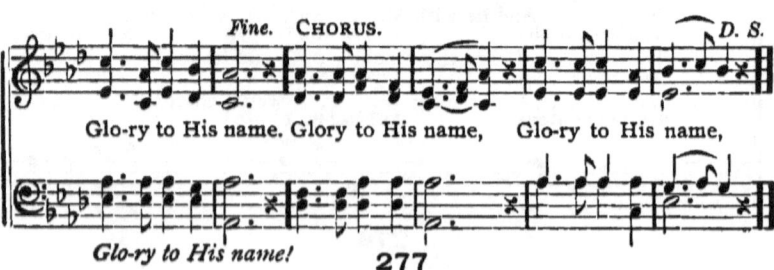

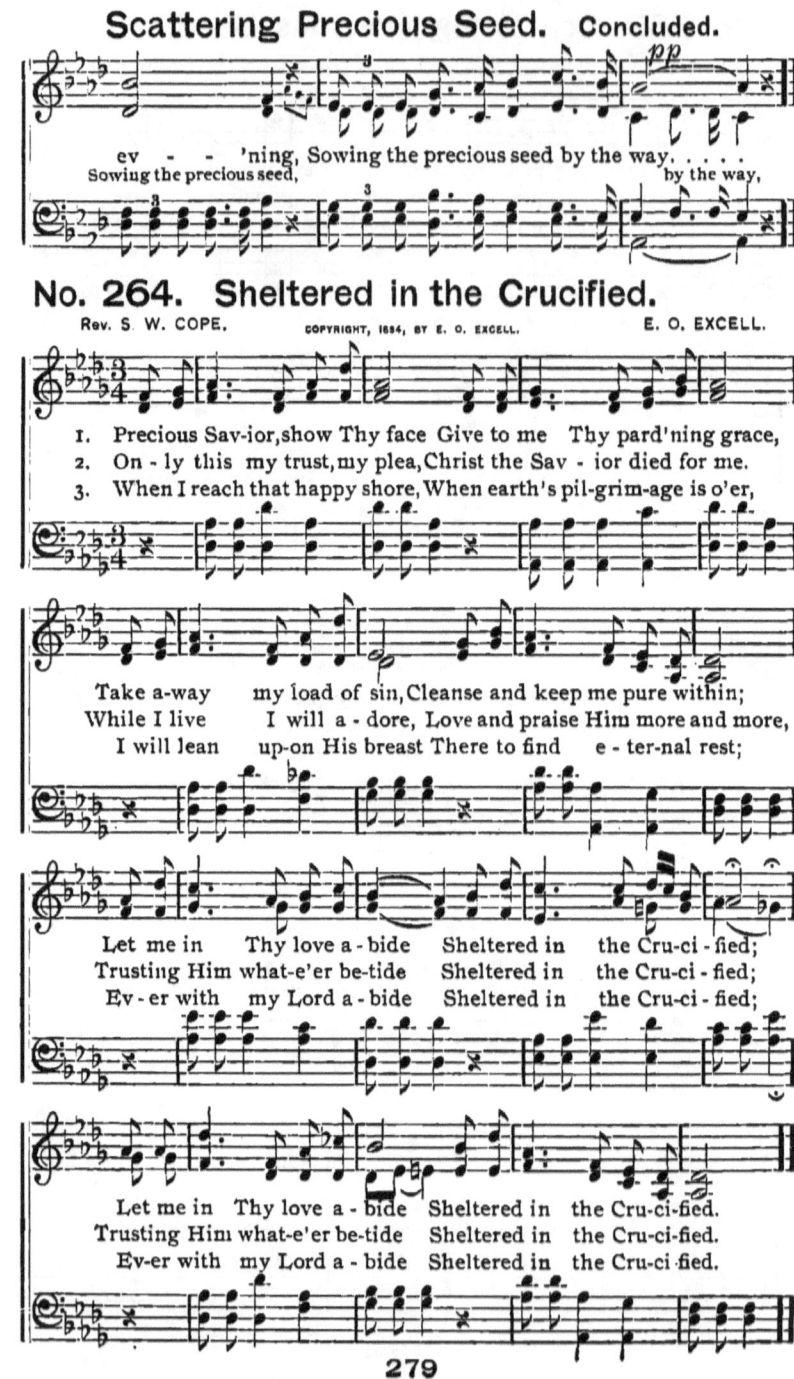

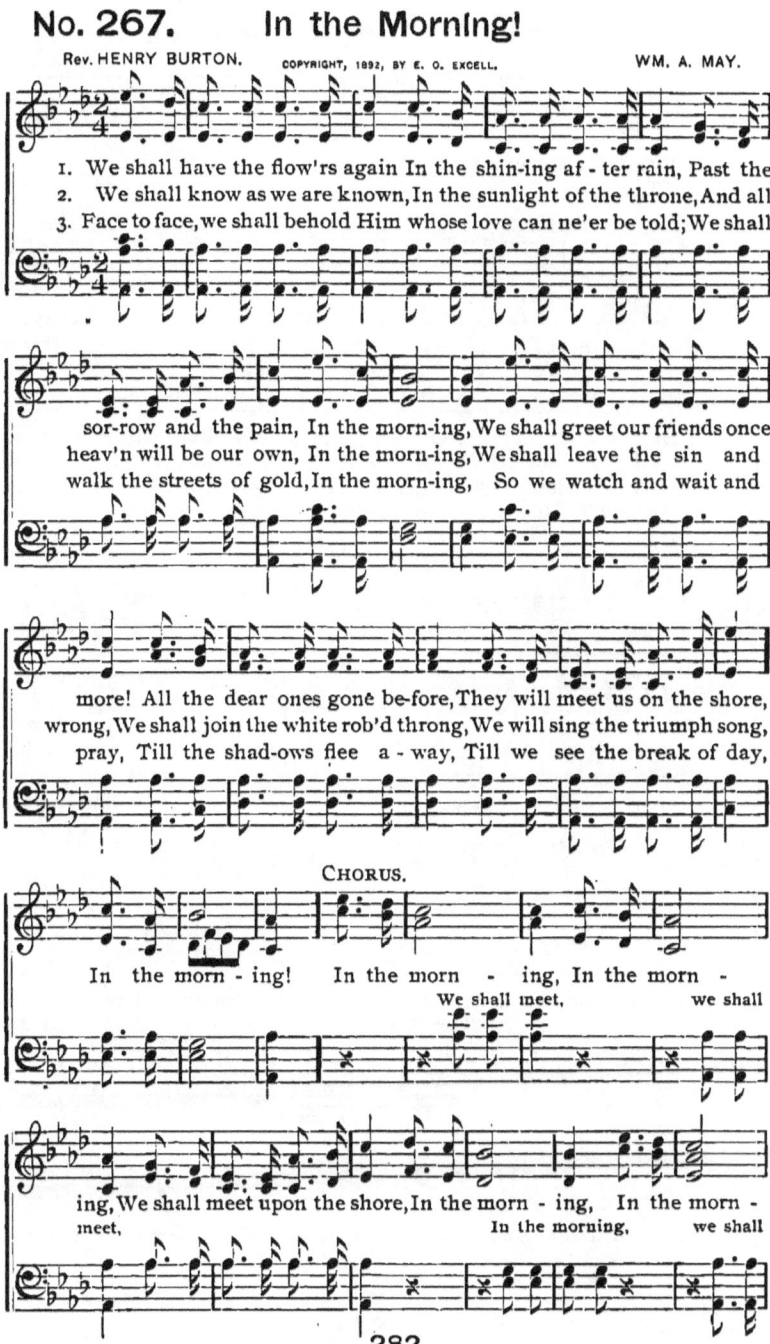

## In the Morning! Concluded.

ing, In the morning! We shall meet upon the golden shore.
meet, the golden shore.

### No. 268. The Temperance Call.
FRANZ ABT.

*Allegro con fuoco.*

1. { Hear the Temp'rance call, Free-men, one and all! Hear your
   { See your na-tive land Lift its beck-'ning hand, (*Omit.*)
2. { Leave the shop and farm, Leave your bright hearths warm; To the
   { Let your lead-ers be True and no-ble, free, (*Omit.*)
3. { Hail! our fa-ther-land! Here thy chil-dren stand, All re-
   { In the Temp'rance cause, Ne'er to faint or pause! (*Omit.*)

coun-try's ear-nest cry! "Sons of free-dom, come ye nigh;
polls! the land to save; Fear-less, temp'rate, good, and brave;
solved, u-nit-ed, true, This our pur-pose is, and vow;

Chase the monster from our shore, Let his cru-el reign be
Chase the monster from our shore, Let his

o'er; Chase the monster from our shore, Let his cruel reign be o'er.
cru-el reign be o'er, from our shore,

## How I Love Jesus. Concluded.

### No. 270. Ever Will I Pray.

A. CUMMINGS.     BY PERMISSION.     J. H. TENNEY.

1. Fa-ther, in the morn-ing Un-to Thee    I pray, Let Thy lov-ing
2. At the busy noon-tide, Press'd with work and care, Then I'll wait with
3. When the evening shadows Chase away    the light, Fa-ther, then I'll
4. Thus in life's glad morning, In its bright noon-day, In the shad-owy

**CHORUS.**

kind-ness Keep me thro'    this day.     I will pray,     I will pray,
Je-sus Till He hear    my pray'r.
pray Thee, Bless Thy child    to-night.
eve-ning, Ev-er will    I pray.     I will pray,     I will pray,

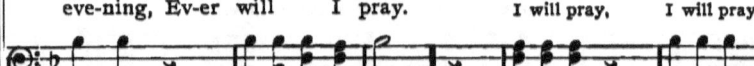

Ev-er will I pray; Morning, noon and evening Unto Thee I'll pray.
Ever will I pray;                                         Unto Thee I'll pray.

# No. 271. "Let Us Alone."

T. P. W.     COPYRIGHT, 1894, BY E. O. EXCELL.     THOS. P. WESTENDORF.

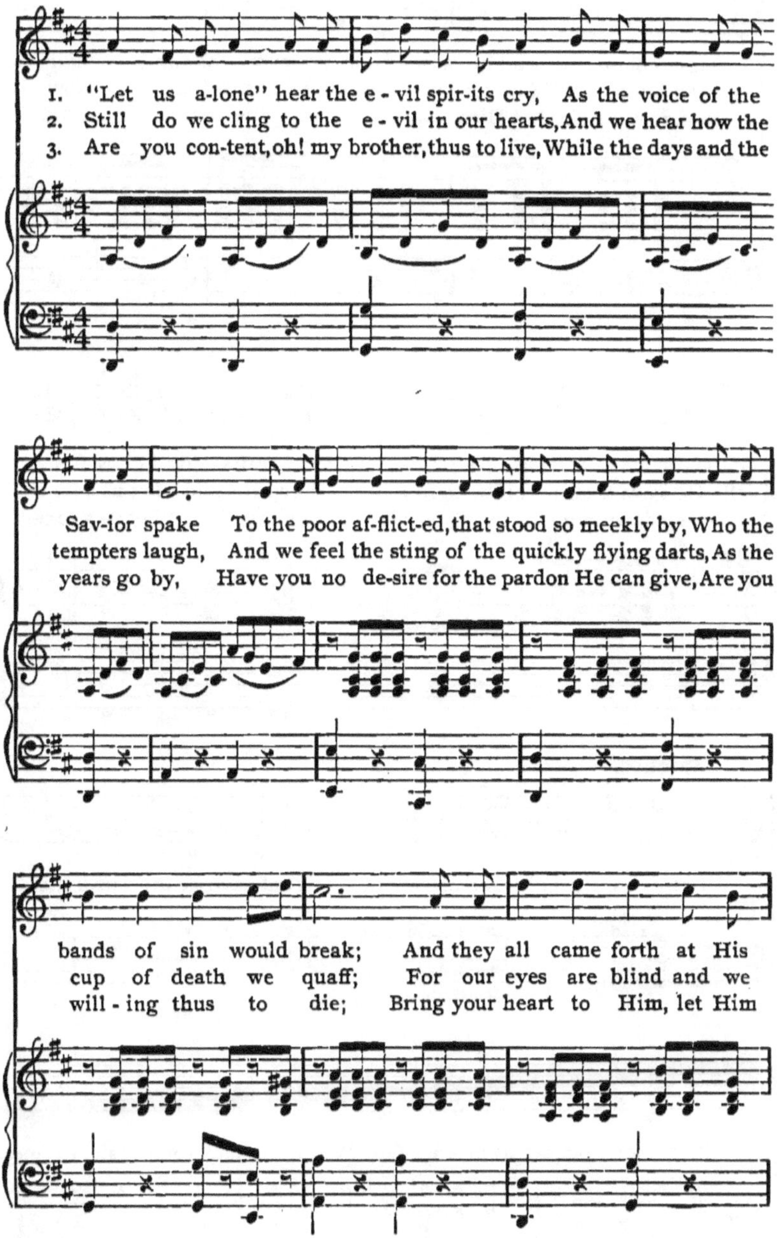

1. "Let us a-lone" hear the e-vil spir-its cry, As the voice of the Sav-ior spake To the poor af-flict-ed, that stood so meekly by, Who the bands of sin would break; And they all came forth at His
2. Still do we cling to the e-vil in our hearts, And we hear how the tempters laugh, And we feel the sting of the quickly flying darts, As the cup of death we quaff; For our eyes are blind and we
3. Are you con-tent, oh! my brother, thus to live, While the days and the years go by, Have you no de-sire for the pardon He can give, Are you will-ing thus to die; Bring your heart to Him, let Him

### No. 272. Rock of Ages.

A. M. TOPLADY.    BY PER. WM. A. POND & CO., OWNERS OF COPYRIGHT.    G. W. WARREN.

Rock of a-ges, cleft for me, Let me hide my-self in thee;
*D. C. While I draw this fleet-ing breath, When mine eye-lids close in death;*

Let the wa-ter and the blood, Let the wa-ter and the blood,
*When I rise to worlds un-known, When I rise to worlds un-known,*

From Thy side, a heal-ing flood, Be of sin the doub-le cure,
*And be-hold Thee on Thy throne, Rock of a-ges, cleft for me,*

Save from wrath and make me pure.
*Let me hide my-self in Thee.*

## An Heir to the Kingdom. Concluded.

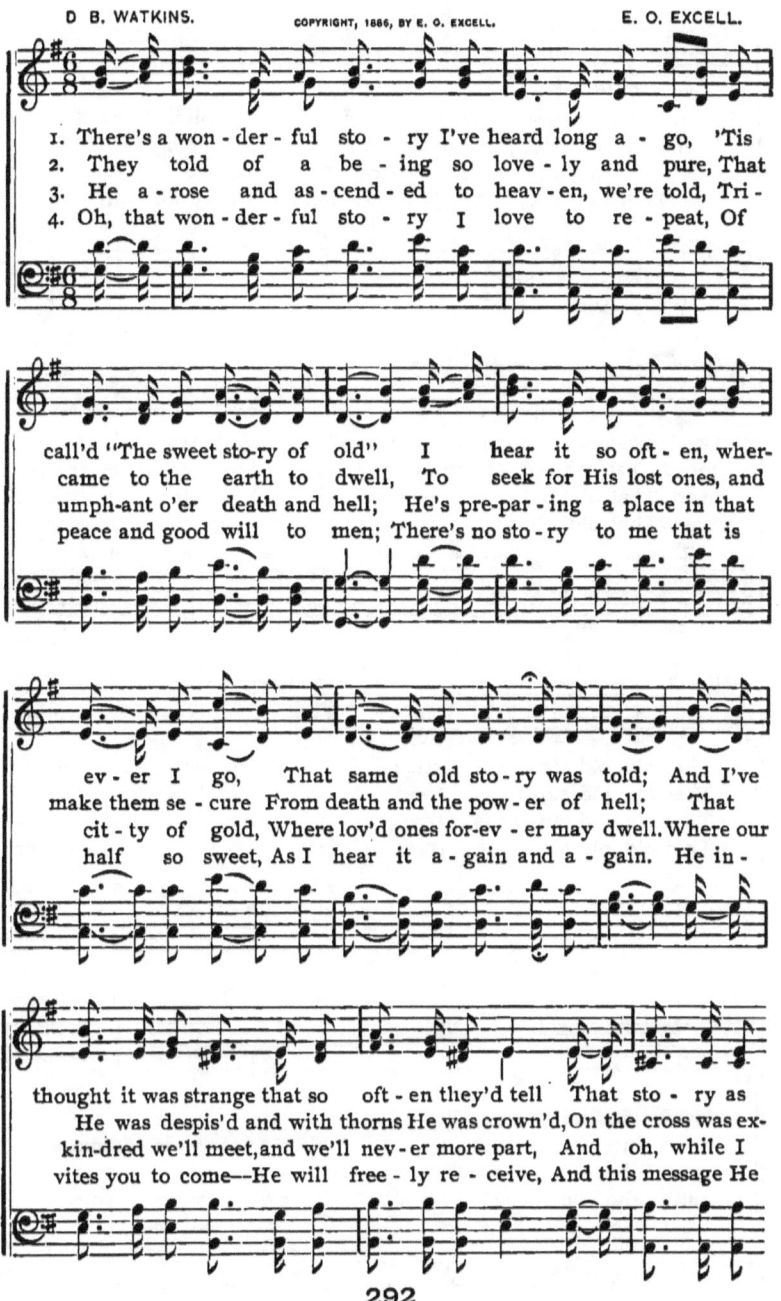

# That Old, Old Story is True. Concluded.

## No. 275. Peace Be Unto You.

Harmonized by T. M. T.  COPYRIGHT, 1894 BY E. O. EXCELL.  Melody and Words by W. E. WATT.

1. When the evening came and the doors were barr'd, They had gather'd there in fear, For the cru-el Jews who had slain their Lord, Might now be lurk-ing near. 'Twas a fear-ful time in Je-
2. There the dear Lord show'd both His hands and side To the friends who loved Him most, Breath'd a mission forth to the world so wide—"Re-ceive ye the Ho-ly Ghost." 'Twas a glo-rious time in Je-
3. There was one a-way from the com-pa-ny When the Lord ap-peared to them, But he said, "Un-less I can feel and see, I will not be-lieve He came." Then the Sav-ior came at the

## The Sinner and the Song. Concluded.

## No. 278. My Father's House.

Rev. G. B. GREIG.     COPYRIGHT, 1894, BY E. O. EXCELL.     J. M. DUNGAN.

Andante.

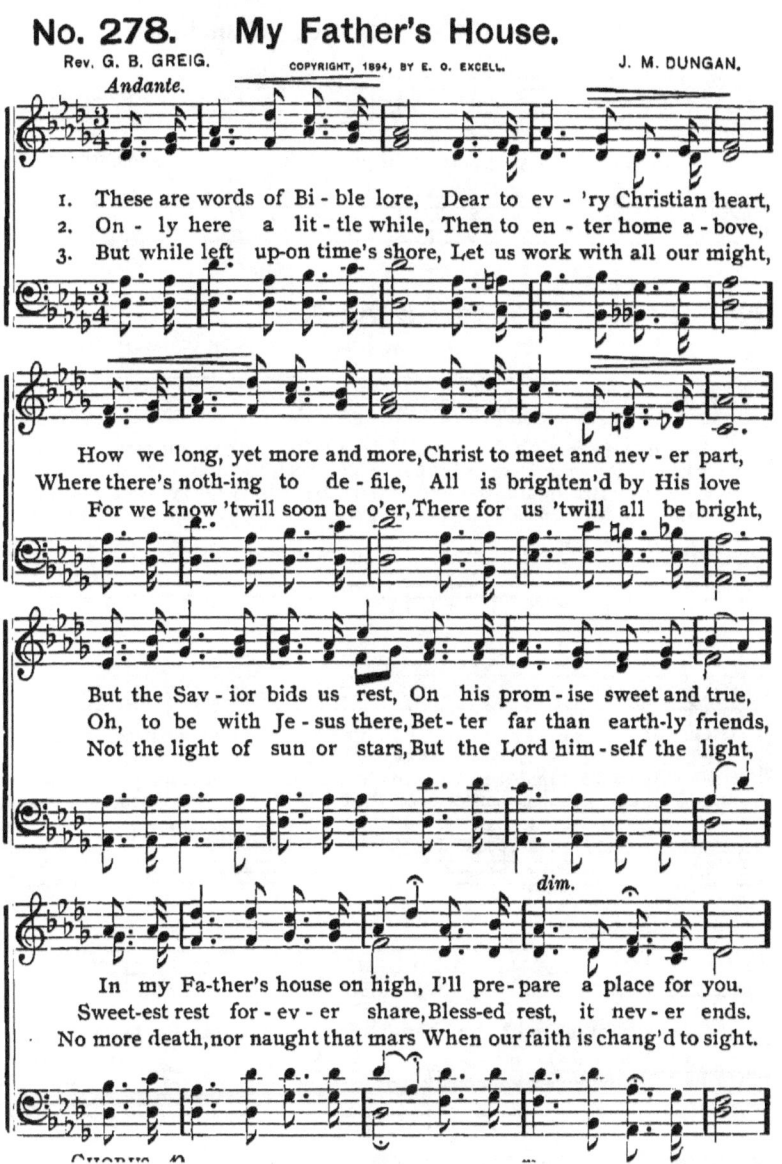

1. These are words of Bi-ble lore, Dear to ev-'ry Christian heart,
2. On-ly here a lit-tle while, Then to en-ter home a-bove,
3. But while left up-on time's shore, Let us work with all our might,

How we long, yet more and more, Christ to meet and nev-er part,
Where there's noth-ing to de-file, All is brighten'd by His love
For we know 'twill soon be o'er, There for us 'twill all be bright,

But the Sav-ior bids us rest, On his prom-ise sweet and true,
Oh, to be with Je-sus there, Bet-ter far than earth-ly friends,
Not the light of sun or stars, But the Lord him-self the light,

In my Fa-ther's house on high, I'll pre-pare a place for you.
Sweet-est rest for-ev-er share, Bless-ed rest, it nev-er ends.
No more death, nor naught that mars When our faith is chang'd to sight.

## No. 282. Blessed Assurance.

F. J. CROSBY.  COPYRIGHT, 1873, BY JOS. F. KNAPP. BY PER.  Mrs. JOS. F. KNAPP.

1. Bless-ed as-sur-ance, Je-sus is mine! Oh, what a fore-taste of glo-ry di-vine! Heir of sal-va-tion, purchase of God, Born of His Spir-it, washed in His blood.
2. Per-fect sub-mis-sion, per-fect de-light, Vis-ions of rap-ture now burst on my sight, An-gels descending, bring from a-bove Ech-oes of mer-cy, whis-pers of love.
3. Per-fect sub-mis-sion, all is at rest, I in my Sav-ior am hap-py and blest, Watching and waiting, look-ing a-bove, Fill'd with His good-ness, lost in His love.

CHORUS.

This is my sto-ry, this is my song, Prais-ing my Sav-ior all the day long; This is my sto-ry, this is my song, Prais-ing my Sav-ior all the day long.

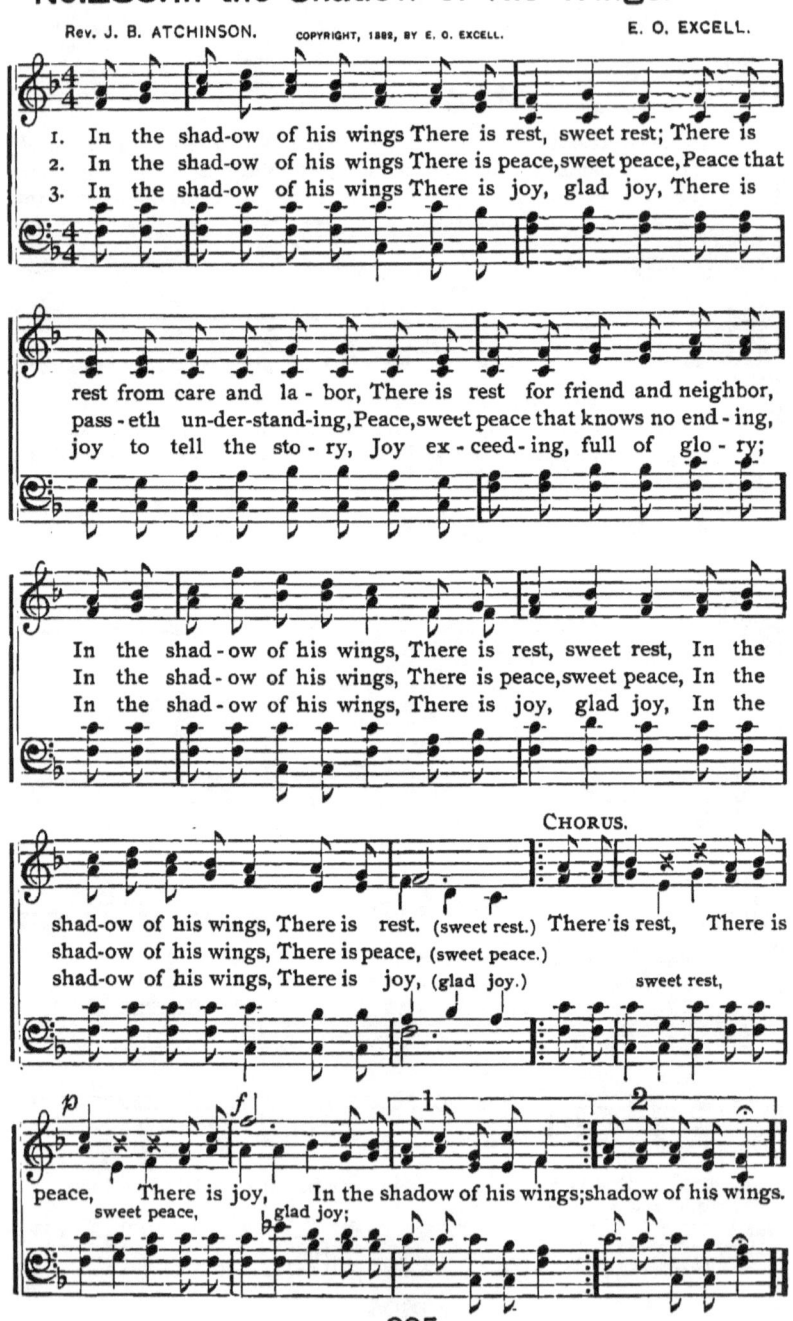

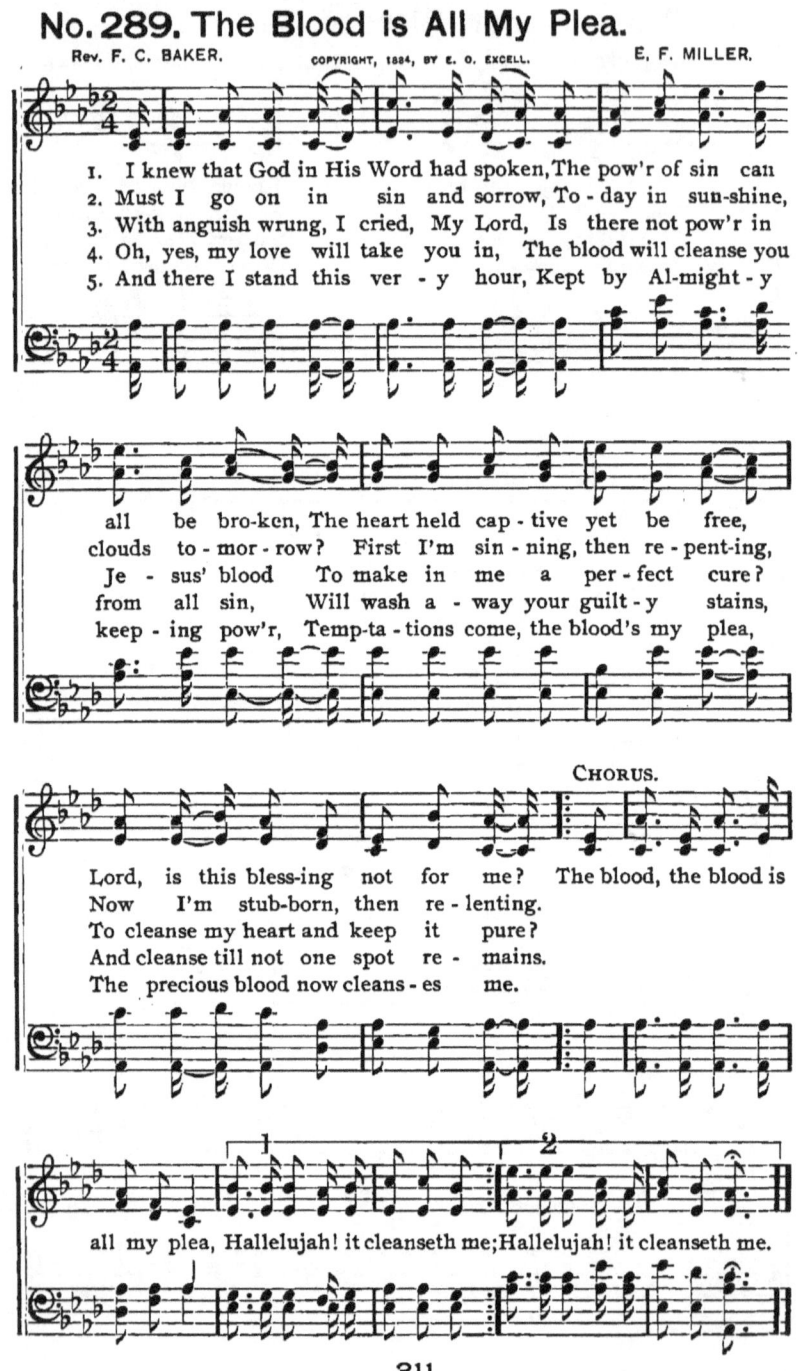

### No. 290. What Will You Do?

E. O. E.  
COPYRIGHT, 1893, BY E. O. EXCELL.  
E. O. EXCELL.

1. What if the watchman should cry a-loud; And proclaim the day of judgment near? What would you do if you heard him say, "You must at the judgment bar ap-pear?" What would you do?
2. What will you do on that dreadful day, As be-fore the Judge you trembling wait? What will you do if the door is shut, And you hear it said "too late, too late?" What will you do?
3. What will you do in that sad, sad hour, When the Judge has said, "de-part" to thee? What will you do as He turns you back, If your soul is lost e-ter-nal-ly? What will you do?

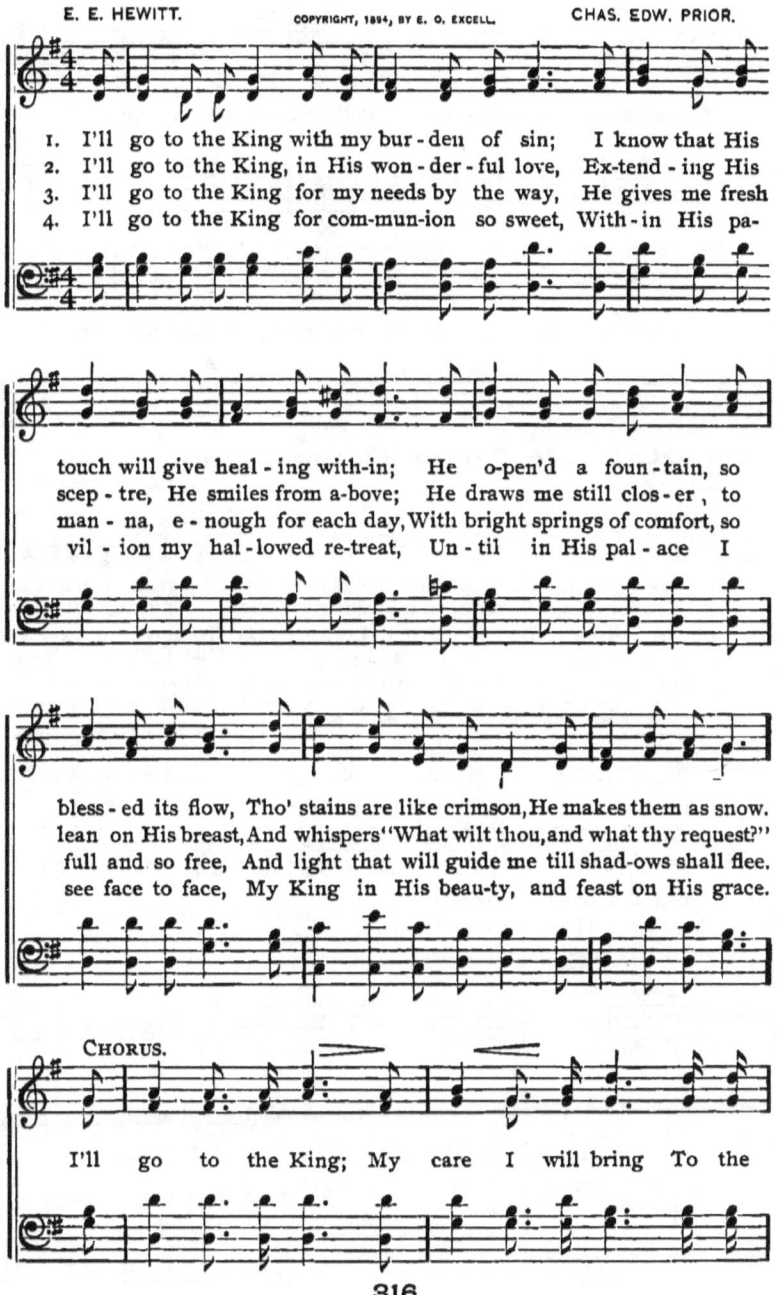

## A Little Talk With Jesus. Concluded.

4. The way is sometimes weary
   To yonder nearing clime,
   But a little talk with Jesus
   Has helped me many a time.
   The more I come to know Him,
   And all His grace explore,
   It sets me ever longing
   To know Him more and more.

## The Vows of God are on You. Concluded.

CHORUS.

The vows of God are on you, Ye are no more your own:
Christ claims Himself to own you, He calls with trumpet tone.

## No. 298. When We Are There.

E. R. LATTA.  COPYRIGHT, 1894, BY E. O. EXCELL.  FRANK M. DAVIS.

1. { There will be a won-drous meet-ing When we are there,
   { There will be a glo-rious greet-ing When we are there.
2. { There will be no earth-ly loss-es When we are there,
   { There will be no heav-y cross-es When we are there.
3. { There will be no tears or cry-ing When we are there,
   { There will be no pains or dy-ing When we are there.

CHORUS.

In the shin-ing man-sions fair, That He promised to pre-pare,
We shall safe-ly dwell for-ev-er, When we are there.

4 There will be no more unkindness,
  When we are there;
  There will be no halt or blindness
  When we are there.

5 There will be no evil near us,
  When we are there;
  But the Lord will keep and cheer us,
  When we are there.

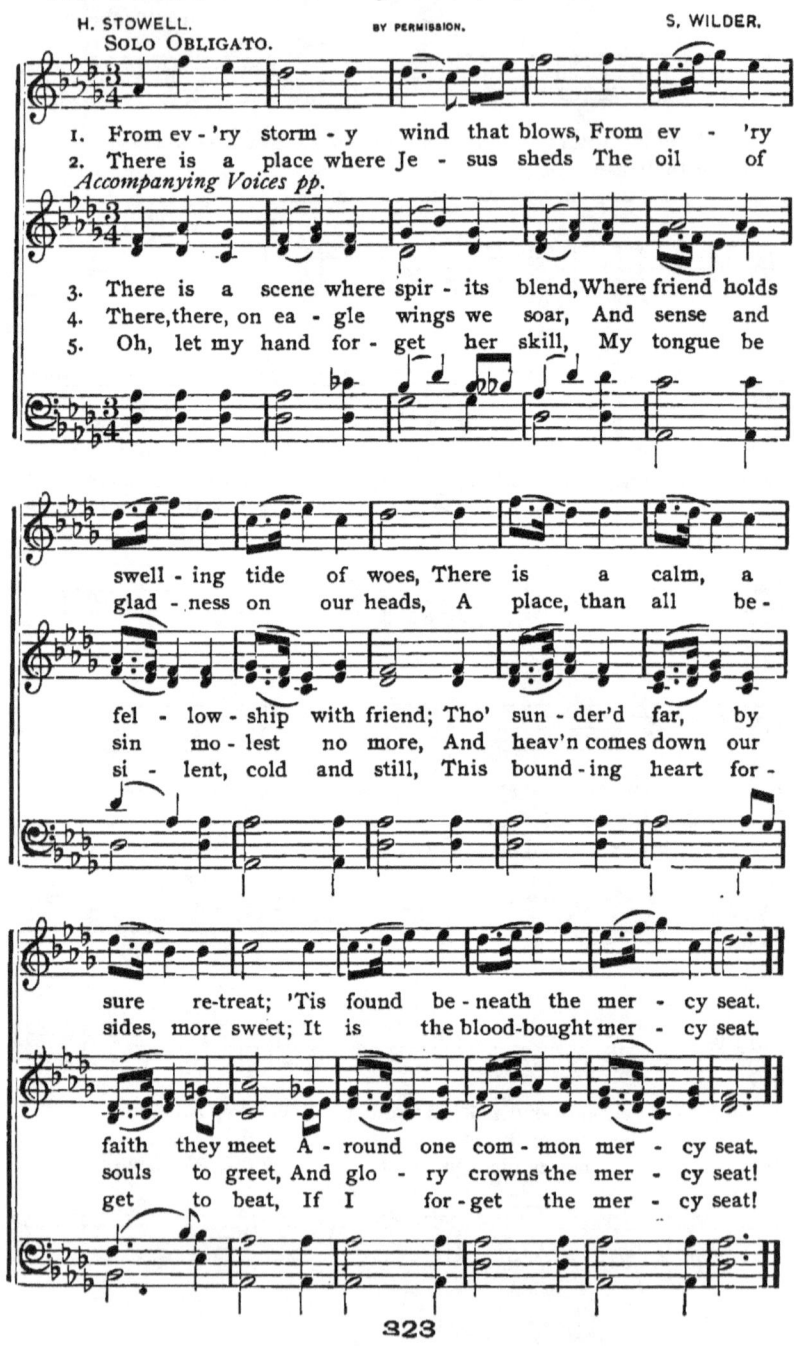

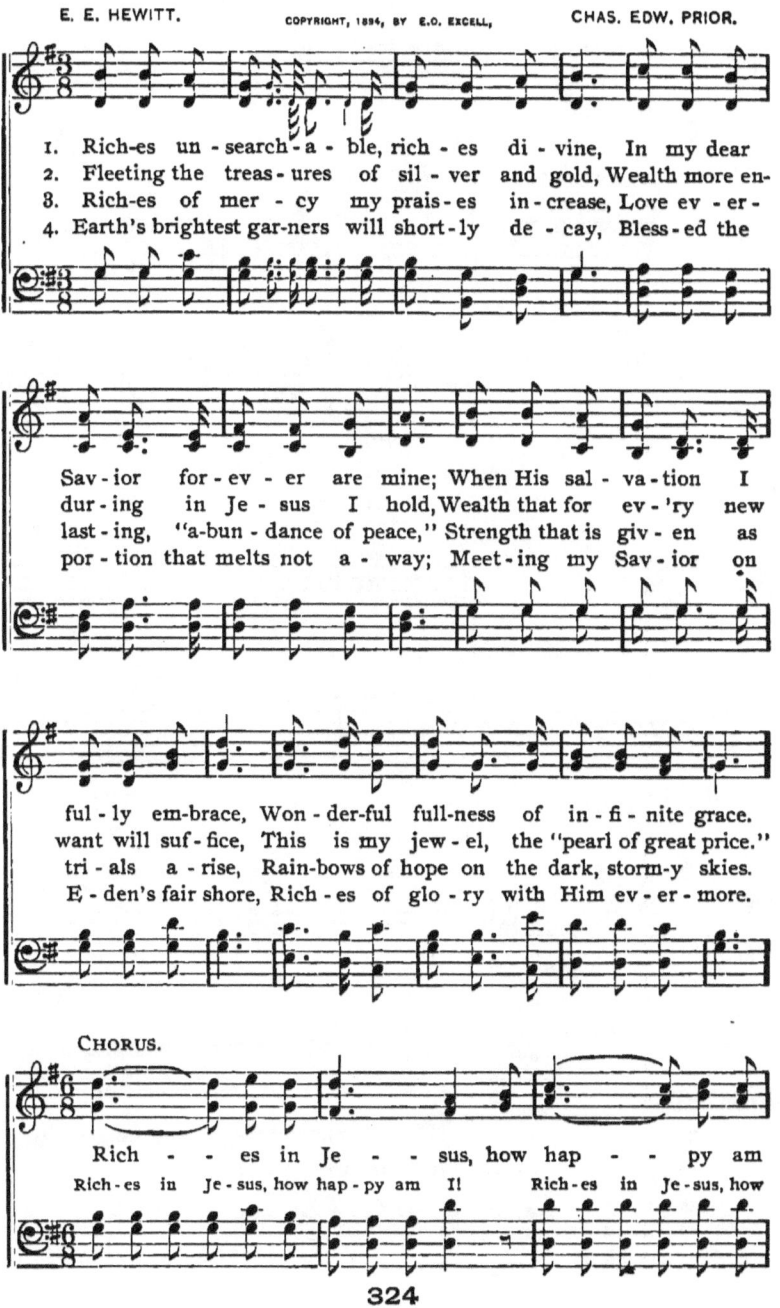

## Riches Unsearchable. Concluded.

# In Heavenly Love Abiding. Concluded.

## No. 304. Good News.

E. E. HEWITT.  COPYRIGHT, 1894, BY E. O. EXCELL.  E. O. EXCELL.

1. Have you heard the good news from the coun-try a-far, Where the
2. Have you heard the good news from the land where they say That no
3. Have you heard the good news? will you tell it a-gain? Will you
4. Have you heard the good news from the Sav-ior we love? Nev-er-

an-gels of God and the glo-ri-fied are? That a mansion of joy is pre-
shadow of night dims its beau-ti-ful day, Not a sor-row shall darken its
speed on the word to the children of men? For the Lord who has gone to pre-
more is it far to that Coun-try a-bove! For our union with Him brings its

pared there for you If your trust is in Je-sus, "the Faithful and True."
por-tals so fair, And no sin dare invade, for the King dwelleth there.
pare you a place, Has a wel-come for all, thro' His won-der-ful grace.
glo-ries so near, That we fan-cy its grand hal-le-lu-jahs we hear.

## No. 308. Over There.

EBEN E. REXFORD.     COPYRIGHT, 1894, BY E. O. EXCELL.     CHAS. EDW. PRIOR.

1. O-ver there what rest is wait-ing, For earth's trials com-pen-sa-ting,
2. O-ver there we shall know Je-sus, In the home from which He sees us
3. O-ver there! no words can capture All the soul's ex-ul-tant rapt-ure,

When we lay our burdens down, When we lay our bur-dens down;
  When we lay our heav-y burdens down,
Journeying heav'nward day by day, Journeying heav'nward day by day;
  Journeying heav'nward, heav'nward day by day,
When we think of go - ing home, When we think of go - ing home,
  When we think of go - ing, go-ing home,

Nev - er a - ny pain or sor-row, O-ver there in God's to-morrow
We shall feel His arms a-round us, In the mighty love that found us
To the rest and to the glo - ry, Told in song and sa-cred sto - ry,

Where we'll find the victor's crown, Where we'll find the victor's crown.
When we wandered from the way, When we wandered from the way.
Nev - er-more from God to roam, Nev-er-more from God to roam.

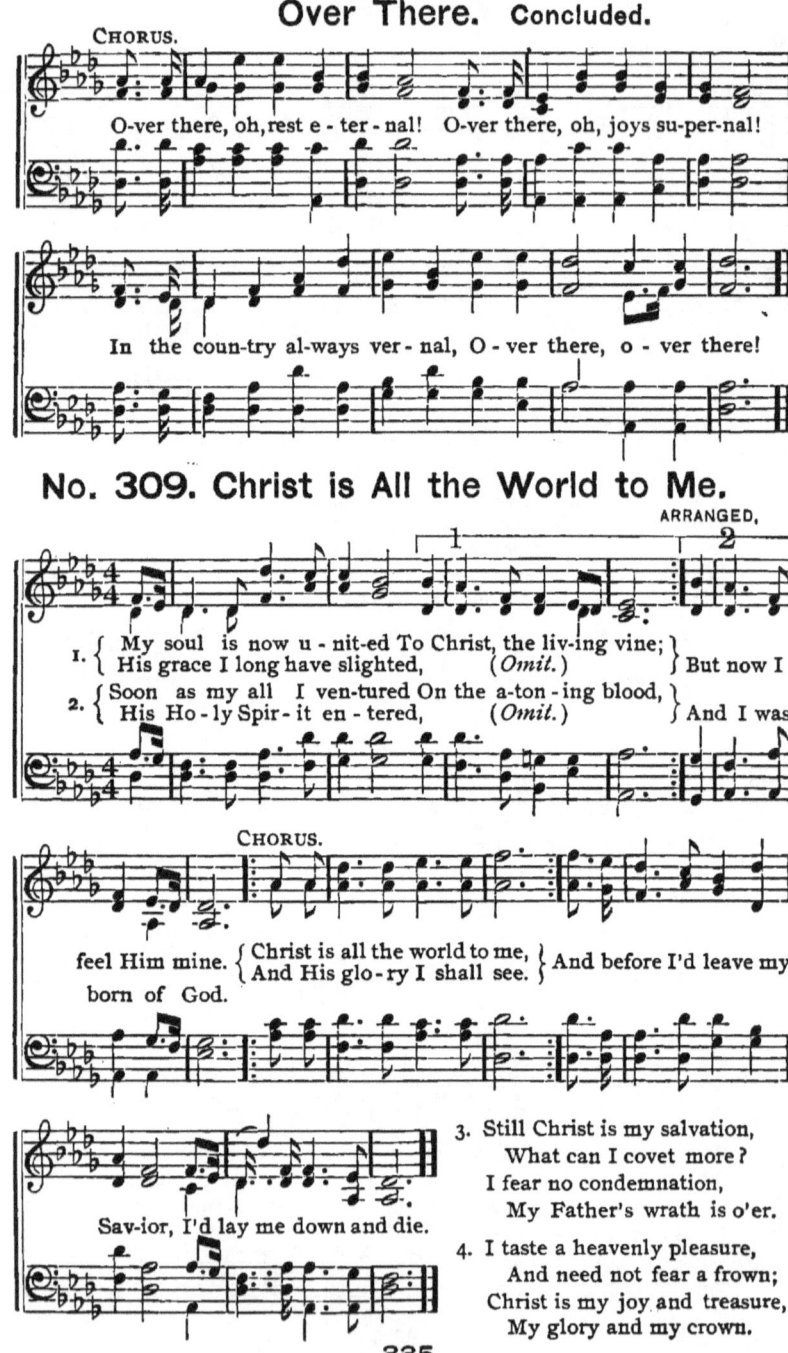

## Over There. Concluded.

O-ver there, oh, rest e-ter-nal! O-ver there, oh, joys su-per-nal! In the coun-try al-ways ver-nal, O-ver there, o-ver there!

## No. 309. Christ is All the World to Me.

ARRANGED.

1. My soul is now u-nit-ed To Christ, the liv-ing vine;
His grace I long have slighted, (*Omit.*) But now I feel Him mine.

2. Soon as my all I ven-tured On the a-ton-ing blood,
His Ho-ly Spir-it en-tered, (*Omit.*) And I was born of God.

CHORUS.
Christ is all the world to me, And His glo-ry I shall see. And before I'd leave my Sav-ior, I'd lay me down and die.

3. Still Christ is my salvation,
What can I covet more?
I fear no condemnation,
My Father's wrath is o'er.

4. I taste a heavenly pleasure,
And need not fear a frown;
Christ is my joy and treasure,
My glory and my crown.

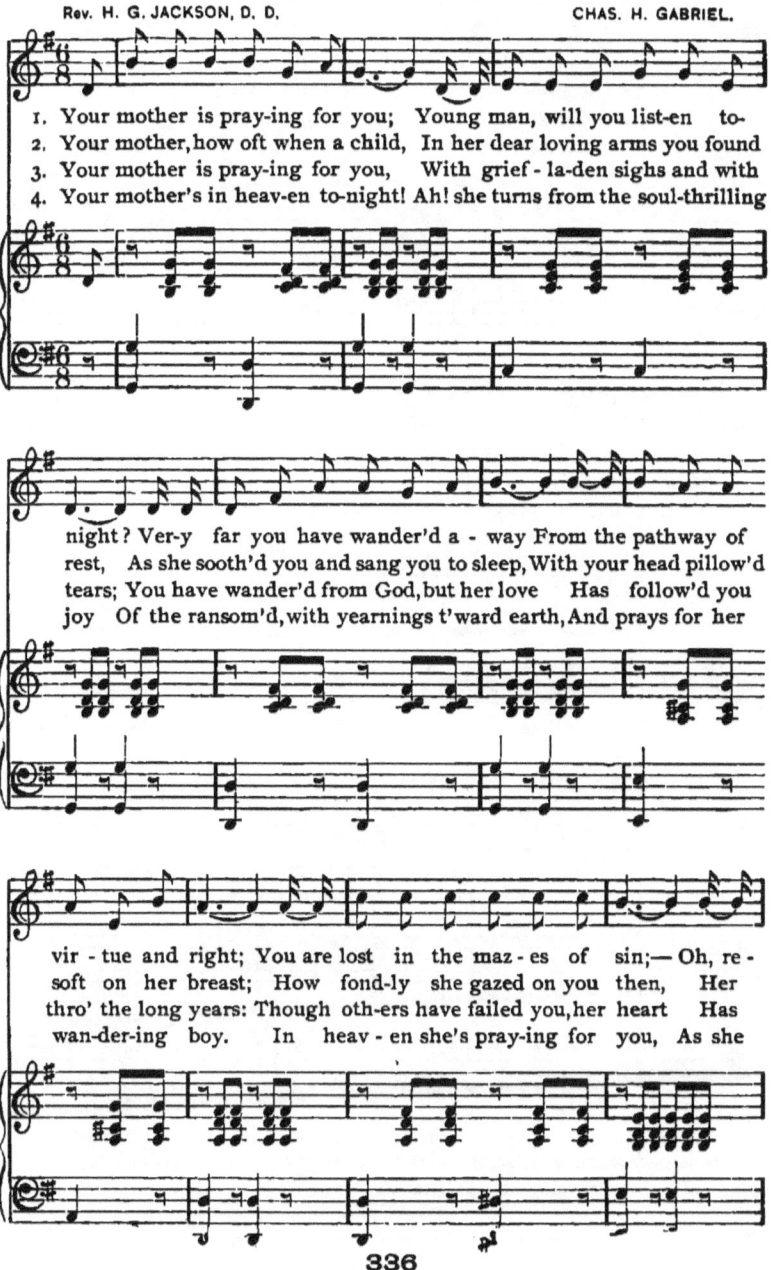

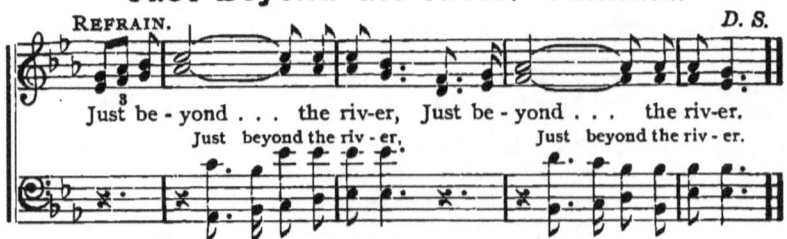

### No. 317. The Wonderful Word.

*To Rev. W. D. Parr, D. D.*

M. E. J.   COPYRIGHT, 1894, BY E. O. EXCELL.   M. EDWIN JOHNSON.

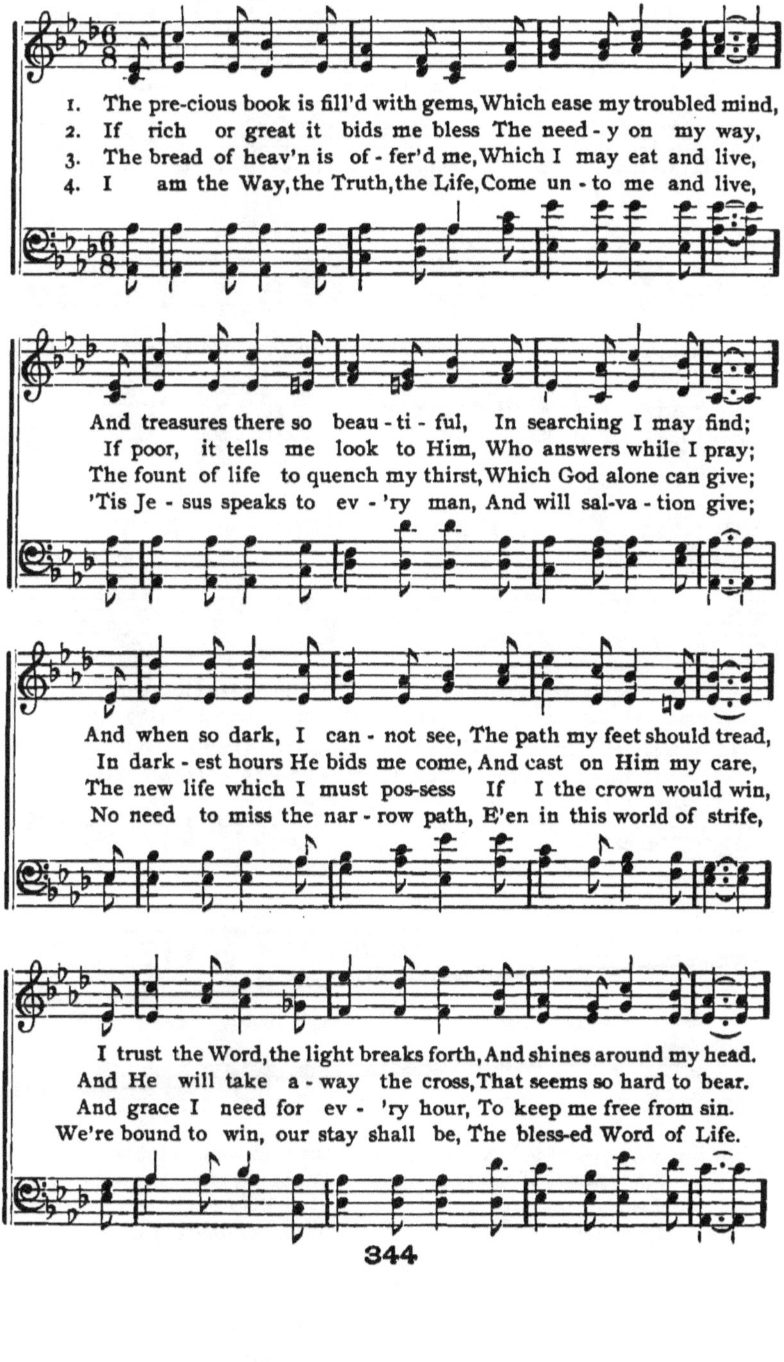

1. The precious book is fill'd with gems, Which ease my troubled mind,
2. If rich or great it bids me bless The needy on my way,
3. The bread of heav'n is offer'd me, Which I may eat and live,
4. I am the Way, the Truth, the Life, Come unto me and live,

And treasures there so beautiful, In searching I may find;
If poor, it tells me look to Him, Who answers while I pray;
The fount of life to quench my thirst, Which God alone can give;
'Tis Jesus speaks to ev'ry man, And will salvation give;

And when so dark, I cannot see, The path my feet should tread,
In darkest hours He bids me come, And cast on Him my care,
The new life which I must possess If I the crown would win,
No need to miss the narrow path, E'en in this world of strife,

I trust the Word, the light breaks forth, And shines around my head.
And He will take away the cross, That seems so hard to bear.
And grace I need for ev'ry hour, To keep me free from sin.
We're bound to win, our stay shall be, The bless-ed Word of Life.

## The Wonderful Word. Concluded.

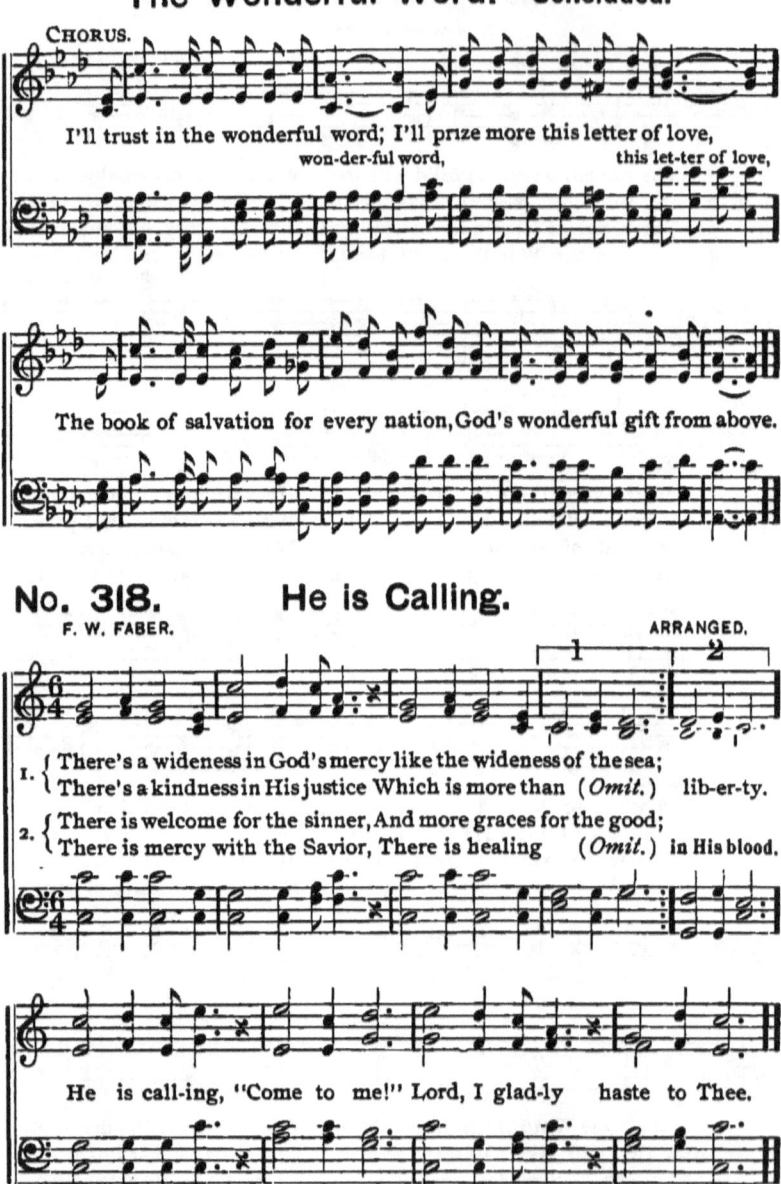

I'll trust in the wonderful word; I'll prize more this letter of love,
won-der-ful word,  this let-ter of love,

The book of salvation for every nation, God's wonderful gift from above.

---

### No. 318.  He is Calling.

F. W. FABER.  ARRANGED.

1. { There's a wideness in God's mercy like the wideness of the sea;
     There's a kindness in His justice Which is more than (*Omit.*) lib-er-ty.
2. { There is welcome for the sinner, And more graces for the good;
     There is mercy with the Savior, There is healing (*Omit.*) in His blood.

He is call-ing, "Come to me!" Lord, I glad-ly haste to Thee.

3 For the love of God is broader
  Than the measure of man's mind;
  And the heart of the Eternal
  Is most wonderfully kind.

4 If our love were but more simple,
  We should take Him at His word;
  And our lives would be all sunshine,
  In the sweetness of our Lord.

## No. 319. Sitting at the Feet of Jesus.

A. A. ARMEN.   COPYRIGHT, 1891, BY THE RUEBUSH-KIEFFER CO. BY PER.   A. A. ARMEN.

1. My heart has found a resting place—Sitting at the feet of Jesus;
2. Here all my doubts and fears depart—Sitting at the feet of Jesus;
3. Here I take coun-sel how to live,— Sitting at the feet of Jesus;
4. Here I am e'er su-preme-ly blest—Sitting at the feet of Jesus;

'Tis where I share the richest grace,—Sitting at the feet of Je - sus.
Here Christ's own blood doth cleanse my heart,—Sitting at the feet of Jesus.
Such wis-dom God a-lone can give,— Sitting at the feet of Je - sus.
When worn and wea-ry I find rest,— Sitting at the feet of Je - sus.

CHORUS.

Oh, hap - py bliss - ful rest! Oh, how my soul is blest!

Of all the world 'tis best; Sit-ting at the feet of Je - sus

5 Here I enjoy communion sweet,—
  Sitting at the feet of Jesus; [greet,
  The Lord comes down my soul to
  Sitting at the feet of Jesus.

6 Here I shall ever safely hide,—
  Sitting at the feet of Jesus;
  For, God, with me, forever abide,—
  Sitting at the feet of Jesus.

## In the Secret of His Presence. Concluded.

## No. 328. I'll Live For Him.

R. E. HUDSON.  COPYRIGHT, 1882, BY R. E. HUDSON. USED BY PER.  C. R. DUNBAR.

1. My life, my love I give to Thee, Thou Lamb of God, who died for me;
2. I now believe Thou dost receive, For Thou hast died that I might live;
3. Oh, Thou, who died on Cal-va-ry To save my soul and make me free,

CHO. I'll live for Him who died for me, How hap-py then my life shall be!

Oh, may I ev-er faith-ful be, My Sav-ior and my God!
And now henceforth I'll trust in Thee, My Sav-ior and my God!
I'll con-se-crate my life to Thee, My Sav-ior and my God!

I'll live for Him who died for me, My Sav-ior and my God!

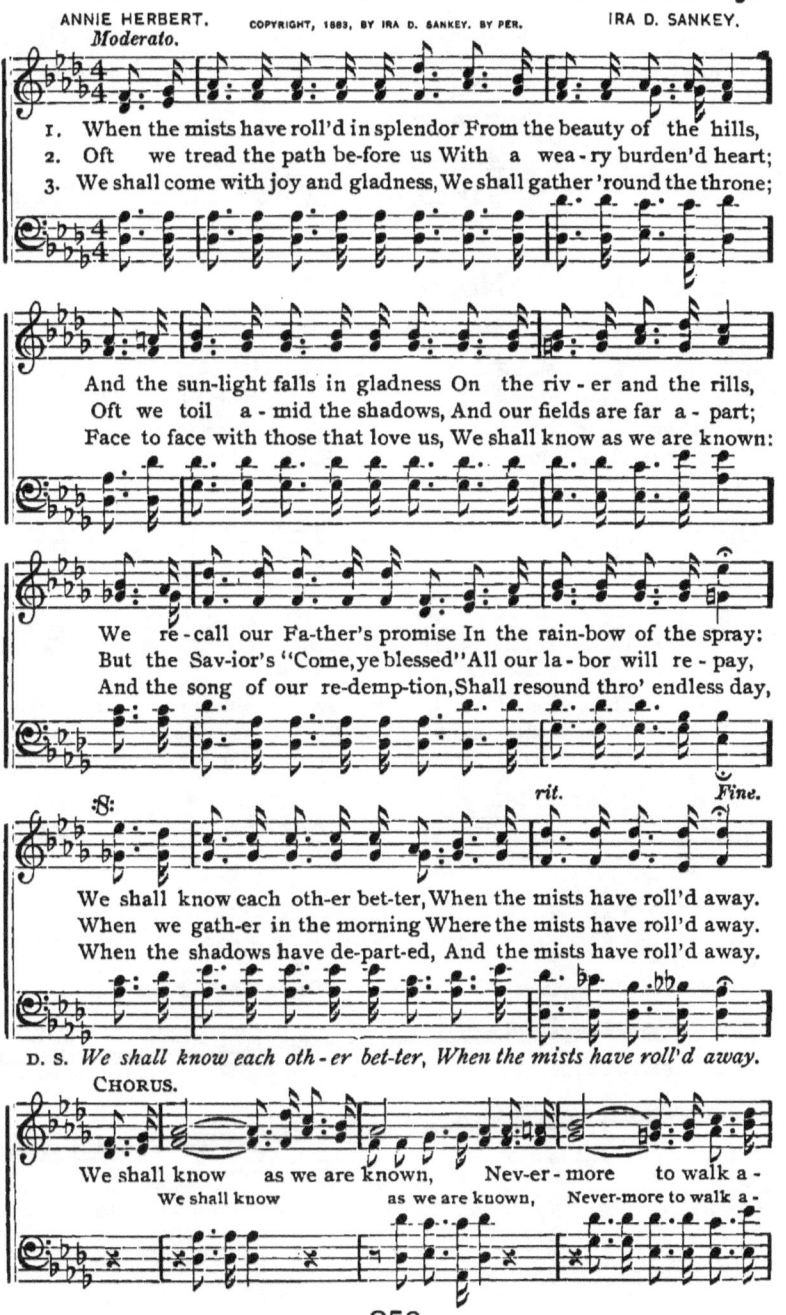

## When the Mists Have Rolled Away. Concluded.

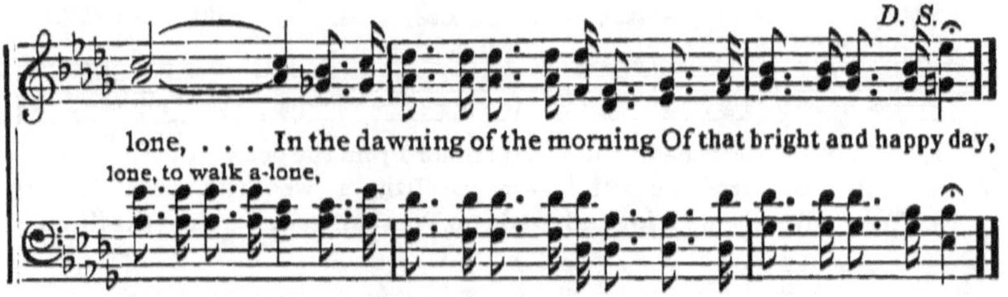

lone, ... In the dawning of the morning Of that bright and happy day,
lone, to walk a-lone,

---

### No. 330. Nearer Thee.

Alt. from F. L. S.     COPYRIGHT, 1894, BY E. O. EXCELL.     CHAS. H. GABRIEL.

1. "Nearer Thee" oh, precious feel-ing! Near-er Thee in gain and loss;
2. Near-er Thee, when love descending Falls in bless-ing on my head;
3. Near-er Thee in joy, or sor-row, 'Tis the same wher-e'er I roam;

Near-er Thee, when I am kneeling, In the shadow of the cross!
Near-er Thee, when I am bend-ing O'er the graves that hide my dead.
Near-er Thee, to-day, to-morrow, Oh, my King, my Christ, my Home.

**CHORUS.**

Near-er Thee, O precious Sav-ior, Draw me near-er to Thee;

Let me feel Thy blessed fa-vor, Nearer, nearer, Lord, to Thee.

## Coming Unto Jesus. Concluded.

glo - ries shine; Sing His wondrous mer-cies, Sing His love di - vine.

## No. 334. Come, Sinner, Come.

E. L. A.    COPYRIGHT, 1894, BY E. O. EXCELL.    E. L. ASHFORD.

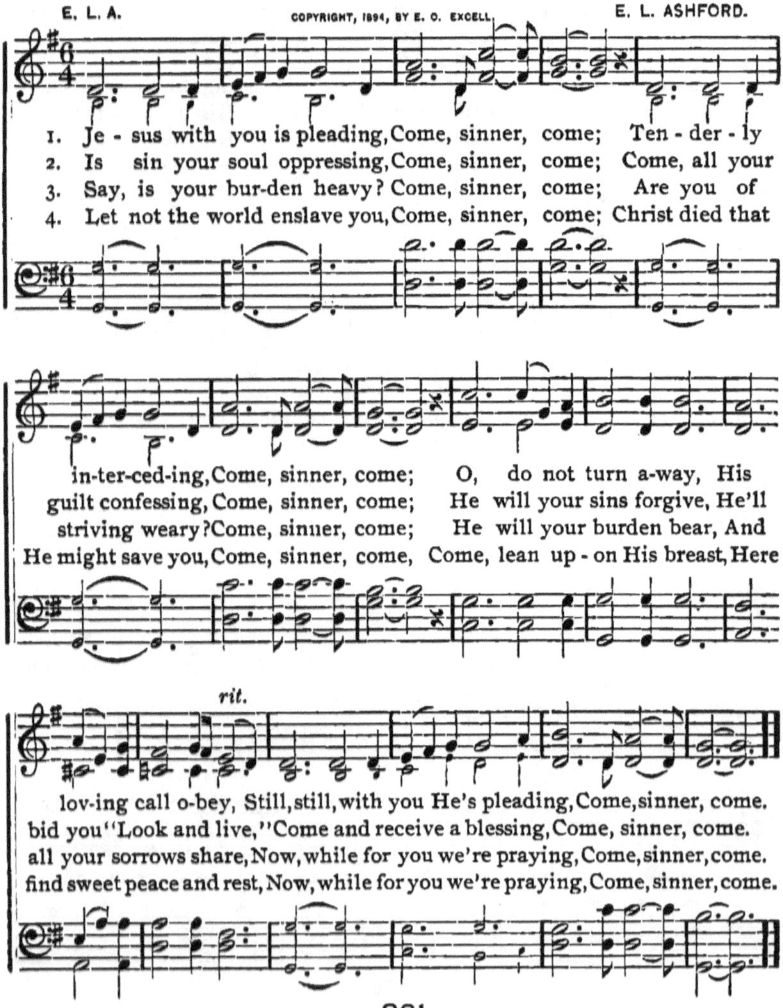

1. Je - sus with you is pleading, Come, sinner, come; Ten - der - ly
2. Is sin your soul oppressing, Come, sinner, come; Come, all your
3. Say, is your bur-den heavy? Come, sinner, come; Are you of
4. Let not the world enslave you, Come, sinner, come; Christ died that

in-ter-ced-ing, Come, sinner, come; O, do not turn a-way, His
guilt confessing, Come, sinner, come; He will your sins forgive, He'll
striving weary? Come, sinner, come; He will your burden bear, And
He might save you, Come, sinner, come, Come, lean up - on His breast, Here

*rit.*

lov-ing call o-bey, Still, still, with you He's pleading, Come, sinner, come.
bid you "Look and live," Come and receive a blessing, Come, sinner, come.
all your sorrows share, Now, while for you we're praying, Come, sinner, come.
find sweet peace and rest, Now, while for you we're praying, Come, sinner, come.

## Ring Out the Tidings. Concluded.

Ring out the tid - ings, Je-sus is might - y to save.
Ring out the tid - ings, Je-sus is might-y, is might - y to save.

---

### No. 336. He Loved Me So.

E. O. E.  
COPYRIGHT, 1894, BY E. O. EXCELL.  
E. O. EXCELL.

1. By faith the Lamb of God I see, Ex-pir-ing on the cross for me;
2. For me the Fa-ther sent His Son; For me the vic-to-ry He won;
3. So glad I am that He is mine, So glad that I with Him shall shine;
4. O Lamb of God, that made me free, I con-se-crate my all to Thee;
5. And when my Lord shall bid me come, To join the lov'd ones round the throne,

He paid the might-y debt I owe; He died because He lov'd me so.
To save my soul from endless woe, He died because He lov'd me so.
I'll trust in Him, for this I know, He died because He lov'd me so.
My all,—for this I sure-ly know, He died because He lov'd me so.
I'll sing, as thro' the gates I go, He died because He lov'd me so.

REFRAIN.

He lov'd me so, He lov'd me so, He died because He lov'd me so.
He lov'd me so, He lov'd me so,

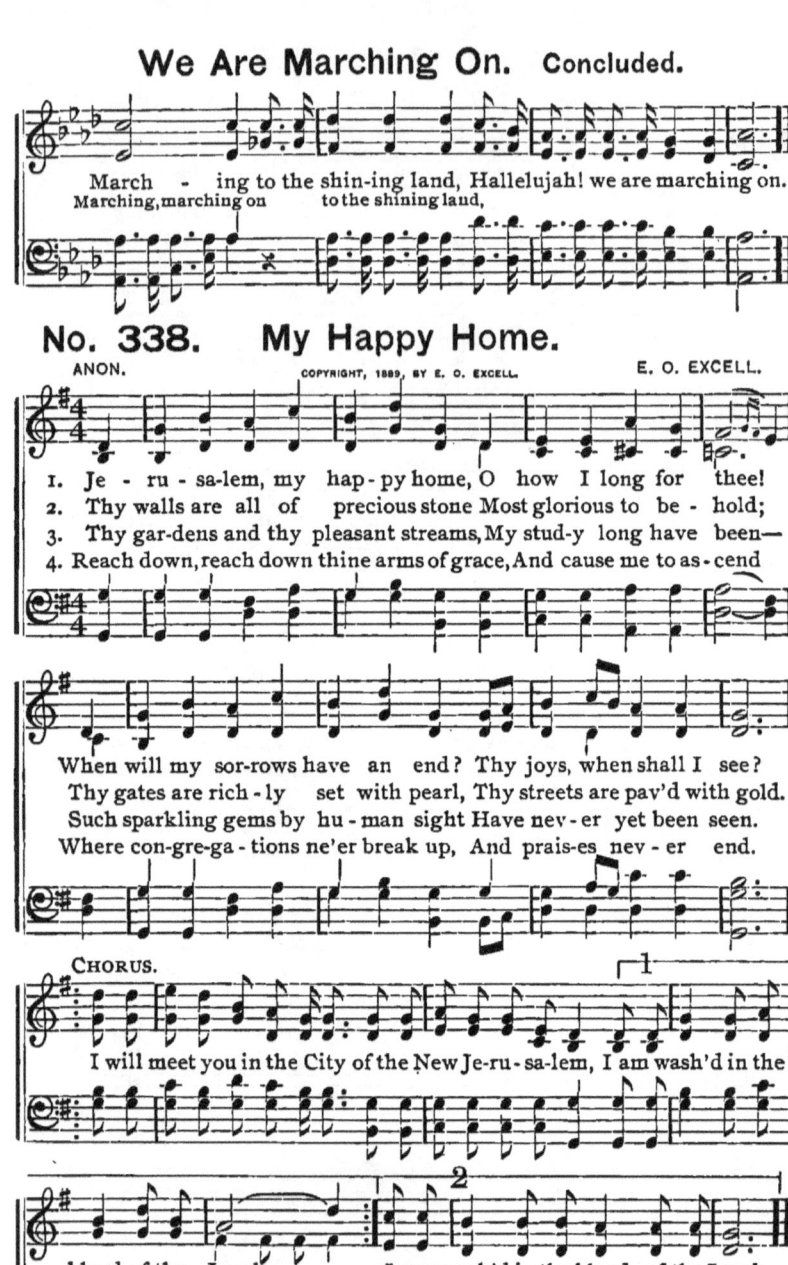

## Lend a Hand! Concluded.

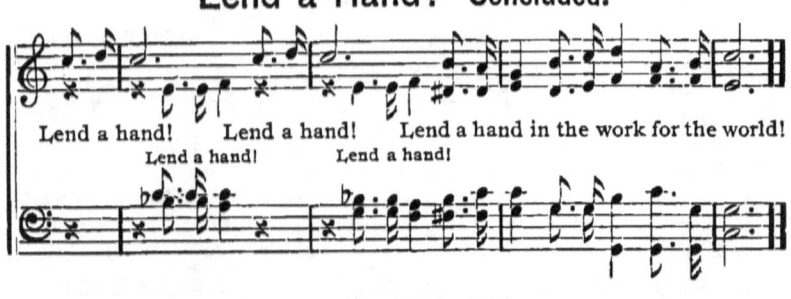

Lend a hand! Lend a hand! Lend a hand in the work for the world!
Lend a hand! Lend a hand!

### No. 340. Jesus Saved Others.

E. E. HEWITT.  COPYRIGHT, 1894, BY E. O. EXCELL.  CHAS. H. GABRIEL.

1. Je - sus saved oth - ers; burden'd, oppress'd, Throng'd they around Him
2. Je - sus saved oth - ers; life they obtained, Par - don and cleansing,
3. Je - sus saved oth - ers; trusting Him here, Mul - ti - tudes yon - der

find-ing sweet rest; Num - ber - less sin - ners seek - ing His face,
free - ly they gained; Might - y sal - va - tion!— al - ways the same,
spot - less ap - pear; Give Him the glo - ry, joy - ful - ly say:—

CHORUS.

Now are re - joic - ing, prais - ing His grace. Je - sus saved oth - ers,
None ev - er per - ish pleading His name.
He who saved oth - ers, saves me to - day.

Mer - cy is free! Sing Hal - le - lu - jah! Je - sus saves me!

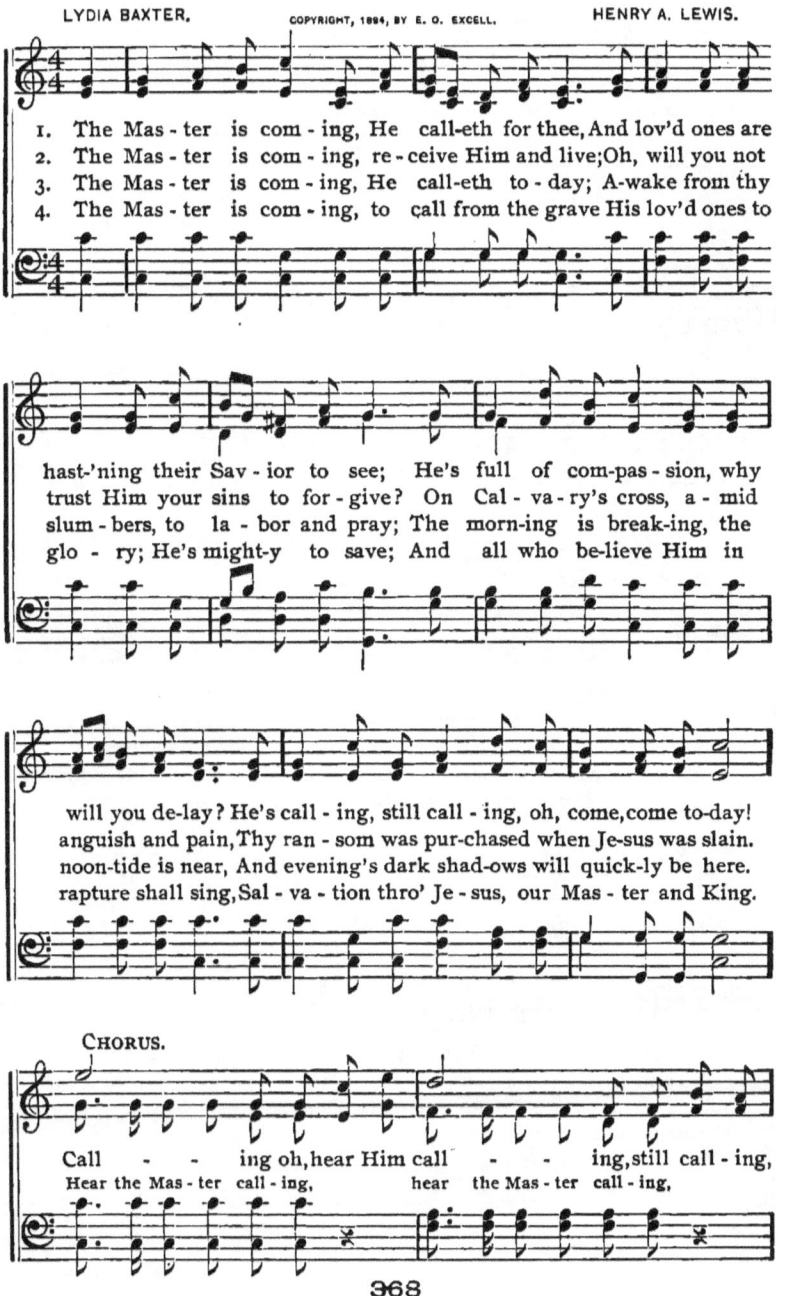

## Hear the Master Calling. Concluded.

Why, O why will you de-lay, Oh, hear Him call - - ing, so sweet-ly
Hear the Mas-ter call-ing

call - - ing, hear Him, Hear the Master calling, come, oh, come to-day.
call-ing, still He's calling, Hear the Master call-ing,

## No. 342. The Angels are Looking on Me.

Rev. JOHN PARKER.  COPYRIGHT, 1889, BY E. C. AVIS. BY PER.  ARRANGED.

1. Like Ja-cob, in his Beth-el rest, The an-gels are looking on me;
2. Each night I lay me down to sleep, The an-gels are looking on me;
3. And when I wake, new toils to meet, The an-gels are looking on me;
4. A pil-grim to the heav'nly land, The an-gels are looking on me;
5. And till I reach my home at last, The an-gels are looking on me;

REFRAIN. *All night, all night, The an-gels are look-ing on me;*

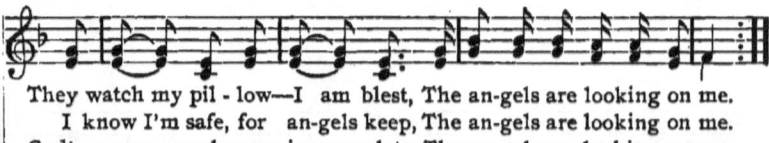

They watch my pil - low—I am blest, The an-gels are looking on me.
I know I'm safe, for an-gels keep, The an-gels are looking on me.
God's presence makes my joy complete, The an-gels are looking on me.
My steps are kept by God's command, The an-gels are looking on me.
With ev - 'ry tear and tri - al past, The an-gels are looking on me.

*All night, all night, The an-gels are look-ing on me.*

## Let Me in the Life-boat. Concluded.

stand the rag-ing storm, Let me in the life-boat,
let me in the life-boat, She will bear my spir-it home.

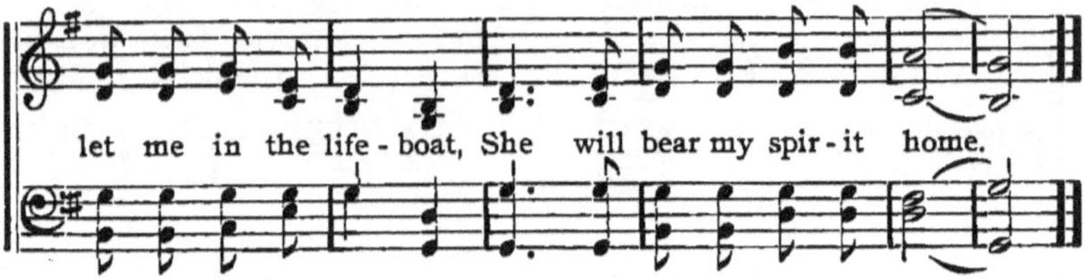

## No. 344. Have Faith in God.

E. A. H.  COPYRIGHT, 1894, BY E. O. EXCELL.  Rev. E. A. HOFFMAN.

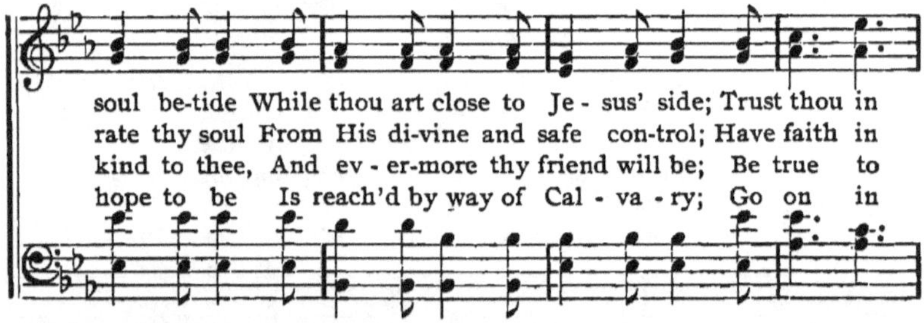

1. Trust thou in God! Trust thou in God! No e-vil can thy soul be-tide While thou art close to Je-sus' side; Trust thou in God! Trust thou in God! A-long life's road trust thou in God!
2. Have faith in God! Have faith in God! And naught can sep-a-rate thy soul From His di-vine and safe con-trol; Have faith in God! Have faith in God! A-long life's road have faith in God!
3. Be true to God! Be true to God! He has been good and kind to thee, And ev-er-more thy friend will be; Be true to God! Be true to God! A-long life's road be true to God!
4. Go on in faith, in trust-ing faith! The heav'n where soon we hope to be Is reach'd by way of Cal-va-ry; Go on in faith, a-long life's road; The goal is reach'd by trust in God!

## Onward! Concluded.

go dear Sav-ior, Thou art our God, we ful-ly trust in Thee.

### No. 346. Come to Me.
(TRIO, FOR MALE VOICES.)

Mrs. J. C. YULE.  COPYRIGHT, 1886, BY E. O. EXCELL.  E. O. EXCELL.

1. Wea-ry soul, by sin op-press'd, Wouldst thou find a place of rest,
2. Hun-gry soul, why pine and die, With ex-haust-less stores so nigh?
3. Thirst-y soul, earth's sweetest rill, Mocks thee with its prom-ise still?
4. Heav'nly bread and heav'nly wine, Liv-ing wa-ters, all are mine,

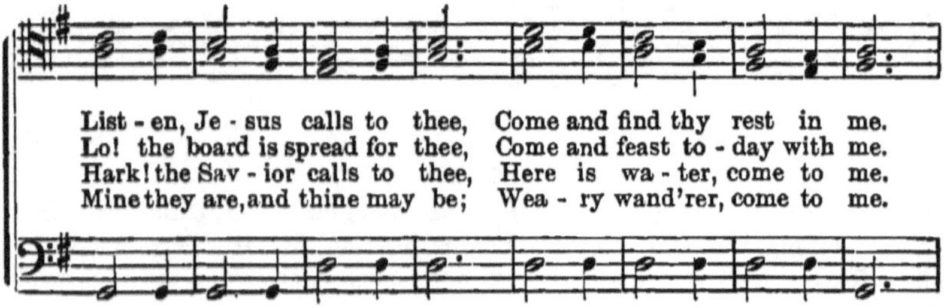

List-en, Je-sus calls to thee, Come and find thy rest in me.
Lo! the board is spread for thee, Come and feast to-day with me.
Hark! the Sav-ior calls to thee, Here is wa-ter, come to me.
Mine they are, and thine may be; Wea-ry wand'rer, come to me.

**CHORUS.** *Repeat pp.*

Come to me, come to me, Come and find thy rest in me.
Come to me, come to me, Come and feast to-day with me.
Come to me, come to me, Here is wa-ter, come to me.
Come to me, come to me, Wea-ry wand'rer, come to me.

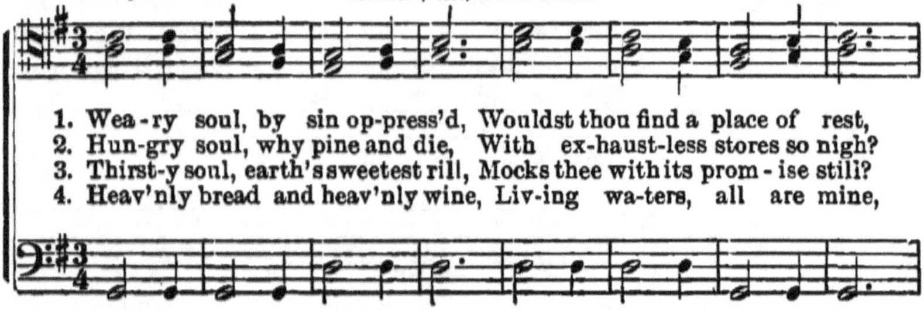

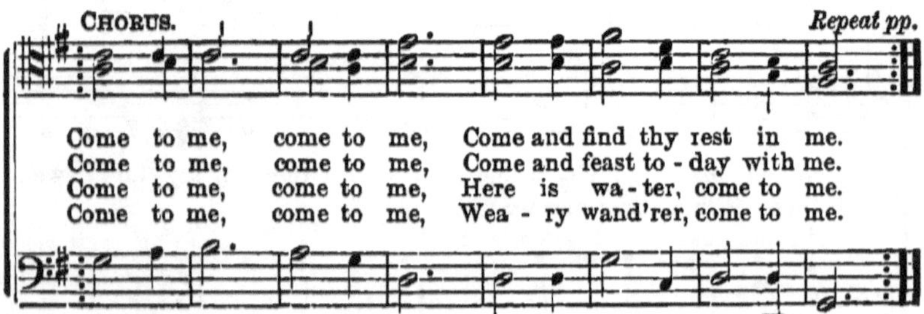

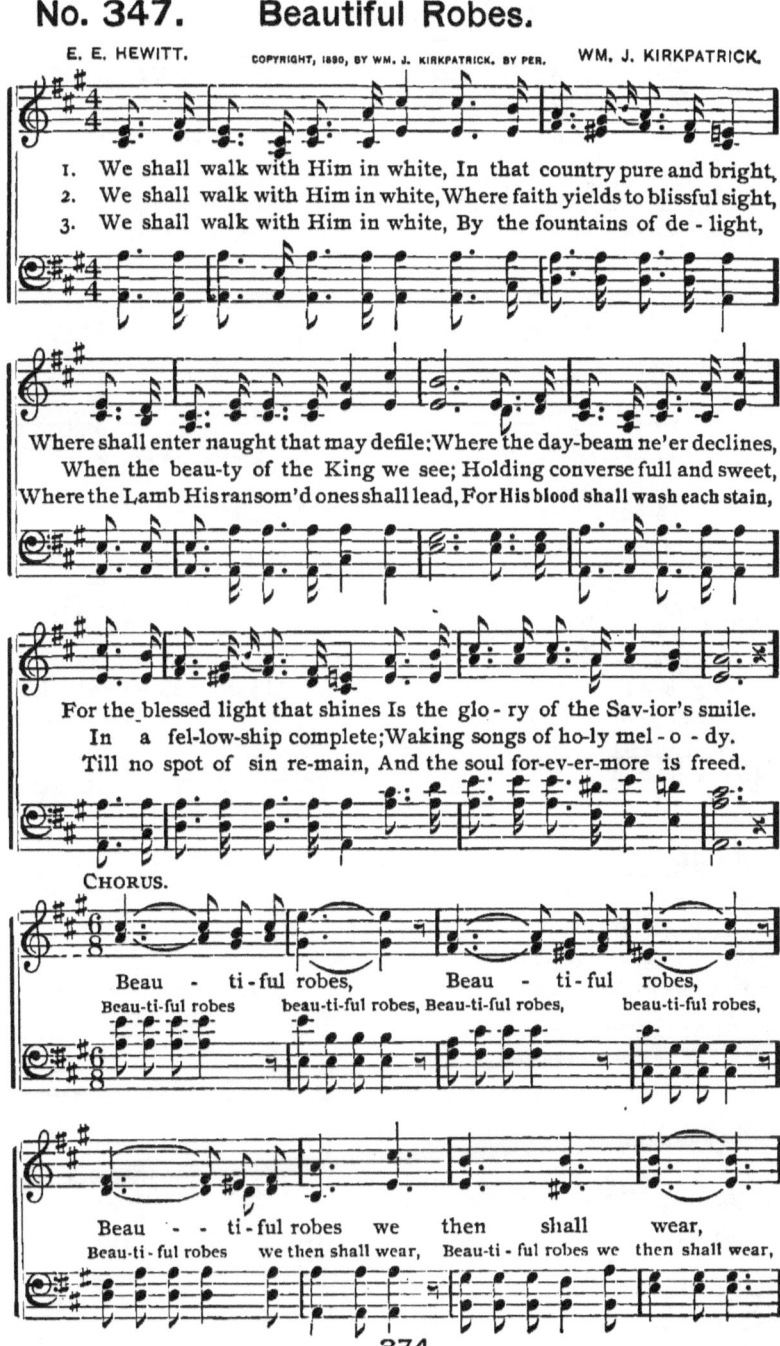

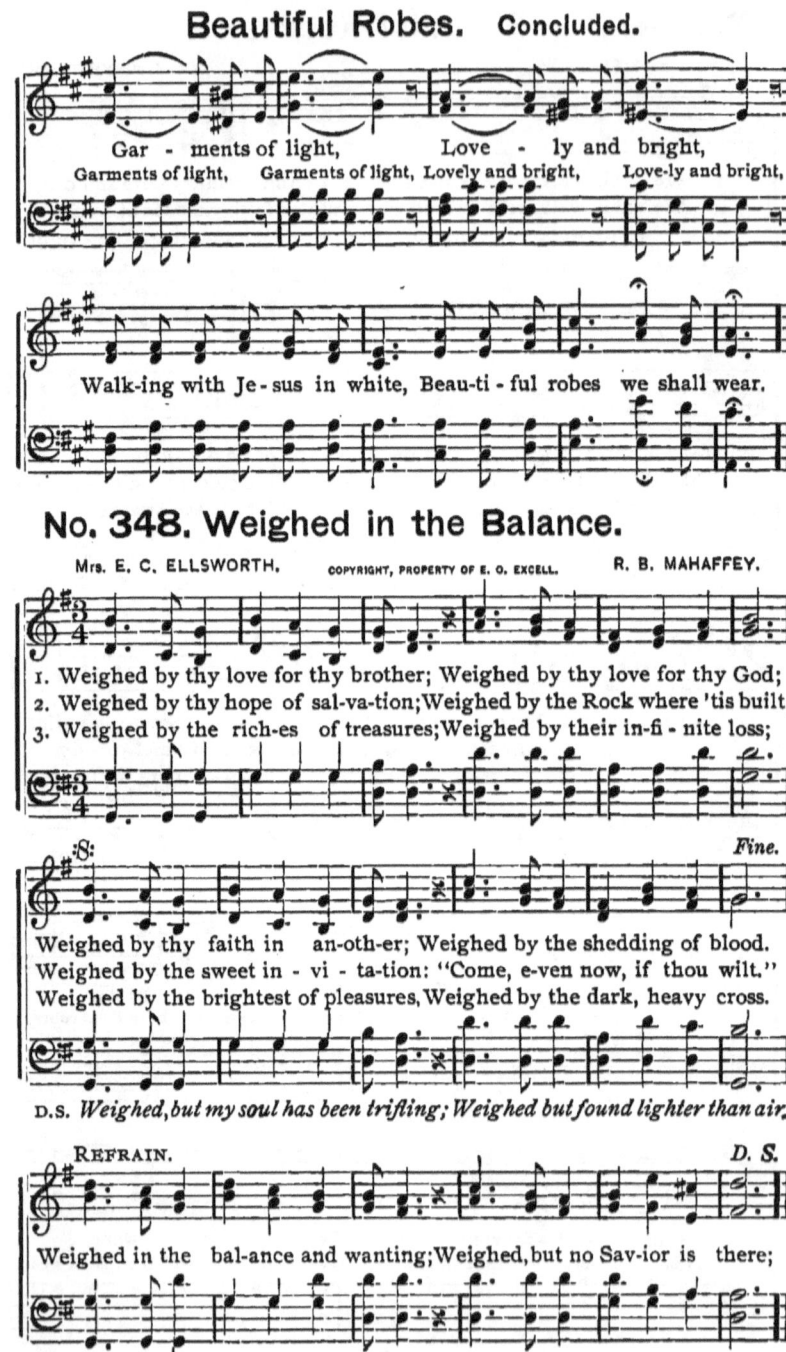

## We Shall Stand Before the King. Concluded.

lu - jah, We shall stand ..... be-fore the King.
Hal - le - lu - jah, We shall stand

---

### No. 350.  Tell it all to Jesus.

F. M. D.  
COPYRIGHT, 1889, BY E. O. EXCELL.  
FRANK M. DAVIS.

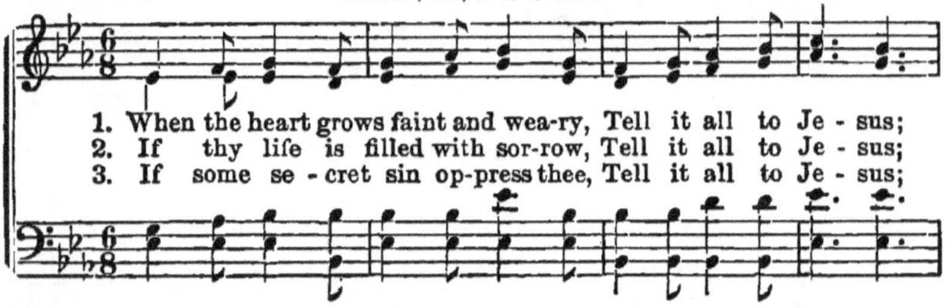

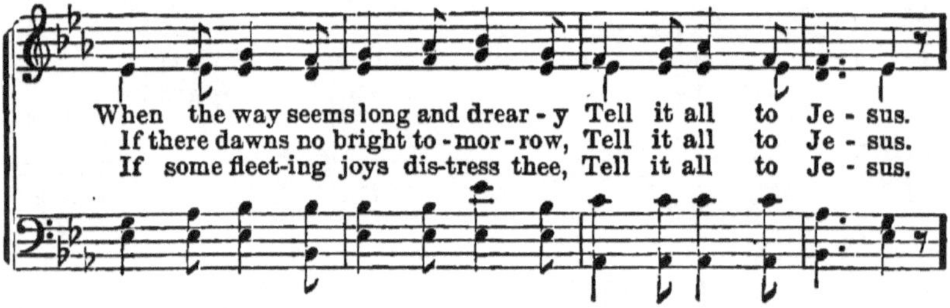

1. When the heart grows faint and wea-ry, Tell it all to Je-sus;
2. If thy life is filled with sor-row, Tell it all to Je-sus;
3. If some se-cret sin op-press thee, Tell it all to Je-sus;

When the way seems long and drear-y Tell it all to Je-sus.
If there dawns no bright to-mor-row, Tell it all to Je-sus.
If some fleet-ing joys dis-tress thee, Tell it all to Je-sus.

**Chorus.**

Tell it all to Je-sus, Tell it all to Je-sus;

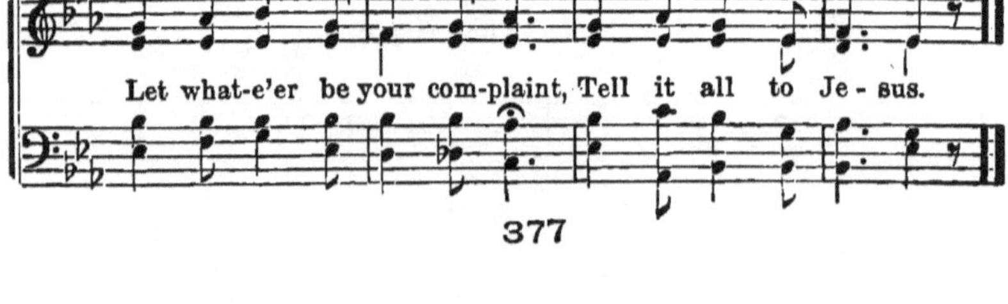

Let what-e'er be your com-plaint, Tell it all to Je-sus.

### No. 352. Wine is a Mocker.

COPYRIGHT, 1894, BY E. O. EXCELL.

EDWIN SHERRETT.

## Wine is a Mocker. Continued.

## The Heavenly Gate. Concluded.

384

## No. 354. This Uttermost Salvation.

GRACE WEISER DAVIS. COPYRIGHT, 1894, BY E. O. EXCELL. CHAS. H. GABRIEL.

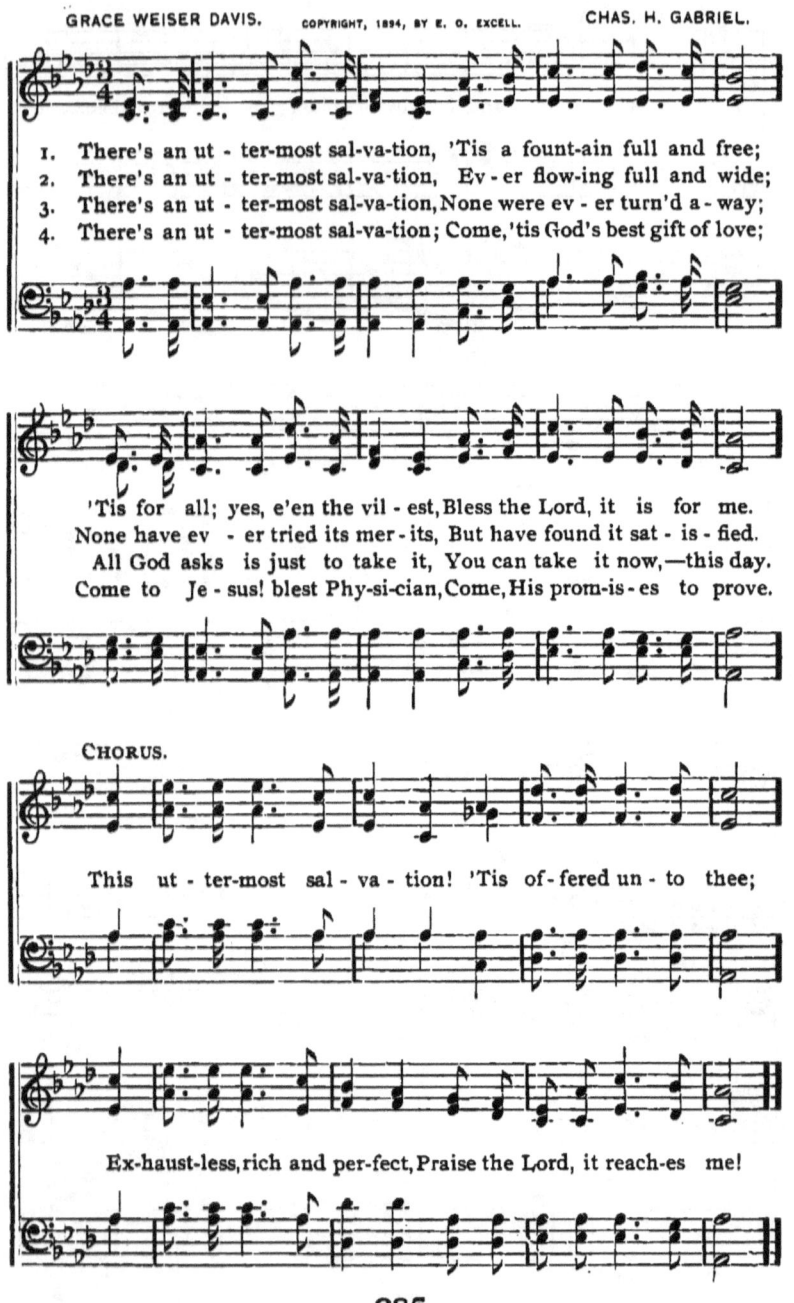

1. There's an ut-ter-most sal-va-tion, 'Tis a fount-ain full and free;
2. There's an ut-ter-most sal-va-tion, Ev-er flow-ing full and wide;
3. There's an ut-ter-most sal-va-tion, None were ev-er turn'd a-way;
4. There's an ut-ter-most sal-va-tion; Come,'tis God's best gift of love;

'Tis for all; yes, e'en the vil-est, Bless the Lord, it is for me.
None have ev-er tried its mer-its, But have found it sat-is-fied.
All God asks is just to take it, You can take it now,—this day.
Come to Je-sus! blest Phy-si-cian, Come, His prom-is-es to prove.

CHORUS.

This ut-ter-most sal-va-tion! 'Tis of-fered un-to thee;

Ex-haust-less, rich and per-fect, Praise the Lord, it reach-es me!

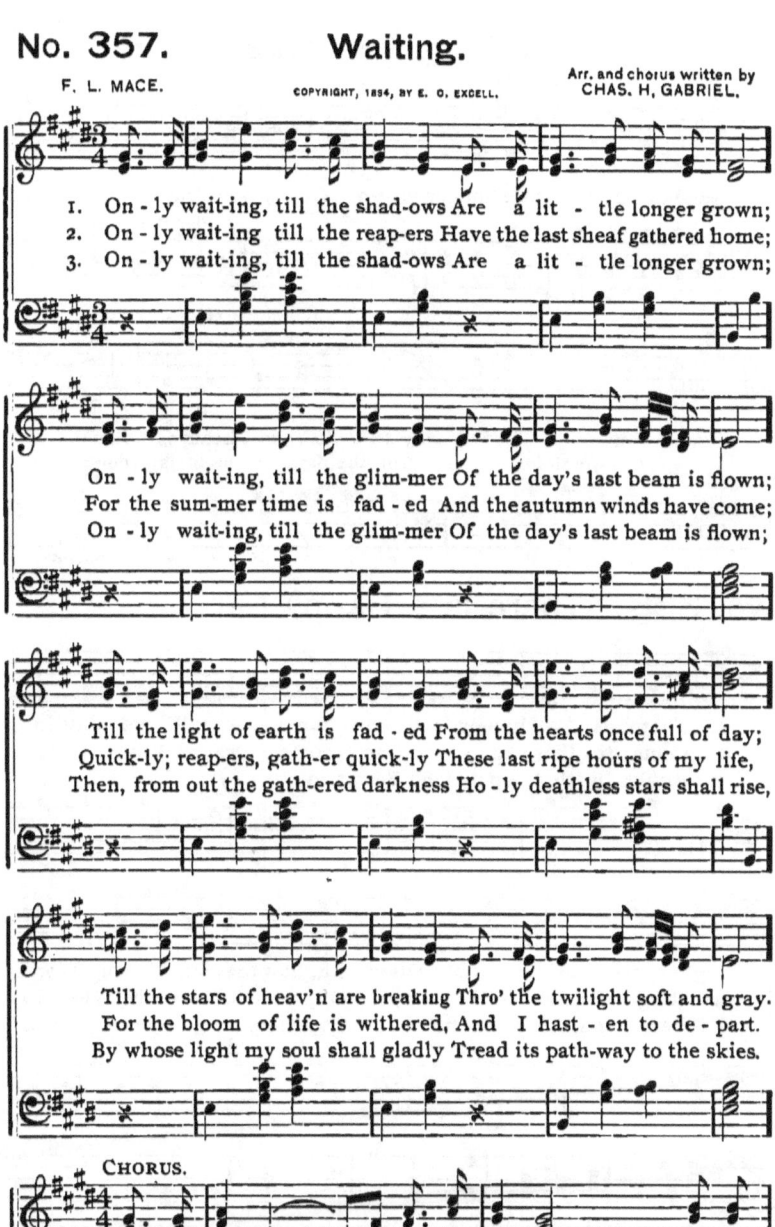

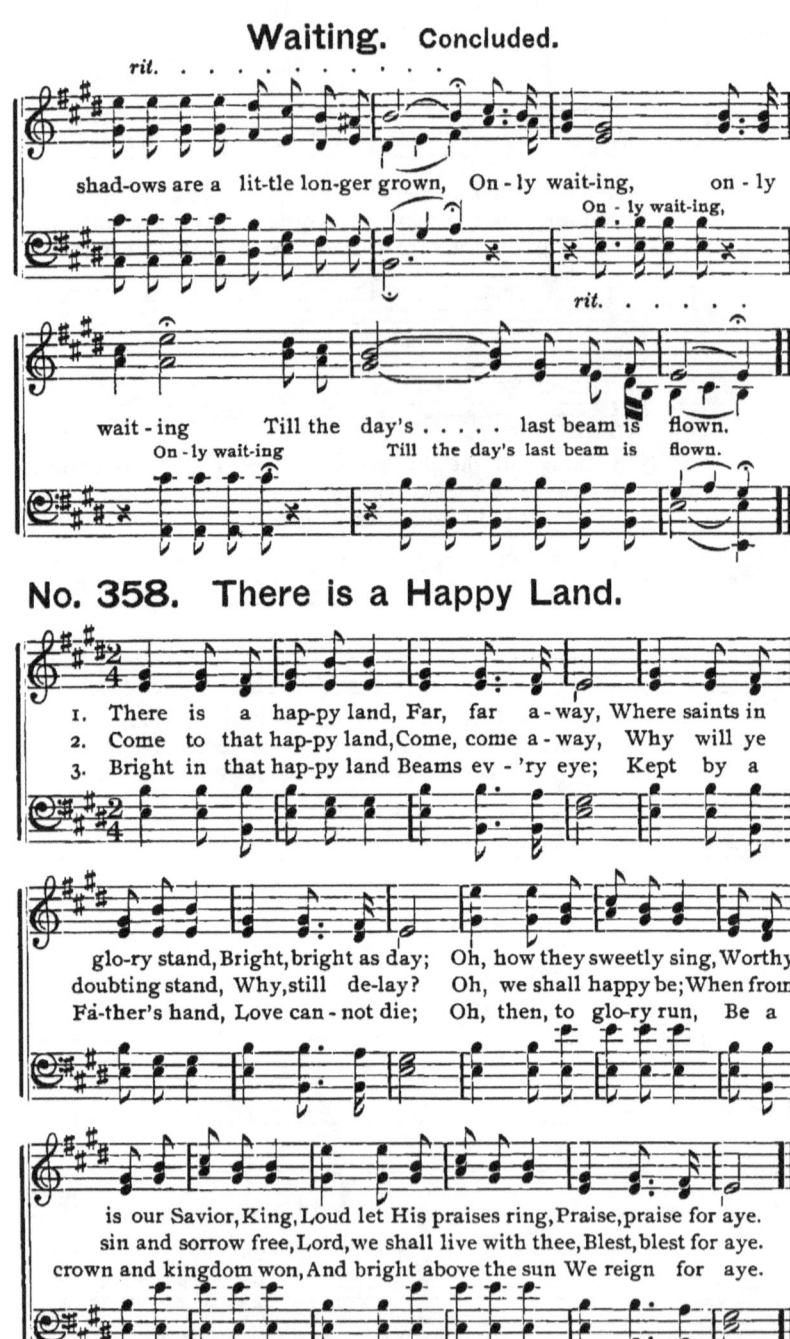

## Waiting. Concluded.

shad-ows are a lit-tle lon-ger grown, On-ly wait-ing, on-ly wait-ing  Till the day's last beam is flown.
On-ly wait-ing  Till the day's last beam is flown.

### No. 358. There is a Happy Land.

1. There is a hap-py land, Far, far a-way, Where saints in glo-ry stand, Bright, bright as day; Oh, how they sweetly sing, Worthy is our Savior, King, Loud let His praises ring, Praise, praise for aye.
2. Come to that hap-py land, Come, come a-way, Why will ye doubting stand, Why, still de-lay? Oh, we shall happy be; When from sin and sorrow free, Lord, we shall live with thee, Blest, blest for aye.
3. Bright in that hap-py land Beams ev-'ry eye; Kept by a Fa-ther's hand, Love can-not die; Oh, then, to glo-ry run, Be a crown and kingdom won, And bright above the sun We reign for aye.

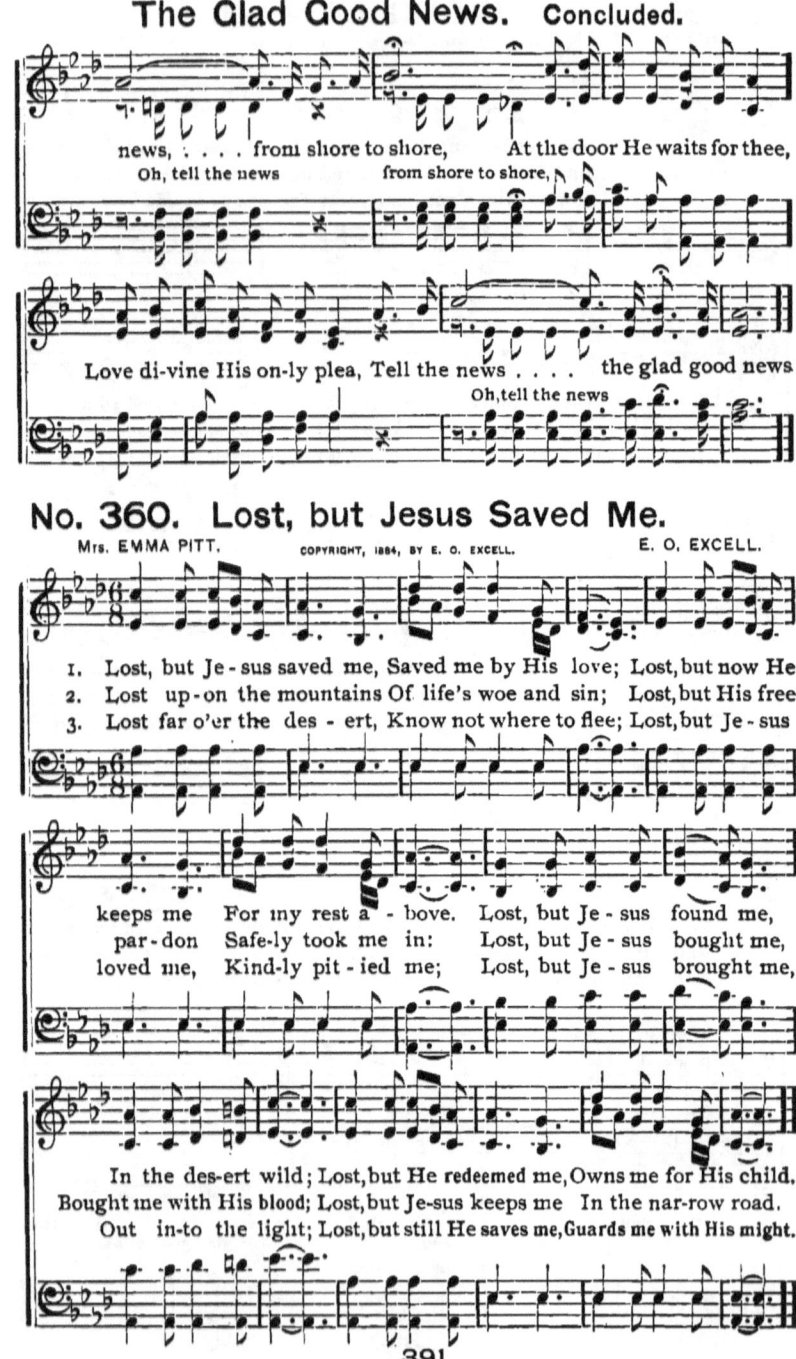

## No. 362. Companionship with Jesus.

MARY D. JAMES.  COPYRIGHT, 1875, BY WM. J. KIRKPATRICK.  WM. J. KIRKPATRICK.

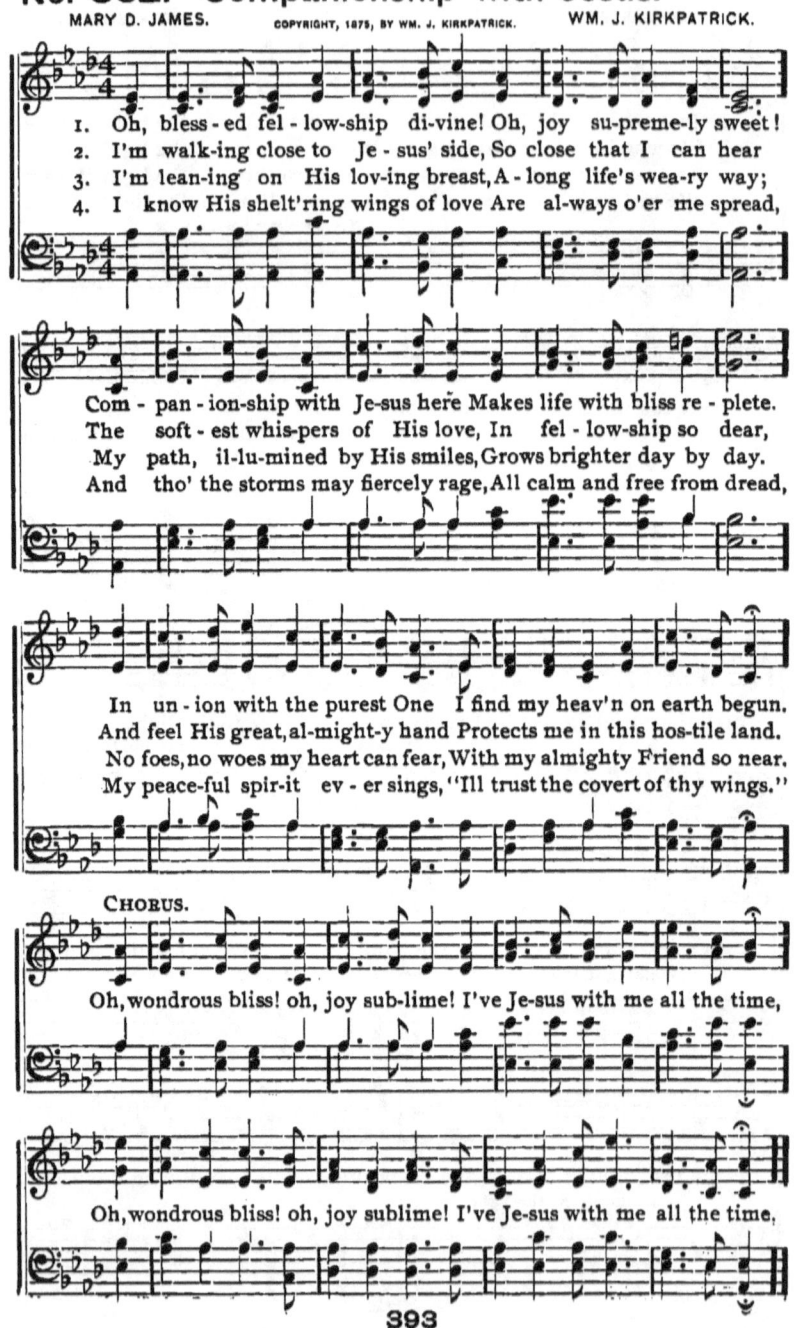

1. Oh, bless-ed fel-low-ship di-vine! Oh, joy su-preme-ly sweet!
2. I'm walk-ing close to Je-sus' side, So close that I can hear
3. I'm lean-ing on His lov-ing breast, A-long life's wea-ry way;
4. I know His shelt'ring wings of love Are al-ways o'er me spread,

Com-pan-ion-ship with Je-sus here Makes life with bliss re-plete.
The soft-est whis-pers of His love, In fel-low-ship so dear,
My path, il-lu-mined by His smiles, Grows brighter day by day.
And tho' the storms may fierce-ly rage, All calm and free from dread,

In un-ion with the purest One I find my heav'n on earth begun.
And feel His great, al-might-y hand Protects me in this hos-tile land.
No foes, no woes my heart can fear, With my almighty Friend so near.
My peace-ful spir-it ev-er sings, "I'll trust the covert of thy wings."

CHORUS.

Oh, wondrous bliss! oh, joy sub-lime! I've Je-sus with me all the time,

Oh, wondrous bliss! oh, joy sublime! I've Je-sus with me all the time,

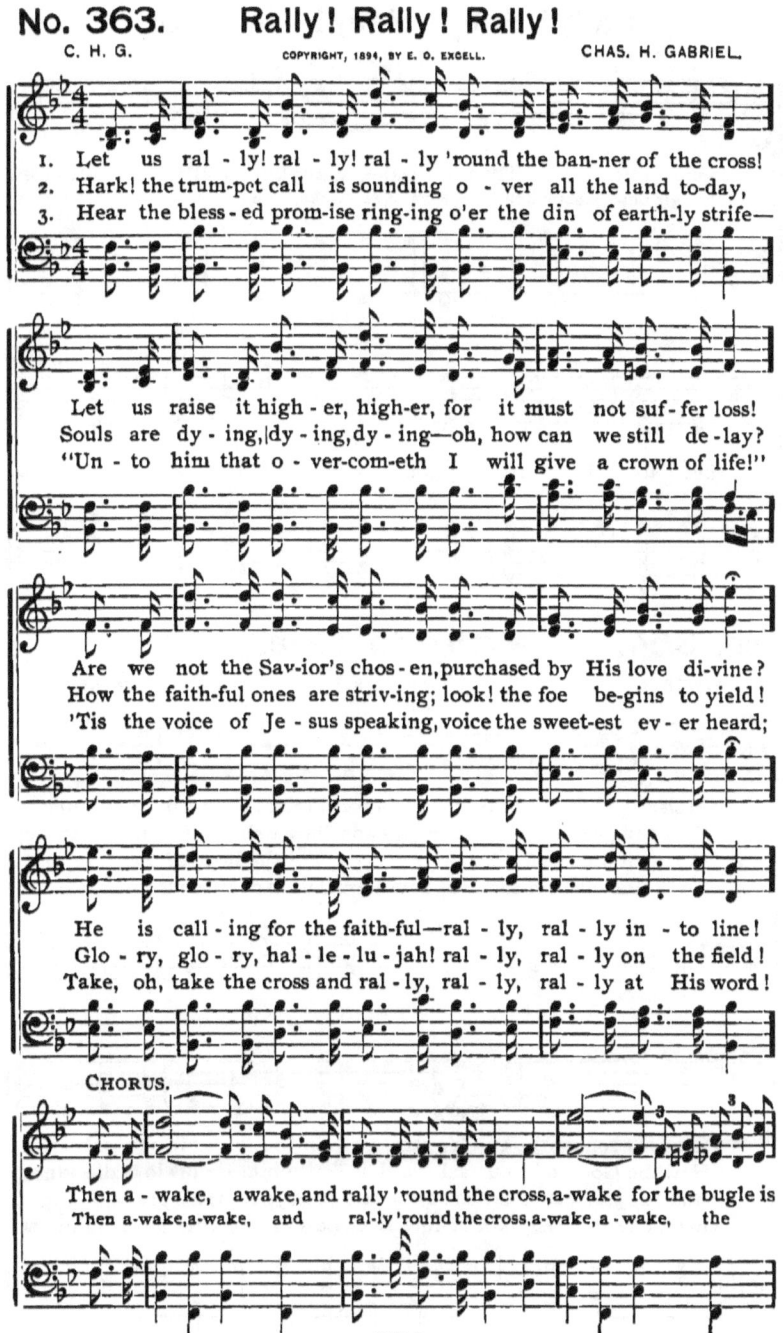

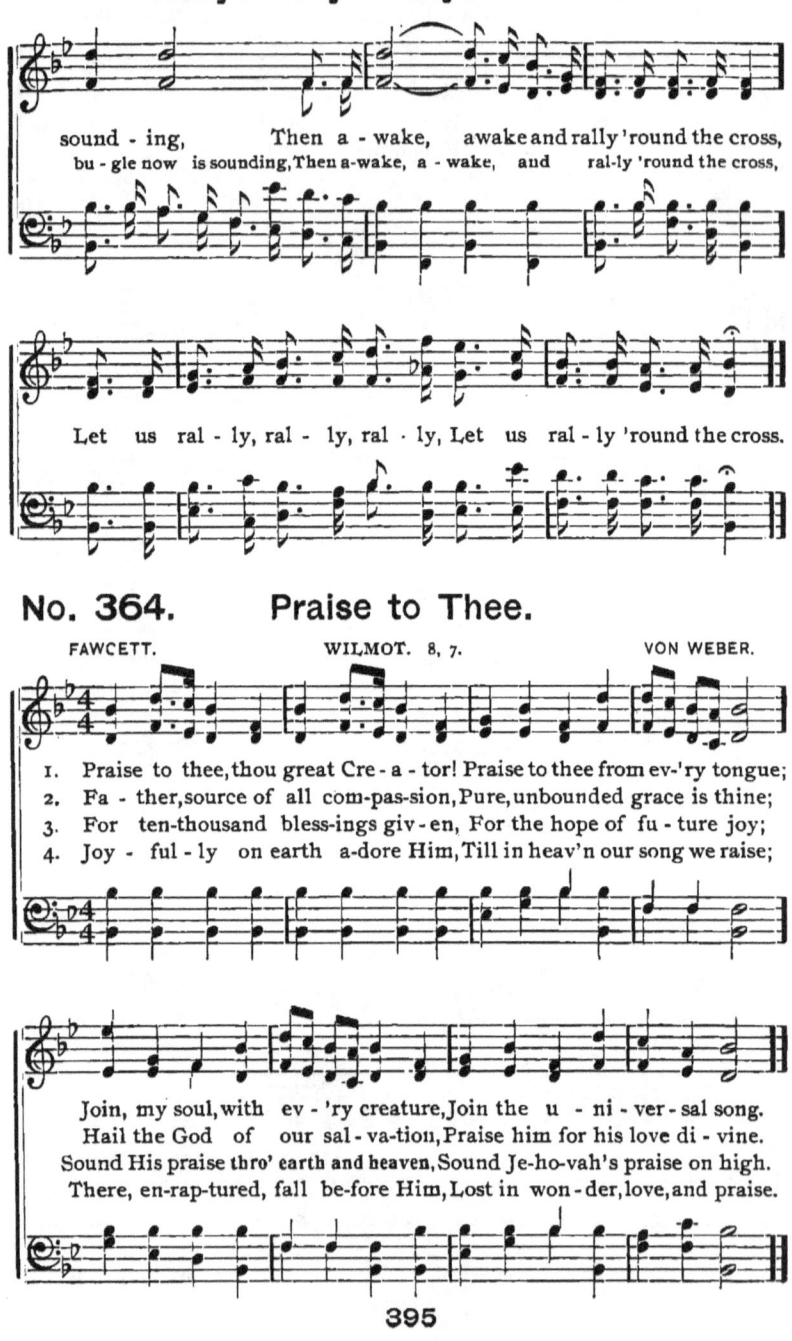

## No. 366. Call Them In,

E. O E.     COPYRIGHT, 1884, BY E. O. EXCELL.     E. O. EXCELL.

1. Hear the Sav-ior sweet-ly say-ing, Call them in, make no de-lay;
2. Hear Him say, let no one lin-ger, Call them in from out the cold,
3. Call them in, I can-not leave them, Call them in, I can-not go;

Call them in, say *all* are wel-come, Bid them come to me to-day.
Call them in, the lit-tle chil-dren, Bid them come with-in the fold.
Oh, make haste for souls are dying, Snatch them from the brink of woe.

CHORUS.

Call them in, . . . . . . . . . Bid them come, . . . . . . . . .,
Call them in, oh, call them in, Bid them come, oh, bid them come!

Hear the Sav-ior sweetly say-ing, "Call them in, oh, call them in."

## The Judgment, Concluded.

## No. 370. I Know that My Redeemer Lives.

CHARLES WESLEY.     BRADFORD. C. M.     HANDEL.

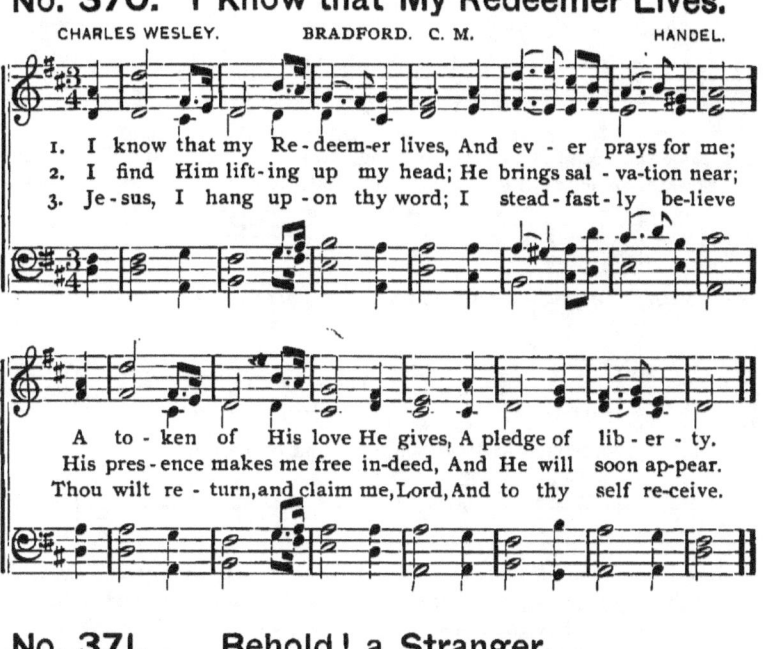

1. I know that my Re-deem-er lives, And ev-er prays for me;
2. I find Him lift-ing up my head; He brings sal-va-tion near;
3. Je-sus, I hang up-on thy word; I stead-fast-ly be-lieve

A to-ken of His love He gives, A pledge of lib-er-ty.
His pres-ence makes me free in-deed, And He will soon ap-pear.
Thou wilt re-turn, and claim me, Lord, And to thy self re-ceive.

## No. 371. Behold! a Stranger.

JOSEPH GRIGG.     FEDERAL STREET. L. M.     H. K. OLIVER.

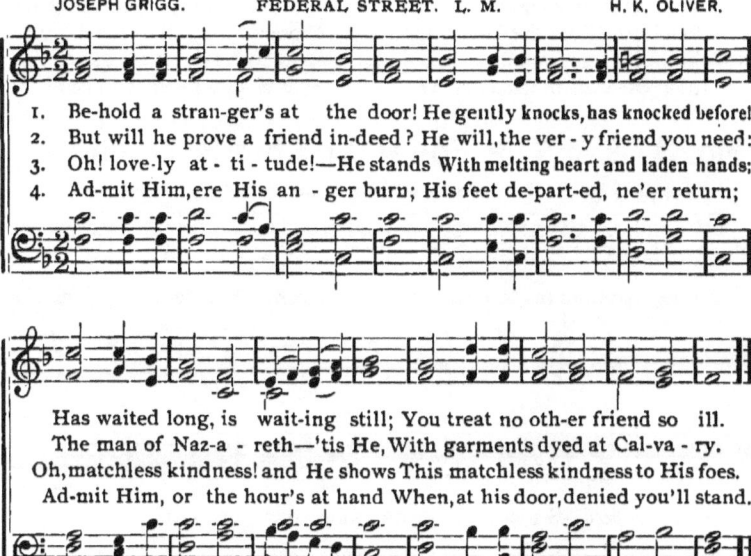

1. Be-hold a stran-ger's at the door! He gently knocks, has knocked before!
2. But will he prove a friend in-deed? He will, the ver-y friend you need:
3. Oh! love-ly at-ti-tude!—He stands With melting heart and laden hands;
4. Ad-mit Him, ere His an-ger burn; His feet de-part-ed, ne'er return;

Has waited long, is wait-ing still; You treat no oth-er friend so ill.
The man of Naz-a-reth—'tis He, With garments dyed at Cal-va-ry.
Oh, matchless kindness! and He shows This matchless kindness to His foes.
Ad-mit Him, or the hour's at hand When, at his door, denied you'll stand.

## No. 372. Come Thou Fount.

ROBINSON. UNKNOWN.

2. Here I'll raise my Ebenezer,
   Hither by Thy help I'll come;
   And I hope, by Thy good pleasure,
   Safely to arrive at home.
   Jesus sought me when a stranger,
   Wandering from the fold of God
   He to rescue me from danger,
   Interposed his precious blood.

3. Oh, to grace, how great a debtor,
   Daily I'm constrained to be!
   Let thy goodness, like a fetter,
   Bind my wandering heart to Thee;
   Prone to wander, Lord, I feel it—
   Prone to leave the God I love—
   Here's my heart, oh, take and seal it,
   Seal it for Thy courts above.

## No. 373. *The Fountain Stands Open.

COPYRIGHT, 1894, BY E. O. EXCELL. Arr. by E. O. E.

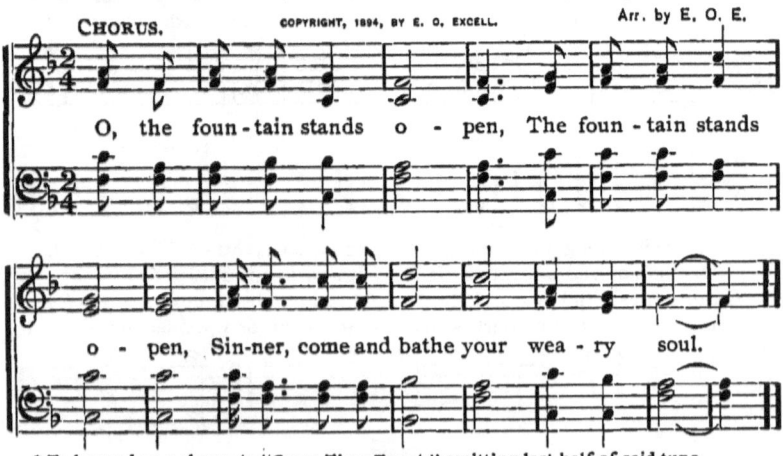

* To be used as a chorus to "Come Thou Fount," omitting last half of said tune.

## No. 374. Happy Day.

PHILIP DODDRIDGE.

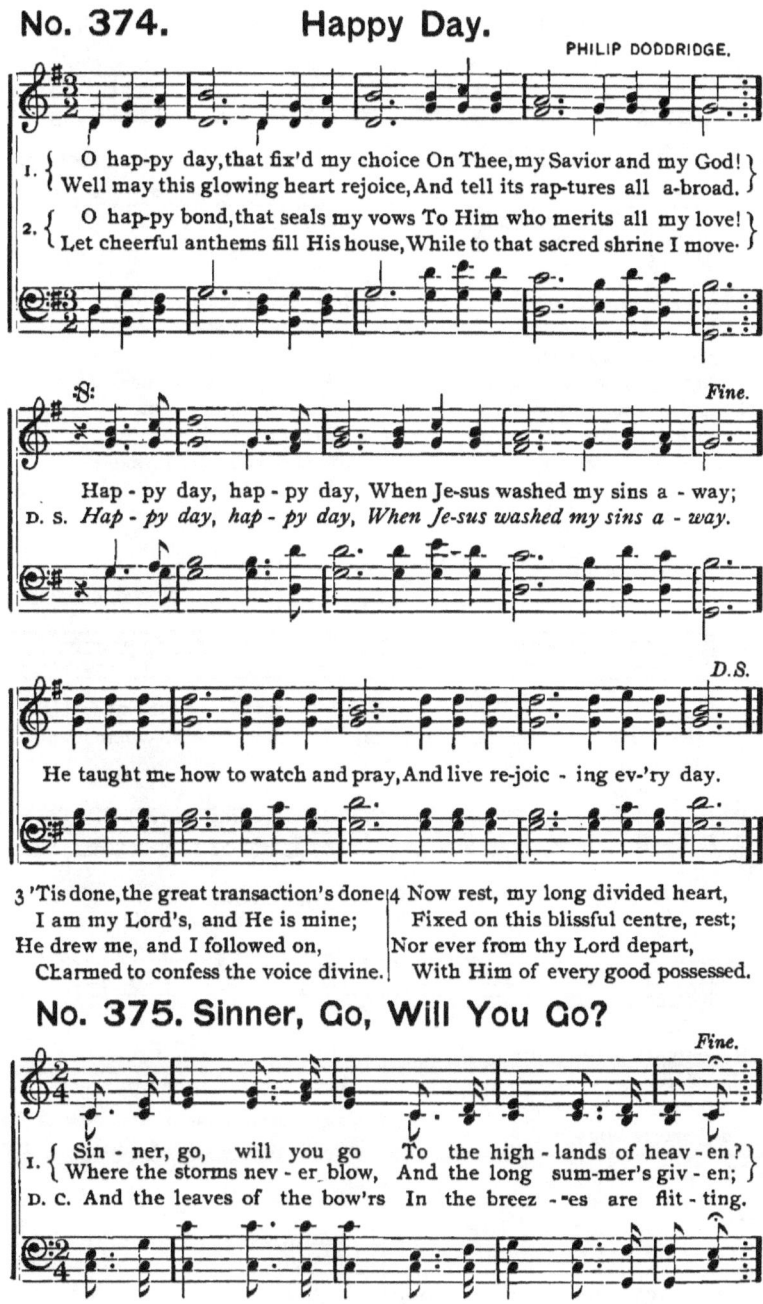

1. O happy day, that fix'd my choice On Thee, my Savior and my God!
Well may this glowing heart rejoice, And tell its raptures all abroad.

2. O happy bond, that seals my vows To Him who merits all my love!
Let cheerful anthems fill His house, While to that sacred shrine I move.

Happy day, happy day, When Jesus washed my sins away;
D. S. *Happy day, happy day, When Jesus washed my sins away.*

He taught me how to watch and pray, And live rejoicing ev'ry day.

3 'Tis done, the great transaction's done,
I am my Lord's, and He is mine;
He drew me, and I followed on,
Charmed to confess the voice divine.

4 Now rest, my long divided heart,
Fixed on this blissful centre, rest;
Nor ever from thy Lord depart,
With Him of every good possessed.

## No. 375. Sinner, Go, Will You Go?

1. Sinner, go, will you go To the highlands of heav-en?
Where the storms never blow, And the long summer's giv-en;
D. C. And the leaves of the bow'rs In the breezes are flitting.

## Sinner, Go, Will You Go? Concluded.

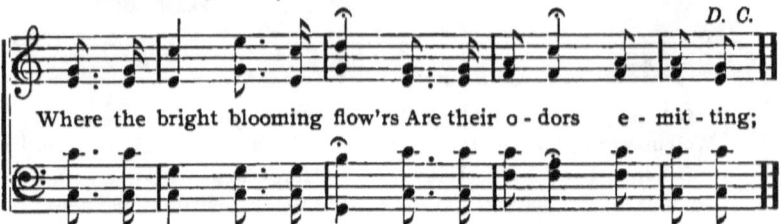

Where the bright blooming flow'rs Are their o-dors e-mit-ting;

2 Where the saints, robed in white,
   Cleansed in life's flowing fountain,
  Shining beauteous and bright,
   They inhabit the mountain;
  Where no sin nor dismay,
   Neither trouble nor sorrow,
  Will be felt for a day,
   Nor be feared for the morrow.

3 He's prepared thee a home,—
   Sinner, canst thou believe it?
  And invites thee to come,—
   Sinner, wilt thou receive it?
  Oh, come, sinner come,
   For the tide is receding;
  And the Savior will soon
   And forever cease pleading.

## No. 376.  The Road to Heaven.

COPYRIGHT, 1887, BY E. O. EXCELL.

E. O. EXCELL.

1. { The road to heav'n by Christ was made, With heav'nly truth the rails are laid;
     From earth to heav'n the line extends, To life e-ter-nal where it ends. }

CHORUS

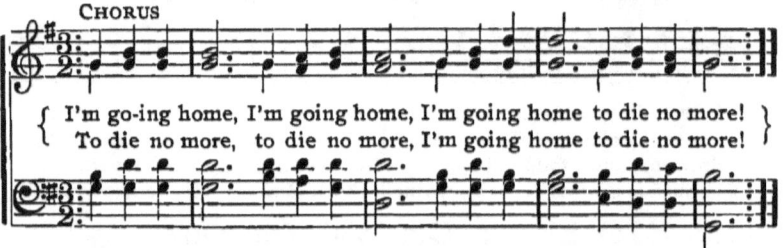

{ I'm go-ing home, I'm going home, I'm going home to die no more!
  To die no more, to die no more, I'm going home to die no more! }

2 Repentance is the station, then,
   Where passengers are taken in;
  No fee for them is there to pay,
   For Jesus is himself the way.

3 The Bible is the engineer—
   It points the way to heaven so clear,
  Thro' tunnels dark and dreary here—
   It does the way to glory steer.

4 God's love the fire, his truth the steam
   Which drives the engine and the train;

All you who would to glory ride,
Must come to Christ—in him abide.

5 Come, then, poor sinner, now is the time
   At any station on the line;
  If you repent and turn from sin,
   The train will stop and take you in.

6 And then to glory we will go,
   With all on board as white as snow;
  Ring, ring the bell and start the train
   And run it through in Jesus' name.

## No. 377. I am Trusting, Lord, in Thee.

Rev. WM. McDONALD.     WM. G. FISCHER.

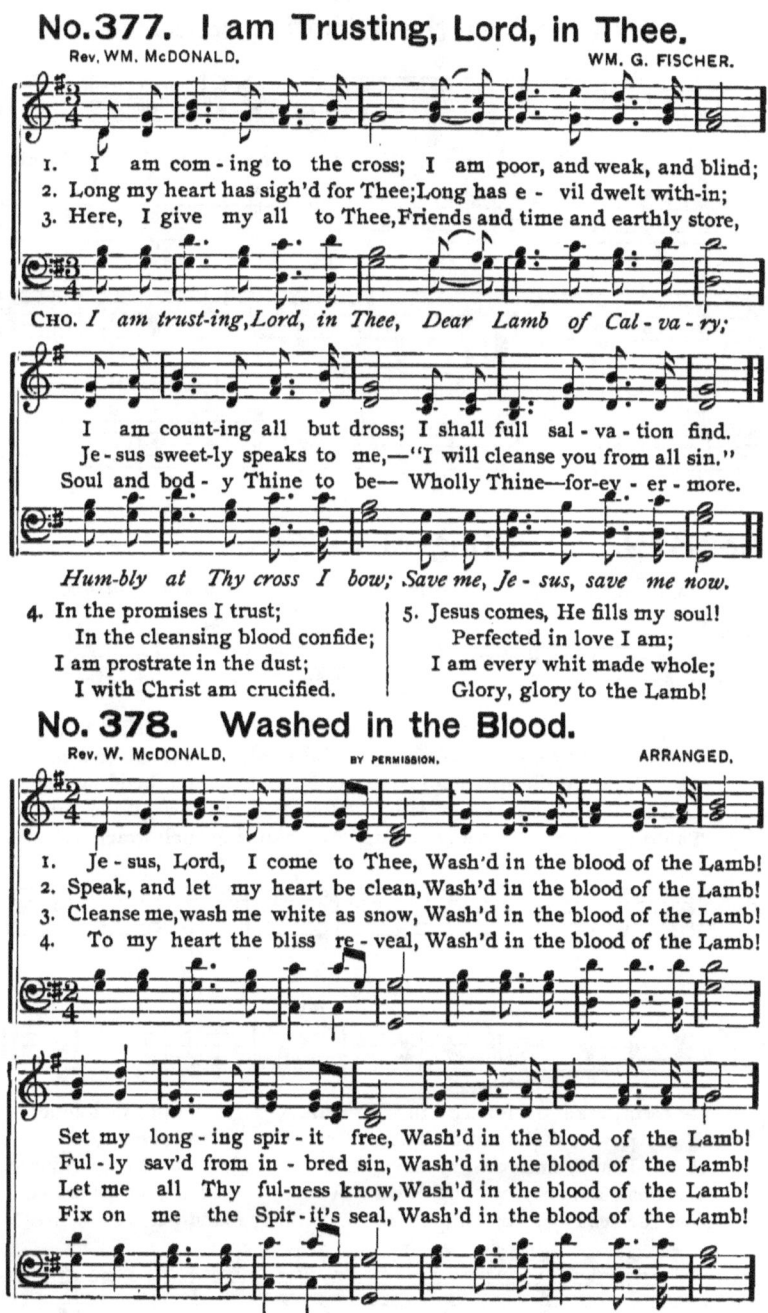

1. I am com-ing to the cross; I am poor, and weak, and blind;
2. Long my heart has sigh'd for Thee; Long has e-vil dwelt with-in;
3. Here, I give my all to Thee, Friends and time and earthly store,

CHO. *I am trust-ing, Lord, in Thee, Dear Lamb of Cal-va-ry;*

I am count-ing all but dross; I shall full sal-va-tion find.
Je-sus sweet-ly speaks to me,—"I will cleanse you from all sin."
Soul and bod-y Thine to be— Wholly Thine—for-ev-er-more.

*Hum-bly at Thy cross I bow; Save me, Je-sus, save me now.*

4. In the promises I trust;
   In the cleansing blood confide;
   I am prostrate in the dust;
   I with Christ am crucified.

5. Jesus comes, He fills my soul!
   Perfected in love I am;
   I am every whit made whole;
   Glory, glory to the Lamb!

## No. 378. Washed in the Blood.

Rev. W. McDONALD.    BY PERMISSION.    ARRANGED.

1. Je-sus, Lord, I come to Thee, Wash'd in the blood of the Lamb!
2. Speak, and let my heart be clean, Wash'd in the blood of the Lamb!
3. Cleanse me, wash me white as snow, Wash'd in the blood of the Lamb!
4. To my heart the bliss re-veal, Wash'd in the blood of the Lamb!

Set my long-ing spir-it free, Wash'd in the blood of the Lamb!
Ful-ly sav'd from in-bred sin, Wash'd in the blood of the Lamb!
Let me all Thy ful-ness know, Wash'd in the blood of the Lamb!
Fix on me the Spir-it's seal, Wash'd in the blood of the Lamb!

## Washed in the Blood. Concluded.

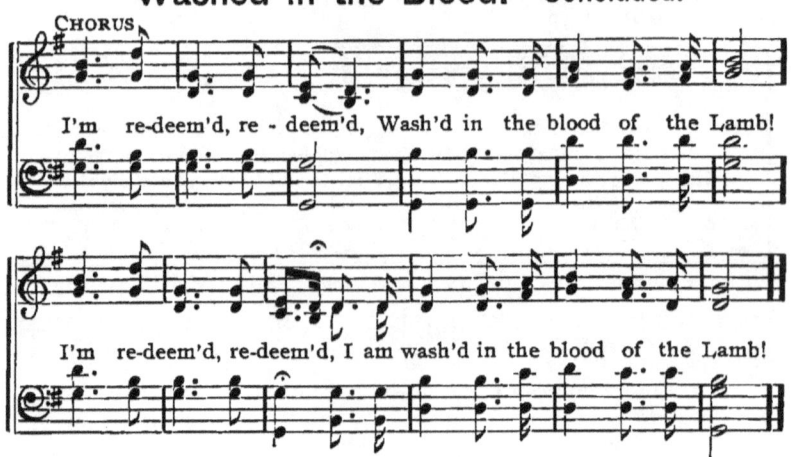

I'm re-deem'd, re-deem'd, Wash'd in the blood of the Lamb!

I'm re-deem'd, re-deem'd, I am wash'd in the blood of the Lamb!

### No. 379. King of Kings.

W. A. MUHLENBERG.     HORTON. 7.     X. S. VON WARTENSEE.

1. King of kings, and wilt thou deign O'er this wayward heart to reign?
2. Then, like heav'n's an-gel-ic bands, Waiting for thine high commands,
3. At thy word my will shall bow, Judgment, reason, bending low;
4. Zeal shall haste on ea-ger wing, Hour-ly some new gift to bring;
5. Tun'd by thee in sweet ac-cord, All shall sing their gracious Lord;

Hence-forth, take it for Thy throne, Rule here, Lord, and rule a-lone.
All my pow'rs shall wait on Thee, Cap-tive, yet di-vine-ly free.
Hope, de-sire, and ev-'ry thought, In-to glad o-be-dience brought.
Wis-dom, hum-bly cast-ing down At thy feet her gold-en crown.
Love the lead-er of the choir, Breathing round her seraph fire.

No. 382. **Come, Ye Sinners.**

HART.        J. INGALLS.

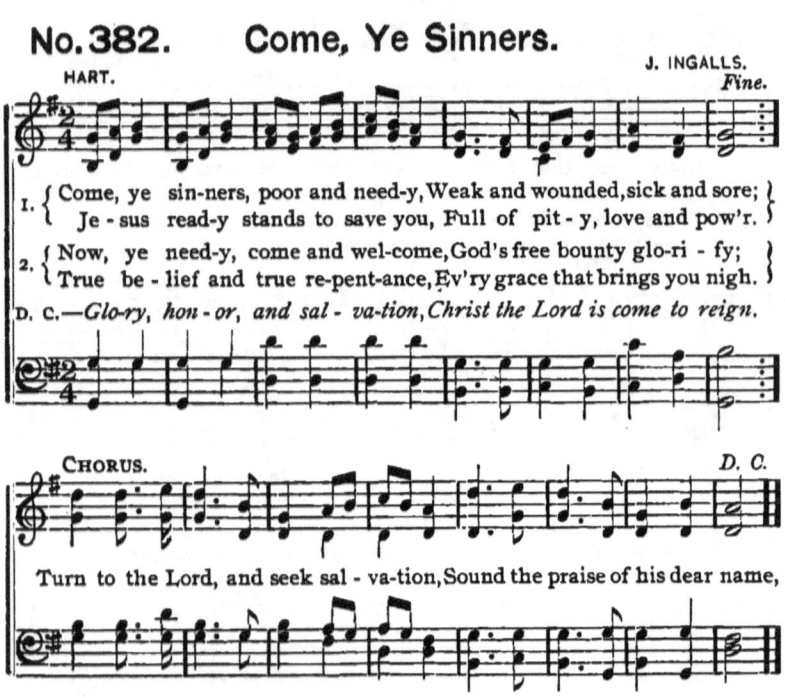

1. Come, ye sin-ners, poor and need-y, Weak and wounded, sick and sore;
   Je-sus read-y stands to save you, Full of pit-y, love and pow'r.
2. Now, ye need-y, come and wel-come, God's free bounty glo-ri-fy;
   True be-lief and true re-pent-ance, Ev'ry grace that brings you nigh.

D. C.—Glo-ry, hon-or, and sal-va-tion, Christ the Lord is come to reign.

CHORUS.

Turn to the Lord, and seek sal-va-tion, Sound the praise of his dear name,

3 Let not conscience make you linger,    4 Come, ye weary, heavy-laden,
   Nor of fitness fondly dream;               Bruised and mangled by the fall,
   All the fitness he requireth,                 If you tarry till you're better,
   Is to feel your need of him.                  You will never come at all.

No. 383. **Come to Jesus.**

1. Come to Je-sus, Come to Je-sus, Come to Je-sus, just now;
   Just now come to Je-sus, Come to Je-sus, just now.

2. He will save you.      5. Call upon Him.      8. He'll forgive you.
3. He is able.             6. He will hear you.    9. Don't reject Him.
4. Only trust Him.       7. Look to Jesus.      10. Hallelujah, Amen.

## No. 384. How I Love Jesus.

FREDERICK WHITFIELD.     Arr. by E O. E.

1. There is a name I love to hear, I love to sing its worth; It sounds like music in mine ear, The (*Omit*) sweetest name on earth, Oh, how I love Jesus, Oh, how I love Jesus, Oh, how I love Jesus, Be- (*Omit*) cause he first lov'd me.

2 It tells me of a Savior's love,
   Who died to set me free;
  It tells me of His precious blood,
   The sinner's perfect plea.

3 It tells me what my Father hath
   In store for every day,

And, tho' I tread a darksome path,
   Yields sunshine all the way.

4 It tells of One, whose loving heart
   Can feel my deepest woe,
  Who in each sorrow bears a part,
   That none can bear below.

## No. 385. Angels Hovering 'Round.

ANON.     UNKNOWN.

1. There are an-gels hov'ring 'round, There are an-gels hov'ring 'round,
2. They will carry the tid-ings home; They will carry the tidings home;

There are an - - gels, an - - gels hov - 'ring 'round.
They will car - - ry, car - - ry the tid - ings home.

3 To the new Jerusalem, etc.
4 Poor sinners are coming home, etc.

5 And Jesus bids them come, etc.
6 There's glory all around, etc.

## No. 386. Jesus Saves Me.

Cho. by G. R. S.     COPYRIGHT, 1894, BY E. O. EXCELL.     ZOLLIE STUART.

1. { Je-sus, my all, to heav'n is gone, Glory hallelujah, Jesus saves me;
   He whom I fix my hopes up-on; Glory hallelujah, Jesus saves me. }
2. { His track I see, and I'll pur-sue Glory hallelujah, Jesus saves me;
   The nar-row way, till Him I view, Glory hallelujah, Jesus saves me. }

He saves me, He saves me, Glo-ry hal-le-lu-jah, Je-sus saves me.

D. S. *saves me, He saves me, Glo-ry hal-le-lu-jah, Je-sus saves me.*

He redeem'd me, forgave me and sanc-ti-fied my soul, And

now I'm hap-py all day long, because He made me whole. He

3 The way the holy prophets went,
   The road that leads from banishment

4 The King's highway of holiness,
   I'll go, for all His paths are peace.

5 This is the way I long have sought,
   And mourned because I found it not.

6 My grief a burden long has been,
   Because I was not saved from sin.

7 The more I strove against its power,
   I felt its weight and guilt the more;

8 Till late I heard my Savior say,
   "Come hither, soul, I am the way."

9 Lo! glad I come; and Thou, blest Lamb
   Shalt take me to Thee, as I am;

10 Nothing but sin have I to give;
   Nothing but love shall I receive.

11 Then will I tell to sinners 'round,
   What a dear Savior I have found,

12 I'll point to Thy redeeming blood,
   And say, "Behold the way to God."

## No. 387. I'm Kneeling at the Mercy-Seat.

*(Use any C. M. Metre Hymn with either Chorus.)* ARRANGED.

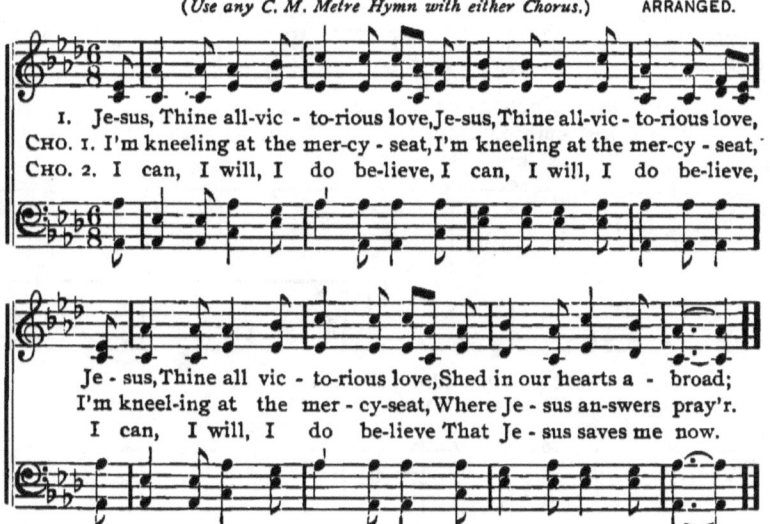

1. Jesus, Thine all-victorious love, Jesus, Thine all-victorious love,
Cho. 1. I'm kneeling at the mercy-seat, I'm kneeling at the mercy-seat,
Cho. 2. I can, I will, I do believe, I can, I will, I do believe,

Jesus, Thine all victorious love, Shed in our hearts abroad;
I'm kneeling at the mercy-seat, Where Jesus answers pray'r.
I can, I will, I do believe That Jesus saves me now.

## No. 388. Jesus, Thine All-victorious.

1 Jesus, Thine all-victorious love
  Shed in my heart abroad;
Then shall my feet no longer rove,
  Rooted and fixed in God.

2 Oh, that in me the sacred fire
  Might now begin to glow;
Burn up the dross of base desire
  And make the mountains flow!

3 Oh, that it now from heav'n might fall
  And all my sins consume!
Come, Holy Ghost, for Thee I call;
  Spirit of burning, come!

4 Refining fire, go thro' my heart,
  Illuminate my soul;
Scatter Thy life through every part,
  And sanctify the whole.

## No. 389. The Cleansing Wave.

Mrs. PHŒBE PALMER.    BY PERMISSION.    Mrs. JOS. F. KNAPP.

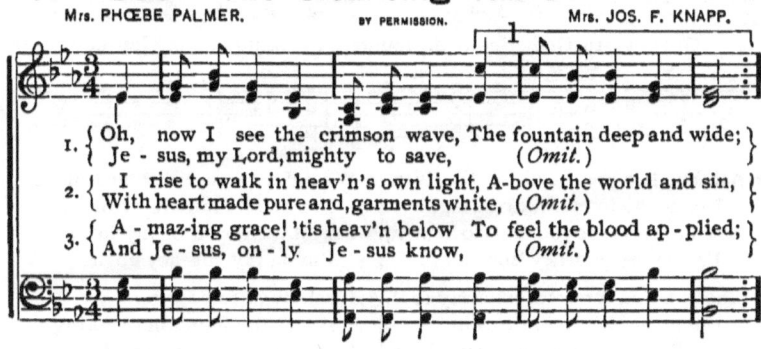

1. { Oh, now I see the crimson wave, The fountain deep and wide;
   Jesus, my Lord, mighty to save,    *(Omit.)* }
2. { I rise to walk in heav'n's own light, Above the world and sin,
   With heart made pure and, garments white, *(Omit.)* }
3. { Amazing grace! 'tis heav'n below To feel the blood applied;
   And Jesus, only Jesus know,    *(Omit.)* }

## The Cleansing Wave. Concluded.

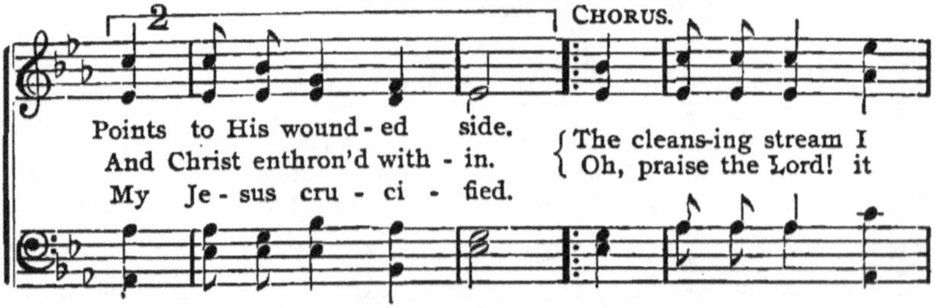

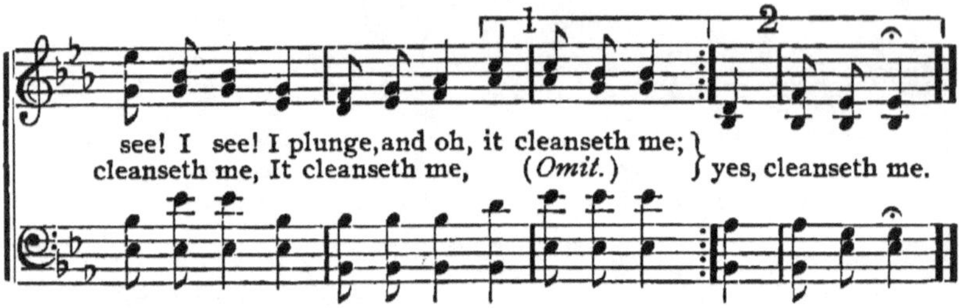

Points to His wound-ed side.
And Christ enthron'd with-in.
My Jesus cru-ci-fied.

The cleans-ing stream I see! I see! I plunge, and oh, it cleanseth me;
Oh, praise the Lord! it cleanseth me, It cleanseth me, (*Omit.*) yes, cleanseth me.

### No. 390. At the Fountain.

OLD MELODY.

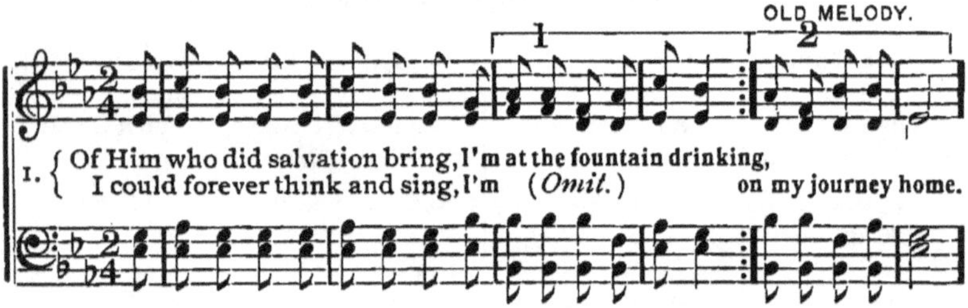

1. Of Him who did salvation bring, I'm at the fountain drinking,
   I could forever think and sing, I'm (*Omit.*) on my journey home.

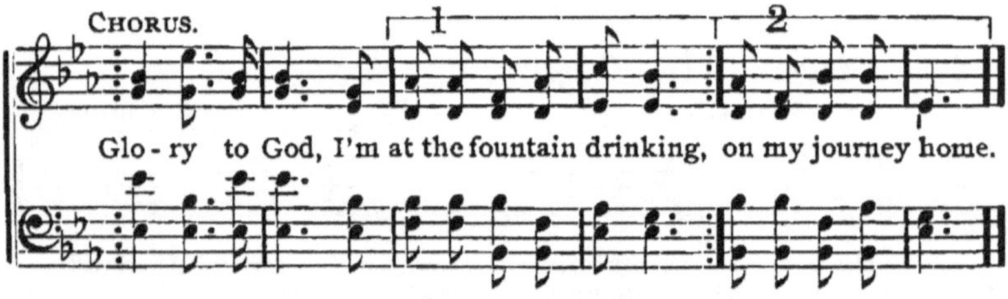

CHORUS.

Glo-ry to God, I'm at the fountain drinking, on my journey home.

2 Ask but His grace and lo! 'tis given,
  I'm at the fountain drinking,
  Ask and He turns your hell to heav'n,
  I'm on my journey home.

3 Tho' sin and sorrow wound my soul,
  I'm at the fountain drinking,
  Jesus, Thy balm will make me whole,
  I'm on my journey home.

4 Where'er I am, where'er I move,
  I'm at the fountain drinking,
  I meet the object of my love,
  I'm on my journey home.

5 Insatiate to this spring I fly,
  I'm at the fountain drinking,
  I drink and yet am ever dry,
  I'm on my journey home

## No. 391. Alas! and Did My Savior Bleed?

ISAAC WATTS.   AVON. C. M.   HUGH WILSON.

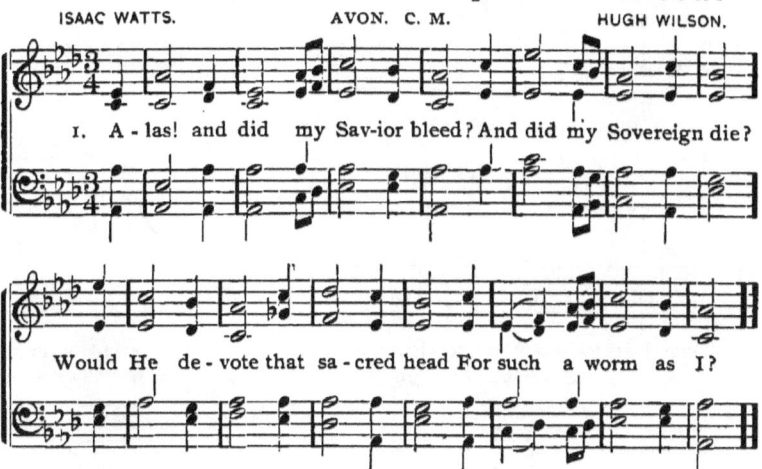

1. A-las! and did my Sav-ior bleed? And did my Sovereign die? Would He de-vote that sa-cred head For such a worm as I?

2 Was it for crimes that I have done,
　He groaned upon the tree?
　Amazing pity! grace unknown!
　And love beyond degree!

3 Well might the sun in darkness hide,
　And shut His glories in,   [died,
　When Christ, the mighty Maker,
　For man, the creature's sin.

4 Thus might I hide my blushing face,
　While His dear cross appears;
　Dissolve my heart in thankfulness,
　And melt mine eyes to tears.

### No. 392.  (See music above.)

1 O for a faith that will not shrink,
　Though pressed by every foe,
　That will not tremble on the brink
　Of any earthly woe!

2 That will not murmur nor complain
　Beneath the chastening rod,
　But, in the hour of grief or pain,
　Will lean upon its God;

3 A faith that shines more bright and
　When tempests rage without;[clear
　That when in danger knows no fear,
　In darkness feels no doubt;

4 That bears, unmoved, the world's dread
　Nor heeds its scornful smile;[frown,
　That seas of trouble cannot drown,
　Nor Satan's arts beguile.

### No. 393.  (See music above.)

1 O for a closer walk with God,
　A calm and heavenly frame;
　A light to shine upon the road
　That leads me to the Lamb!

2 Where is the blessedness I knew,
　When first I saw the Lord?
　Where is the soul-refreshing view
　Of Jesus and His word?

3 Return, O holy Dove, return,
　Sweet messenger of rest![mourn,
　I hate the sins that made Thee
　And drove Thee from my breast.

4 The dearest idol I have known,
　Whate'er that idol be,
　Help me to tear it from Thy throne,
　And worship only Thee.
　　　　　　　　　　WM. COWPER.

### No. 394.  (See music above.)

1 Forever here my rest shall be,
　Close to Thy bleeding side;
　This all my hope and all my plea,
　For me the Savior died.

2 My dying Savior and my God,
　Fountain for guilt and sin,
　Sprinkle me ever with Thy Blood,
　And cleanse and keep me clean.

3 Wash me and make me thus Thine
　Wash me and mine Thou art; [own;
　Wash me, but not my feet alone,—
　My hands, my head, my heart.

4 Th' atonement of Thy blood apply,
　Till faith to sight improve;
　Till hope in full fruition die,
　And all my soul be love.
　　　　　　　　　　CHAS. WESLEY.

## No. 395. Hail, Thou Once Despised.

JOHN BAKEWELL.   AUTUMN. 8, 7, D.

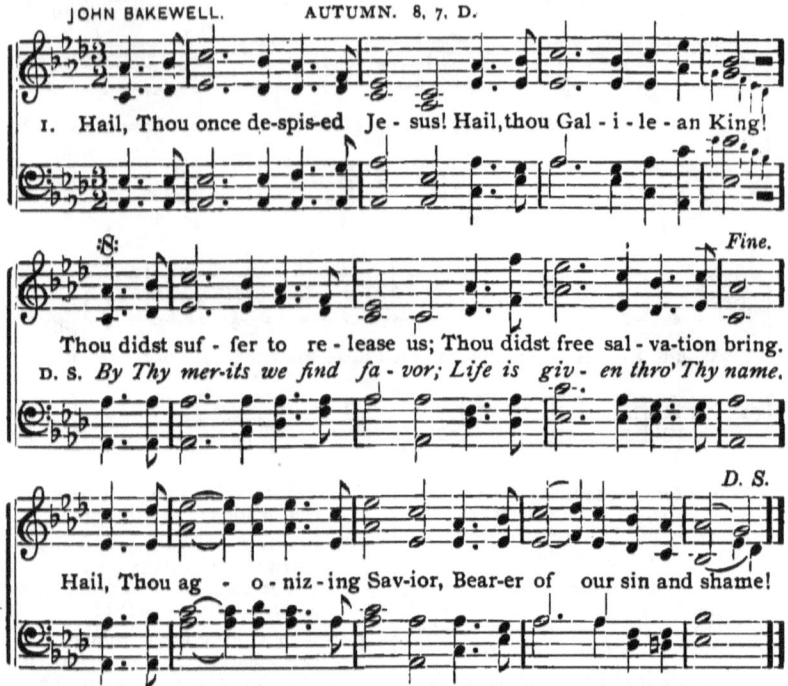

1. Hail, Thou once de-spis-ed Je - sus! Hail, thou Gal - i - le - an King!
Thou didst suf - fer to re - lease us; Thou didst free sal - va-tion bring.
D. S. *By Thy mer-its we find fa - vor; Life is giv - en thro' Thy name.*
Hail, Thou ag - o - niz-ing Sav-ior, Bear-er of our sin and shame!

2 Jesus, hail! enthroned in glory,
  There forever to abide;
All the heavenly hosts adore thee,
  Seated at thy Father's side:
There for sinners thou art pleading,
  There thou dost our place prepare;
Ever for us interceding,
  Till in glory we appear.

3 Worship, honor, power and blessing,
  Thou art worthy to receive;
Loudest praises, without ceasing,
  Meet it is for us to give.
Help, ye bright angelic spirits,
  Bring your sweetest, noblest lays;
Help to sing our Savior's merits;
  Help to chant Immanuel's praise!

### No. 396. *(See music above.)*

1 Gently, Lord, oh, gently lead us
  Through this lonely vale of tears,
Thro' the changes Thou'st decreed us,
  Till our last great change appears;
When temptation's darts assail us,
  When in devious paths we stray,
Let Thy goodness never fail us,
  Lead us in Thy perfect way.

2 In the hour of pain and anguish,
  In the hour when death draws near,
Suffer not our souls to languish,
  Suffer not our souls to fear,
And when mortal life is ended,
  Bid us in Thine arms to rest,
Till by angel bands attended
  We awake among the blest.
  THOS. HASTINGS.

### No. 397. *(See music above.)*

1 Hark, the voice of Jesus calling,
  "Who will go and work to-day?
Fields are white, and harvests waiting.
  Who will bear the sheaves away?"
Loud and long the Master calleth,
  Rich reward He offers free;
Who will answer, gladly saying,
  "Here am I, send me, send me?"

2 Let none hear you idly saying,
  "There is nothing I can do,"
While the souls of men are dying,
  And the Master calls for you:
Take the task He gives you gladly;
  Let His work your pleasure be;
Answer quickly when He calleth,
  "Here am I, send me, send me."
  DANIEL MARCH.

## No. 398. How Firm a Foundation.

GEORGE KEITH. 11s. ANNE STEELE.

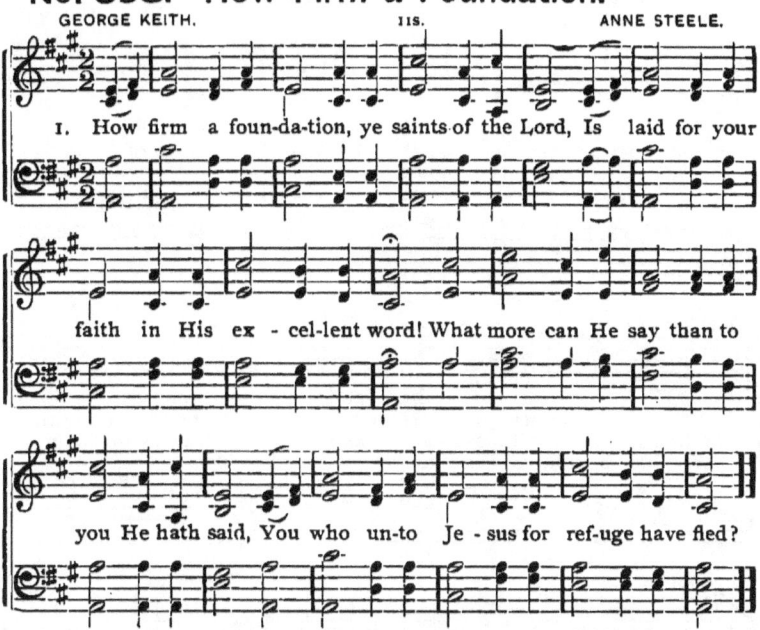

1. How firm a foun-da-tion, ye saints of the Lord, Is laid for your faith in His ex-cel-lent word! What more can He say than to you He hath said, You who un-to Je-sus for ref-uge have fled?

2 In every condition—in sickness, in health; [wealth;
In poverty's vale, or abounding in
At home and abroad; on the land, on the sea—
"As thy days may demand, shall thy strength ever be.

3 "Fear not; I am with thee; O be not dismayed! [aid;
I, I am thy God, and will still give thee
I'll strengthen thee, help thee, and cause thee to stand, [hand.
Upheld by my righteous, omnipotent

4 "When through the deep waters I call thee to go, [flow,
The rivers of woe shall not thee over-
For I will be with thee, thy troubles to bless, [tress.
And sanctify to thee thy deepest dis-

5 "When through fiery trials thy path-way shall lie, [ply:
My grace, all-sufficient, shall be thy sup-
The flame shall not hurt thee—I only design [refine.
Thy dross to consume, and thy gold to

6 "E'en down to old age, all my peo-ple shall prove [love;
My sovereign, eternal, unchangeable

And when hoary hairs shall their tem-ples adorn,
Like lambs they shall still in my bo-som be borne.

7 "The soul that on Jesus still leans for repose,
I will not, I *will* not, desert to his foes;
That soul, though all hell should en-deavor to shake, [sake."
I'll never, *no*, *never*, NO, NEVER for-

---

### No. 399. (*See music above.*)

1 Oh, turn ye, oh, turn ye, for why will ye die,
When God in great mercy is coming so nigh?
Now Jesus invites you, the Spirit says, Come,
And angels are waiting to welcome you home.

2 And now Christ is ready your souls to receive,
Oh! how can you question, if you will believe?
If sin is your burden, why will you not come?
'T is you He bids welcome; He bids you come home.

ANON.

## No. 400. Revive Us Again.

WM. P. MACKAY.  J. J. HUSBAND.

1. We praise Thee, O God! for the Son of Thy love,
2. We praise Thee, O God! for Thy Spir-it of light,
3. All glo-ry and praise to the Lamb that was slain,
4. All glo-ry and praise to the God of all grace,

For Je-sus who died and is now gone a-bove,
Who has shown us our Sav-ior and scat-tered our night,
Who has borne all our sins and has cleansed ev-'ry stain,
Who has bought us, and sought us, and guid-ed our ways,

REFRAIN.
Hal-le-lu-jah! Thine the glory; Hal-le-lu-jah! a-men! Re-vive us a-gain.

### No. 401. God's Love.

*Leader:*—For God so loved the world, that He gave His only begotten Son, that whosoever believeth in him should not perish, but have everlasting life.

*Response:*—In this was manifested the love of God toward us, because that God sent His only begotten Son into the world, that we might live thro' Him.

*Leader:*—Beloved, if God so loved us, we ought also to love one another.

*All sing.* 1st verse No. 400, We praise, etc.

*Leader:*—But the Comforter, which is the Holy Ghost, whom the Father will send in my name, he shall teach you all things and bring all things to your remembrance, whatsoever I have said unto you.

*Response:*—When He, the Spirit of Truth, is come, He will guide you into all truth; for he shall not speak of himself; but whatsoever he shall hear, that shall he speak: and he will show you things to come.

*Leader:*—He shall glorify me: for he shall receive of mine, and shall show it unto you.

*All sing.* 2d verse, We praise Thee, etc.

*Leader:*—And I beheld, and I heard the voice of many angels round about the throne, and the living creatures and the elders; and the number of them was ten-thousand times ten-thousand, and thousands of thousands.

*Response:*—Saying with a loud voice, Worthy is the Lamb that was slain to receive power, and riches, and wisdom, and strength, and honor, and glory, and blessing.

*All Sing.* 3d verse, All glory, etc.

## No. 402. Holy Spirit, Faithful Guide.

M. M. WELLS.

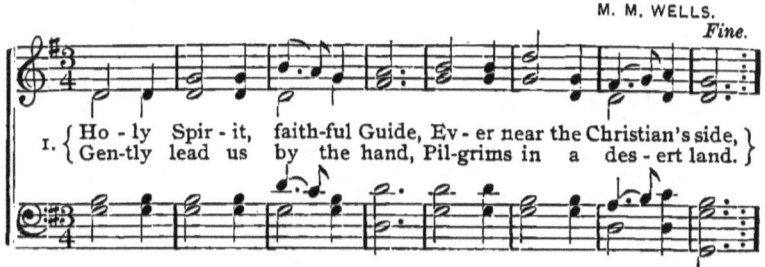

1. Ho-ly Spir-it, faith-ful Guide, Ev-er near the Christian's side,
   Gen-tly lead us by the hand, Pil-grims in a des-ert land.

D. C. Whispering softly, "wanderer, come, Fol-low me, I'll guide thee home."

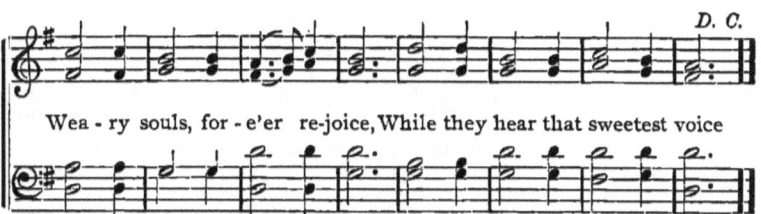

Wea-ry souls, for-e'er re-joice, While they hear that sweetest voice

2 Ever present, truest Friend,
Ever, near Thine aid to lend,
Leave us not to doubt and fear,
Groping on in darkness drear.
When the storms are raging sore,
Hearts grow faint and hopes give o'er
Whisper softly, "wanderer, come,
Follow me, I'll guide thee home."

3 When our days of toil shall cease,
Waiting still for sweet release,
Nothing left but heaven and prayer,
Wondering if our names are there;
Wading deep the dismal flood,
Pleading naught but Jesus' blood;
Whisper softly, "wanderer, come,
Follow me, I'll guide thee home."

---

### No. 403. Holy Spirit, No. I.

*Leader:*—That which is born of the flesh is flesh; and that which is born of the Spirit is spirit.

*Response:*—If any man have not the spirit of Christ, he is none of his.

*Leader;*—As many as are led by the Spirit of God, they are the sons of God.

*Response;*—The Spirit itself beareth witness with our spirit that we are the children of God.

*All Sing;* 1st verse, No. 402, Holy Spirit, etc.

*Leader;*—After that ye believed, ye were sealed with that Holy Spirit of promise, which is the earnest of our inheritance until our redemption of the purchased possessions unto the praise of his glory.

*Response.*—Grieve not the holy Spirit of God, whereby ye are sealed unto the day of redemption.

*Leader;*—The Comforter, which is

### Holy Spirit. Concluded.

the Holy Ghost, whom the Father will send in my name, he shall teach you all things and bring all things to your remembrance whatsoever I have said unto you.

*Response;*—The Spirit also helpeth our infirmities, for we know not what we should pray for as we ought, but the Spirit itself maketh intercession for us.

*All Sing;* 2d verse, Ever present, etc.

*Leader;*—The fruit of the Spirit is love, joy, peace, long suffering, gentleness, goodness, faith, meekness, temperance; if we live in the Spirit, let us also walk in the Spirit.

*Response;*—He that soweth to the flesh shall of the flesh reap corruption, but he that soweth to the Spirit, shall of the Spirit reap life everlasting.

*All sing;* 3d verse, When our days, etc.

## No. 404. How Gentle God's Commands.

PHILIP DODDRIDGE.  DENNIS. S. M.  GEO. NAEGELI.

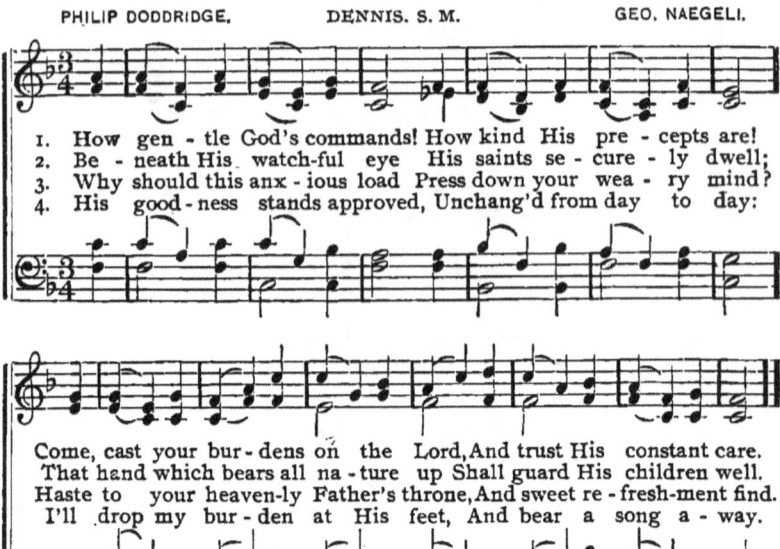

1. How gen-tle God's commands! How kind His pre-cepts are!
2. Be-neath His watch-ful eye His saints se-cure-ly dwell;
3. Why should this anx-ious load Press down your wea-ry mind?
4. His good-ness stands approved, Unchang'd from day to day:

Come, cast your bur-dens on the Lord, And trust His constant care.
That hand which bears all na-ture up Shall guard His children well.
Haste to your heaven-ly Father's throne, And sweet re-fresh-ment find.
I'll drop my bur-den at His feet, And bear a song a-way.

---

### No. 405. Wisdom.

*Leader:*—Remember now thy Creator in the days of thy youth. Serve him with gladness, and magnify his name forever!

*Response:*—What shall I render unto the Lord for all his benefits towards me? I will take the cup of salvation and call upon the name of the Lord.

*Leader:*—Give us, O Lord, the wisdom from above, which is first pure, then peaceable, gentle, easy to be entreated, full of mercy and good fruits, without partiality, and without hypocrisy.

*Response:*—Whence then cometh wisdom? and where is the place of understanding?

*Leader:*—Behold, the fear of the Lord, that is wisdom, and to depart from evil is understanding.

*Response:*—Happy is the man that findeth wisdom, and the man that getteth understanding.

*Leader:*—The merchandise of it is better than the merchandise of silver, and the gain thereof than fine gold.

*Response:*—She is more precious than rubies.

*Leader:*—And all things thou canst desire are not to be compared unto her.

*Response:*—Length of days is in her right hand: and in her left hand riches and honor.

*Leader:*—Her ways are ways of pleasantness, and all her paths are peace.

*Response:*—She is a tree of life to them that lay hold upon her; and happy is every one that retaineth her.

*Leader:*—And beside this, giving all diligence, add to your knowledge temperance.

*Response:*—And to temperance, patience.

*Leader:*—And to patience, godliness.

*Response:*—And to godliness, brotherly kindness.

*Leader:*—And to brotherly kindness, charity.

*All Sing:* 1st and 2d verses, No. 404. How gentle God's commands! etc.

## No. 406.    Holy, Holy, Holy!

NICEA, 11, 12, 10. (M. H. 136.)    Rev. JOHN B. DYKES.

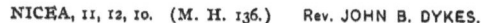

1. Ho-ly, ho-ly, ho - ly! Lord God Al-might-y! Ear-ly in the morn - ing, Our songs shall rise to Thee; Ho-ly, ho-ly, ho - ly! Mer - ci-ful and Might-y! God in three Per-sons, Blessed Trin-i - ty!

2 Holy, holy, holy!
All the saints adore Thee,
Casting down their golden crowns
Around the glassy sea;
Cherubim and Seraphim
Falling down before Thee,
Which wert and art and
Evermore shalt be.

3 Holy, holy, holy!
Lord God Almighty!
All Thy work shall praise Thy name
In earth and sky and sea:
Holy, holy, holy!
Merciful and Mighty!
God in three Persons,
Blessed Trinity!

---

### No. 407.   Holy. Holy!

*Leader:*—Holy, holy, holy, is the Lord of hosts; the whole earth is full of his glory.

*All Sing:* 1st verse, No. 406, Holy, holy, holy! Lord God Almighty! etc.

*Leader:*—For thou art not a God that hath pleasure in wickedness: neither shall evil dwell with Thee.

*Response:*—But thou art holy, O thou that inhabitest the praises of Israel.

*All Sing:* 2d verse, Holy, holy, holy! All the saints adore thee, etc.

### Holy, Holy! Concluded.

*Leader:*—Exalt ye the Lord our God and worship at his footstool; for he is holy.

*Response:*—And the four beasts had each of them six wings about him, and they were full of eyes within, and they rest not day and night, saying, Holy, holy, holy! Lord God Almighty, which was, and is, and is to come!

*All Sing:* 3d verse, Holy, holy, holy! Lord God Almighty! etc.

## No. 408. My Faith Looks Up.

RAY PALMER.    OLIVET. (M. H. 762.)    LOWELL MASON.

1. My faith looks up to Thee, Thou Lamb of Calvary, Savior divine! Now hear me while I pray, Take all my guilt away, Oh, let me from this day Be wholly Thine.

2 May thy rich grace impart
Strength to my fainting heart,
My zeal inspire;
As thou hast died for me,
Oh, may my love to thee,
Pure, warm, and changeless be,
A living fire.

3 While life's dark maze I tread,
And griefs around me spread,
Be thou my Guide:
Bid darkness turn to day,
Wipe sorrow's tears away,
Nor let me ever stray
From thee aside.

4 When ends life's transient dream,
When death's cold sullen stream,
Shall o'er me roll;
Blest Savior, then, in love,
Fear and distrust remove;
Oh, bear me safe above,
A ransomed soul!

---

## No. 409. Faith.

*All Sing:* 1st verse No 408, My faith, etc.

*Leader:*—As many as received him, to them gave he power to become the sons of God, even to them that believe on his name.

*Response:*—He that believeth on him is not condemned; but he that believeth not, is condemned already, because he hath not believed in the name of the only begotten Son of God.

*Leader:*—He that believeth on the Son hath everlasting life; and he that believeth not the Son, shall not see life; but the wrath of God abideth on him.

*Response:*—If ye believe not that I am he, ye shall die in your sins.

*All Sing:* 2d verse, May Thy rich, etc.

*Leader:*—And whosoever liveth, and

## Faith. Concluded.

believeth in me, shall never die.

*Response:*—Gracious is the Lord, and righteous; yea, our God is merciful.

*Leader:*—Even when we were dead in sins, hath he quickened us together with Christ; (by grace ye are saved.)

*Response:*—That in the ages to come he might show the exceeding riches of his grace in his kindness towards us, through Christ Jesus.

*All Sing:* 3d verse, While life's dark, etc.

*Leader:*—Being justified freely by his grace, through the redemption that is in Christ Jesus.

*Response.*—And if by grace, then it is no more of works; otherwise grace is no more grace.

*All Sing:* 4th verse, When ends life's etc.

## No. 410. What a Friend.

H. BONAR.     8s, 7s, D. (M. H. 728.)     C. C. CONVERSE.

1. What a friend we have in Je - sus, All our sins and griefs to bear!
What a priv - i - lege to car - ry Ev - 'ry thing to God in pray'r!
*D. S. All be-cause we do not car - ry, Ev - 'ry thing to God in pray'r!*
Oh, what peace we oft - en for - feit, Oh, what needless pain we bear,

2 Have we trials and temptations?
Is there trouble anywhere?
We should never be discouraged,
Take it to the Lord in prayer.
Can we find a friend so faithful,
Who will all our sorrows share?
Jesus knows our every weakness,
Take it to the Lord in prayer.

3 Are we weak and heavy laden,
Cumbered with a load of care,
Precious Savior, still our refuge,
Take it to the Lord in prayer;
Do thy friends despise, forsake thee?
Take it to the Lord in prayer,
In His arms He'll take and shield thee
Thou wilt find a solace there.

## No. 411. Prayer. No. 1.

*Leader:*—If my people, which are called by my name, shall humble themselves and pray, and seek my face, and turn from their wicked ways, then will I hear from heaven, and will forgive their sin.

*Response:*—And whatsoever ye shall ask in my name, that will I do, that the Father may be glorified in the Son.

*All Sing:* 1st verse, No. 410, What a, etc.

*Leader:*—In everything by prayer and supplication with thanksgiving let your requests be made known unto God.

*Response:*—The Spirit also helpeth our infirmities, for we know not what we should pray for as we ought; but the Spirit itself maketh intercession for us with groanings which cannot be uttered.

*All Sing:* 2d verse, Have we trials, etc.

## Prayer. Concluded.

*Leader:*—Confess your faults one to another, and pray one for another, that ye may be healed. The effectual fervent prayer of a righteous man availeth much.

*Response:*—The sacrifice of the wicked is an abomination to the Lord; but the prayer of the upright is His delight.

*All Sing:* 3d verse, Are we weak, etc.

*Leader:*—After this manner therefore pray ye:

*All:*—Our Father which art in heaven, hallowed be thy name. Thy kingdom come. Thy will be done in earth as it is in heaven. Give us this day our daily bread. And forgive us our debts, as we forgive our debtors. And lead us not into temptation, but deliver us from evil. For thine is the kingdom, and the power, and the glory, forever. Amen.

No. 412.      Rock of Ages.

A. M. TOPLADY.       TOPLADY. 7s.       THOS. HASTINGS.

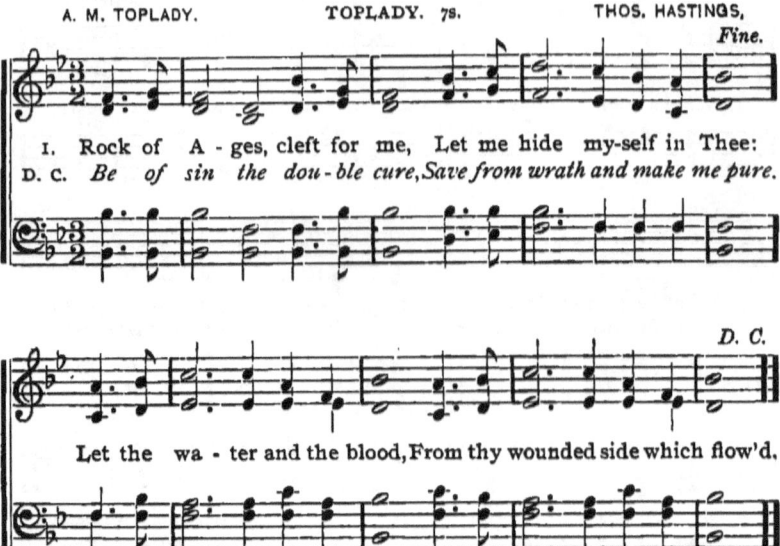

1. Rock of A-ges, cleft for me, Let me hide my-self in Thee:
D. C. *Be of sin the dou-ble cure, Save from wrath and make me pure.*

Let the wa-ter and the blood, From thy wounded side which flow'd.

2 Could my tears forever flow,
   Could my zeal no languor know,
   These for sin could not atone,
   Thou must save, and Thou alone:
   In my hand no price I bring,
   Simply to Thy cross I cling.

3 While I draw this fleeting breath,
   When my eyes shall close in death,
   When I rise to worlds unknown,
   And behold Thee on Thy throne,
   Rock of Ages, cleft for me,
   Let me hide myself in Thee.

---

### No. 413.  Rock of Ages.

*Leader:*—Behold the Lamb of God who taketh away the sins of the world.

*Response:*—He was wounded for our transgressions. He was bruised for our iniquity. The chastisement of our peace was upon him, and with his stripes we are healed.

*Leader:*—Thou shalt call his name Jesus, for he shall save his people from their sins.

*All Sing:* 1st verse, No. 412, Rock of Ages.

*Leader:*—The blood of Jesus Christ, his Son, cleanseth us from all sin.

*Response:*—Neither is there salvation in any other, for there is none other name given under heaven among men whereby we must be saved.

*Leader:*—Without shedding of blood is no remission.

### Rock of Ages. Concluded.

*Response:*—The eternal God is thy refuge and underneath are the everlasting arms.

*All sing;* 2d verse, Could my tears, etc.

*Leader:*—The gift of God is eternal life, through Jesus Christ, our Lord.

*Response:*—By grace are ye saved through faith, and that not of yourselves; it is the gift of God.

*Leader:*—How shall we escape if we neglect so great salvation.

*All.*—When thou passest through the waters I will be with thee and through the rivers, they shall not overflow thee; when thou walkest through the fire thou shalt not be burned, neither shall the flame kindle upon thee.

*All Sing:* 3d verse, While I draw, etc.

## No. 414. Jesus, Lover of My Soul.

CHARLES WESLEY.     MARTYN. 7 D. (M. H. 656.)     S. B. MARSH.

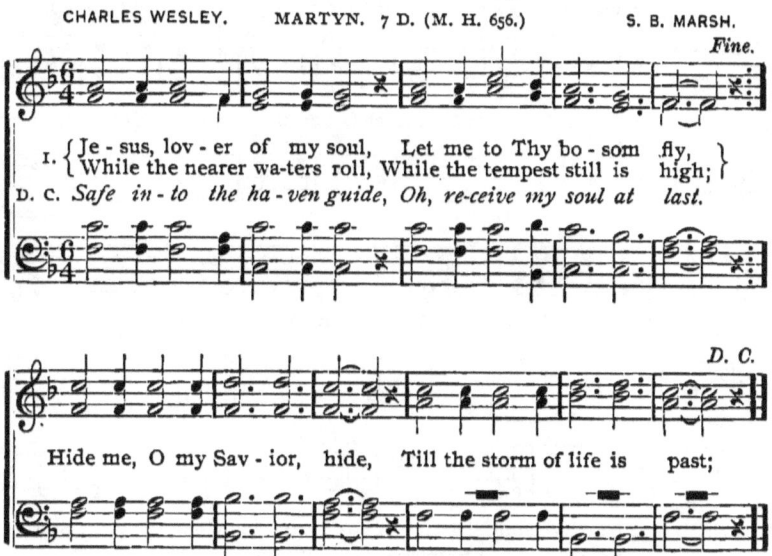

1. Je-sus, lov-er of my soul, Let me to Thy bo-som fly,
While the nearer wa-ters roll, While the tempest still is high;
D. C. *Safe in-to the ha-ven guide, Oh, re-ceive my soul at last.*

Hide me, O my Sav-ior, hide, Till the storm of life is past;

2 Other refuge have I none,
  Hangs my helpless soul on Thee;
Leave, oh, leave me not alone,
  Still support and comfort me.
All my trust on Thee is stayed,
  All my help from Thee I bring;
Cover my defenseless head
  With the shadow of Thy wing.

3 Thou, O Christ, art all I want,
  More than all in Thee I find;
Raise the fallen, cheer the faint,
  Heal the sick and lead the blind.
Just and holy is Thy name;
  I am all unrighteousness;
Vile and full of sin I am,
  Thou art full of truth and grace.

---

### No. 415. Refuge.

*Leader:*—I will lift up mine eyes unto the hills from whence cometh my help. My help cometh from the Lord who made heaven and earth.

*Response:*—He shall be as an hiding place from the wind, and a covert from the tempest; as rivers of water in a dry place, as the shadow of a great rock in a weary land.

*Leader:*—Peace I leave with you, my peace I give unto you. Let not your heart be troubled, neither let it be afraid.

*All Sing.* 1st verse, No. 414, Jesus, lover, etc:

*Leader:*—Come unto me all ye that labor and are heavy laden and I will give you rest.

*Response;*—I will both lay me down in peace and sleep, for thou Lord only maketh me to dwell in safety.

### Refuge. Concluded.

*Leader:*—The Lord will be a refuge for the oppressed, a refuge in time of trouble.

*Response:*—What time I am afraid I will trust in thee.

*All Sing.* 2d verse, Other refuge have, etc.

*Leader:*—Behold he that keepeth Israel shall neither slumber nor sleep.

*Response:*—The name of the Lord is a strong tower. The righteous runneth into it, and is safe.

*Leader:*—Thou wilt keep him in perfect peace whose mind is stayed on thee because he trusteth in thee.

*All Sing;* 3d verse, Thou, O Christ, etc.

## No. 416. Joy to the World.

Rev. ISAAC WATTS.    ANTIOCH. C. M. (M. H. 183)    Arr. by LOWELL MASON.

1. Joy to the world, the Lord is come! Let earth receive her King; Let ev'ry heart pre-pare him room, And heav'n and na-ture sing, And heav'n and na-ture sing, And heav'n, and heav'n and na-ture sing.

2 Joy to the earth, the Savior reigns,
Let men their songs employ;
While fields and floods, rocks, hills and plains,
Repeat the sounding joy.

3 No more let sin and sorrow grow,
Nor thorns infest the ground;
He comes to make his blessings flow
Far as the curse is found.

4 He rules the world with truth and grace,
And makes the nations prove
The glories of his righteousness,
And wonders of his love.

## No. 417. Joy.

*All Sing:* 1st verse No. 416, Joy to the, etc.

*Leader.*—Unto us a child is born, unto us a son is given, and the government shall be upon his shoulders; and his name shall be called Wonderful, Counsellor, The mighty God, The everlasting Father, The Prince of Peace.

*Response.*—God also hath highly exalted him, and given him a name which is above every name: That at the name of Jesus every knee should bow, of things in heaven, and things in earth, and things under the earth, and that every tongue should confess that Jesus Christ is Lord, to the glory of God the Father.

*Leader.*—Sing, O heavens, and be joyful, O earth; and break forth into singing, O mountains; for the Lord hath comforted his people, and will have mercy upon his afflicted.

### Joy. Concluded.

*All Sing:* 2d verse, Joy to the earth, etc.

*Leader.*—Hearken unto me, my people, and give ear unto me, O my nation. My righteousness is near; my salvation is gone forth, and mine arms shall judge the people. The isles shall wait upon me, and on mine arms shall they trust.

*Response.*—Therefore the redeemed of the Lord shall return, and come with singing unto Zion; and everlasting joy shall be upon their heads; they shall obtain gladness and joy, and sorrow and mourning shall flee away.

*Leader.*—For ye shall go out with joy, and be led forth with peace; the mountains and the hills shall break forth before you into singing, and all the trees of the field shall clap their hands.

*All Sing:* 3d verse, No more let sin, etc.

## No. 418. The Great Physician.

Rev. WM. HUNTER.  Arr. by Rev. J. H. STOCKTON.

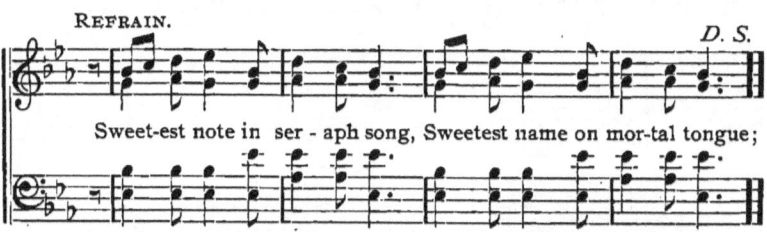

3 All glory to the dying Lamb!
　I now believe in Jesus;
　I love the blessed Savior's name,
　I love the name of Jesus.

4 His name dispels my guilt and fear
　No other name but Jesus;
　Oh! how my soul delights to hear
　The charming name of Jesus.

---

## No. 419. Great Physician.

*Leader.*—And she shall bring forth a son, and thou shalt call his name Jesus; for he shall save his people from their sins.

*Response.*—And they shall call his name Emmanuel, which being interpreted is, God with us.

*Leader.*—He was wounded for our transgressions, he was bruised for our iniquities: the chastisement of our peace was upon him; and with his stripes we are healed.

*All Sing.* 1st verse, No. 418, The Great Physician now is near, etc.

*Leader.*—When the even was come, they brought unto him many that were possessed with devils: and he cast out the spirits with his word, and healed all that were sick.

*Response*—That it might be fulfilled which was spoken by Esaias the prophet, saying, Himself took our infirmities, and bare our sicknesses.

*Leader.*—Glory to God in the highest, and on earth peace, good will toward men.

*All Sing.* 2d verse, Your many sins, etc.

*Leader.*—Him hath God exalted with his right hand to be a Prince and a Savior, for to give repentance to Israel, and forgiveness of sins.

*Response.*—To him give all the prophets witness, that through his name whosoever believeth in him shall receive remission of sins.

*Leader.*—That which we have seen and heard declare we unto you, that ye also may have fellowship with us: and truly our fellowship is with the Father, and with his Son, Jesus Christ.

*Response.*—And these things write we unto you, that your joy may be full.

*All Sing.* 3d verse, All glory to the, etc.

### No. 420.   Oh, Could I Speak.

S. MEDLEY.   Ariel, C. P. M. (M. H. 743.)   Dr. LOWELL MASON.

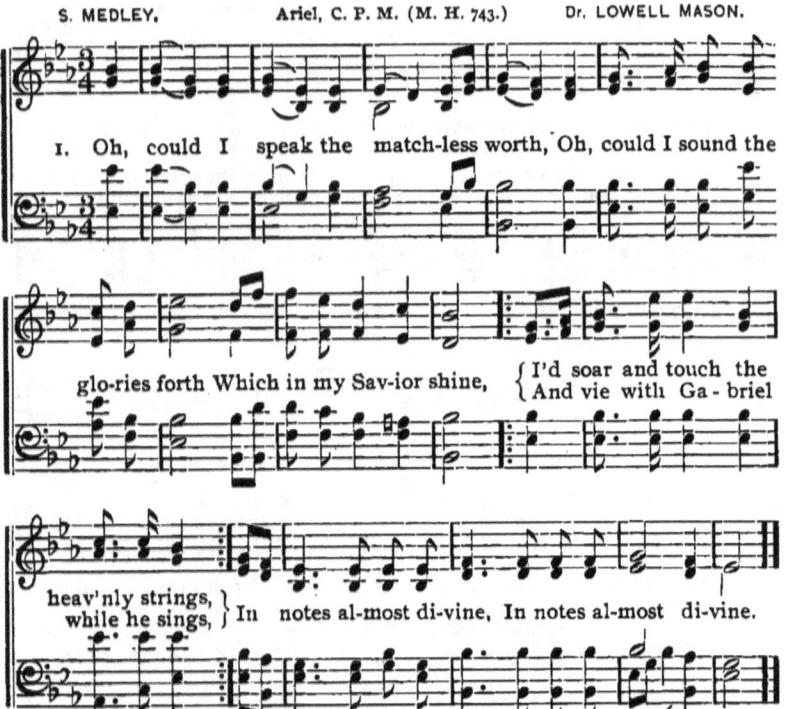

1. Oh, could I speak the match-less worth, Oh, could I sound the glo-ries forth Which in my Sav-ior shine, { I'd soar and touch the heav'nly strings, / And vie with Ga-briel while he sings, } In notes al-most di-vine, In notes al-most di-vine.

2  I'd sing the precious blood he spilt,
My ransom from the dreadful guilt,
Of sin and wrath divine!
I'd sing his glorious righteousness,
In which all perfect heavenly dress
‖: My soul shall ever shine. :‖

3  Well—the delightful day will come,
When my dear Lord will bring me home,
And I shall see his face:
Then with my Savior, Brother, Friend,
A blest eternity I'll spend,
‖: Triumphant in his grace. :‖

---

### No. 421. Praise, No. 1.

*Leader.*—I will praise thee, O Lord, with my whole heart; I will shew forth all thy marvellous works.

*Response.*—O Lord, open thou my lips; and my mouth shall shew forth thy praise.

*Leader.*—Be thou exalted, O God, above the heavens, let thy glory be above all the earth.

*All Sing.*  1st verse No. 420, Oh, could I speak, etc.

*Leader.*—I will wash my hands in innocency, so will I compass thine altar, O Lord.

*Response.*—That I may publish with the voice of thanksgiving, and tell of all thy wondrous works.

### Praise, No. 1. Concluded.

*Leader.*—The Lord redeemeth the soul of his servants; and none of them that trust in him shall be desolate.

*All Sing.*  2nd verse, I'd sing the, etc.

*Leader.*—In my Father's house are many mansions; if it were not so I would have told you; I go to prepare a place for you.

*Response.*—And if I go and prepare a place for you, I will come again and receive you unto myself that where I am, there ye may be also.

*All Sing.*  3d verse, Well, the delight, etc.

## No. 422. Loving Kindness.

1. A-wake, my soul, in joyful lays, And sing my great Redeemer's praise, He just-ly claims a song from me, His lov-ing kind-ness, oh, how free!

Loving kindness, lov-ing kindness, His lov-ing kind-ness, oh, how free!

2 He saw me ruined in the fall,
Yet loved me notwithstanding all;
He saved me from my lost estate,
His loving kindness, oh, how great!
Loving kindness, loving kindness,
Loving kindness, oh, how great!

3 Tho' numerous hosts of mighty foes,
Tho' earth and hell my way oppose,
He safely leads my soul along,
His loving kindness, oh, how strong!
Loving kindness, loving kindness,
His loving kindness, oh, how strong!

## No. 423. Loving Kindness.

*Leader.*—It is a good thing to give thanks unto the Lord, and to sing praises unto thy name, O most High.

*Response.*—For with thee *is* the fountain of life; in thy light shall we see light.

*Leader.*—Continue thy loving kindness unto them that know thee; and thy righteousness to the upright in heart.

*Response.*—To show forth thy loving kindness in the morning, and thy faithfulness every night.

*All Sing.* 1st verse No. 422, Awake my soul, etc.

*Leader.*—How excellent is thy loving kindness, O God! therefore the children of men put their trust under the shadow of thy wings.

*Response.*—Because thy loving kindness is better than life, my lips shall praise thee.

## Loving Kindness. Concluded.

*Leader.*—O praise the Lord, all ye nations; praise him, all ye people.

*Response.*—For his merciful kindness is great toward us; and the truth of the Lord *endureth* forever. Praise ye the Lord.

*All Sing.* 2d verse, He saw me ruined.

*Leader.*—I will mention the loving kindnesses of the Lord, and the praises of the Lord, according to all that the Lord hath bestowed on us, and the great goodness toward the house of Israel.

*Response.*—The Lord hath appeared of old unto me, saying, Yea, I have loved thee with an everlasting love, therefore with loving kindness have I drawn thee.

*Leader.*—And with everlasting kindness will I have mercy on thee, saith the Lord, thy Redeemer.

*All Sing.* 3d verse, Tho' num'rous hosts.

## No. 424. All Hail the Power.

PERRONET.  Coronation. C. M. (M. H. 248.)  OLIVER HOLDEN.

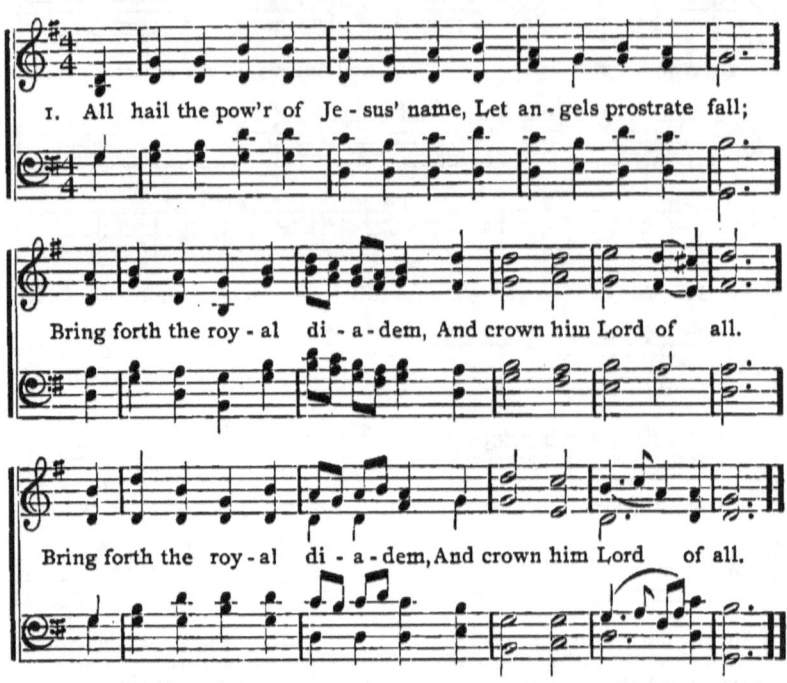

1. All hail the pow'r of Jesus' name, Let angels prostrate fall;
Bring forth the royal diadem, And crown him Lord of all.
Bring forth the royal diadem, And crown him Lord of all.

2 Let every kindred, every tribe,
On this terrestrial ball,
‖:To him all majesty ascribe,
And crown him Lord of all.:‖

3 Oh, that with yonder sacred throng
We at his feet may fall:
‖:We'll join the everlasting song,
And crown him Lord of all.:‖

### No. 425. Coronation.

*Leader.*—And all the angels stood round about the throne, and about the elders and the four beasts, and fell before the throne on their faces and worshiped God.

*Response.*—Saying, Amen: Blessing and glory, and wisdom, and thanksgiving, and honor, and power, and might, be unto our God forever and ever. Amen.

*Leader.*—Thou shalt also be a crown of glory in the hand of the Lord, and a royal diadem in the hand of thy God.

*All Sing:* 1st verse No. 424, All hail the power of, etc.

*Leader.*—And I saw a strong angel proclaiming with a loud voice, Who is worthy to open the book, and loose the seals thereof?

### Coronation. Concluded.

*Response.*—And they sung a new song, saying, Thou art worthy, for thou wast slain and hast redeemed us to God by thy blood out of every kindred and tongue, and people, and nation.

*All Sing.* 2d verse, Let every kindred,

*Leader.*—And after these things I heard a great voice of much people in heaven, saying, Alleluia, salvation, and glory, and honor, and power, unto the Lord, our God.

*Response.*—And they sing the song of Moses the servant of God, and the song of the Lamb, saying, great and marvellous are thy works, Lord God Almighty; just and true are thy ways, thou King of Saints.

*All Sing.* 3d verse, Oh, that with yonder,

## No. 426. Am I a Soldier?

ISAAC WATTS.   ARLINGTON. C. M. (M. H. 593.)   THOS. A. ARNE.

1. Am I a soldier of the cross, A follower of the Lamb,
And shall I fear to own his cause, Or blush to speak his name?

2 Must I be carried to the skies
  On flowery beds of ease,
While others fought to win the prize,
  And sailed through bloody seas?

3 Are there no foes for me to face?
  Must I not stem the flood?

Is this vile world a friend to grace,
  To help me on to God?

4 Since I must fight if I would reign,
  Increase my courage, Lord;
I'll bear the toil, endure the pain,
  Supported by thy word.

---

## No. 427. Soldiers of the Cross.

*Leader.*—Fight the good fight of faith, lay hold on eternal life whereunto thou art called.

*Response.*—Put on the whole armor of God that ye may be able to stand against the wiles of the devil.

*Leader.*—We are troubled on every side, yet not distressed, we are perplexed, but not in despair.

*All Sing.* 1st verse, No. 426, Am I a soldier of the cross, etc.

*Leader.*—Persecuted, but not forsaken; cast down, but not destroyed.

*Response.*—Whosoever, therefore, shall be ashamed of me and of my words, of him also shall the Son of Man be ashamed.

*Leader.*—Blessed are ye when men

## Soldiers of the Cross. Concluded.

shall revile you, and persecute you, and shall say all manner of evil against you falsely, for my sake.

*All Sing.* 2d verse, Must I be carried, etc.

*Leader.*—The fool hath said in his heart, There is no God.

*Response.*—I have set the Lord always before me, because he is at my right hand I shall not be moved.

*Leader.*—Lord, who shall abide in thy tabernacle? who shall dwell in thy holy hill?

*Response.*—He that walketh uprightly, and worketh righteousness and speaketh the truth in his heart.

*All Sing.* 3d verse, Are there no foes, etc.

## No. 428. Guide Me.

W. WILLIAMS.  ZION. 8. 7. 4.  (M. H. 171.)  THOMAS HASTINGS.

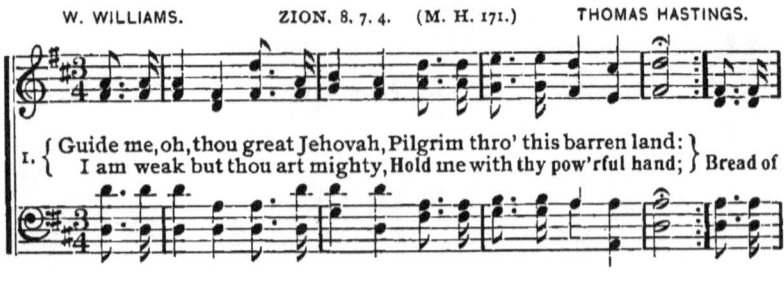

1. Guide me, oh, thou great Jehovah, Pilgrim thro' this barren land:
   I am weak but thou art mighty, Hold me with thy pow'rful hand; Bread of

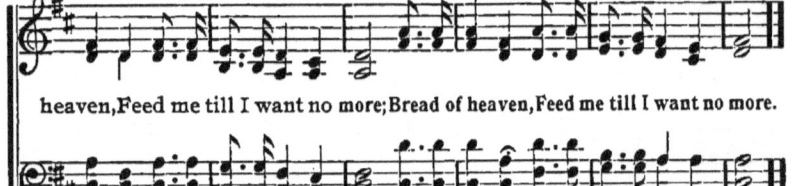

heaven, Feed me till I want no more; Bread of heaven, Feed me till I want no more.

2. Open now the crystal fountain,
   Whence the healing waters flow;
   Let the fiery, cloudy pillar
   Lead me all my journey through:
   ‖: Strong Deliverer,
   Be thou still my strength and shield.:‖

3. When I tread the verge of Jordan,
   Bid my anxious fears subside;
   Bear me thro' the swelling current;
   Land me safe on Canaan's side;
   ‖: Songs of praises
   I will ever give to thee.:‖

---

### No. 429. Guide Me.

*Leader.*—The meek will he guide in judgment; and the meek will he teach his way.

*Response.*—Thou shalt guide me with thy counsel, and afterward receive me to glory.

*Leader.*—If I take the wings of the morning, and dwell in the uttermost parts of the sea, even there shall thy hand lead me, and thy right hand shall hold.

*All Sing.* 1st verse, No. 428, Guide me,

*Leader.*—I am the living bread which came down from heaven; if any man eat of this bread, he shall live forever.

*Response.*—When he, the spirit of truth is come, he will guide you into all truth; for he shall not speak of himself; but whatsoever he shall hear, that shall he speak; and he will show you things to come.

### Guide Me. Concluded.

*All Sing:* 2d verse, Open now the, etc.

*Leader.*—Whosoever drinketh of the water that I shall give him shall never thirst; but the water that I shall give him shall be in him a well of water springing up into everlasting life.

*Response.*—And all the people saw the *cloudy pillar* stand at the tabernacle door; and all the people rose up and *worshiped*; every man in his tent door.

*All.*—My goodness and my *fortress*; my *high tower*, and my *deliverer*; my *shield*, and he in whom I *trust*.

*All Sing:* 3d verse, When I tread the, etc.

## No. 430. Blow Ye the Trumpet, Blow.

CHARLES WESLEY.   LENOX, H. M. (M. H. 331.)

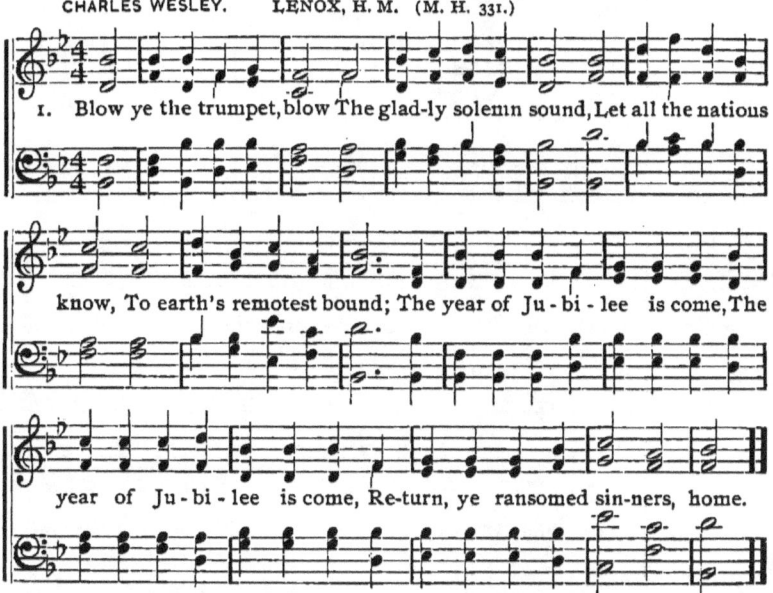

1. Blow ye the trumpet, blow The glad-ly solemn sound, Let all the nations know, To earth's remotest bound; The year of Ju-bi-lee is come, The year of Ju-bi-lee is come, Re-turn, ye ransomed sin-ners, home.

2 Jesus, our great High Priest,
  Has full atonement made;
  Ye weary spirits, rest;
  Ye mourning souls, be glad;
  ||:The year of jubilee is come;:||
  Return, ye ransomed sinners, home.

3 Exalt the Lamb of God,
  The sin atoning Lamb;
  Redemption by his blood
  Through all the world proclaim;
  ||:The year of jubilee is come;:||
  Return, ye ransomed sinners, home.

## No. 431. Missionary.

*Leader.*—Go ye, therefore, and teach all nations baptizing them in the name of the Father, and of the Son, and of the Holy Ghost.

*Response.*—Teaching them to observe whatsoever I have commanded you, and lo, I am with you always even unto the end of the world.

*Leader.*—All the ends of the world shall remember and turn unto the Lord, and all the kindreds of the nations shall worship before him.

*All Sing.* 1st verse, No. 430, Blow ye the trumpet, blow, etc.

*Leader.*—How then shall they call on him in whom they have not believed? and how shall they believe in him of whom they have not heard? and how shall they hear without a preacher, and how shall they preach except they be sent?

*Response.*—As it is written, how beautiful upon the mountains are the feet of them that preach the gospel of peace, that bring glad tidings of good things.

*Leader.*—So shall He sprinkle many nations. He shall see of the travail of His soul and be satisfied for he shall bear their iniquities.

*All Sing.* 2d verse, Jesus, our great, etc.

*Leader.*—The wilderness and the solitary place shall be glad for them and the desert shall rejoice and blossom as the rose. It shall blossom abundantly and rejoice even with joy and singing.

*Response.*—Then shall the lame man leap as an hart and the tongue of the dumb sing, for in the wilderness shall waters break out and streams in the desert.

*Leader.*—The meek also shall increase their joy in the Lord and the poor among men shall rejoice in the Holy One of Israel.

*All Sing.* 3d verse, Exalt the Lamb, etc.

# No. 432. My Jesus, I Love Thee.

LONDON HYMN BOOK.     BY PERMISSION.     A. J. GORDON.

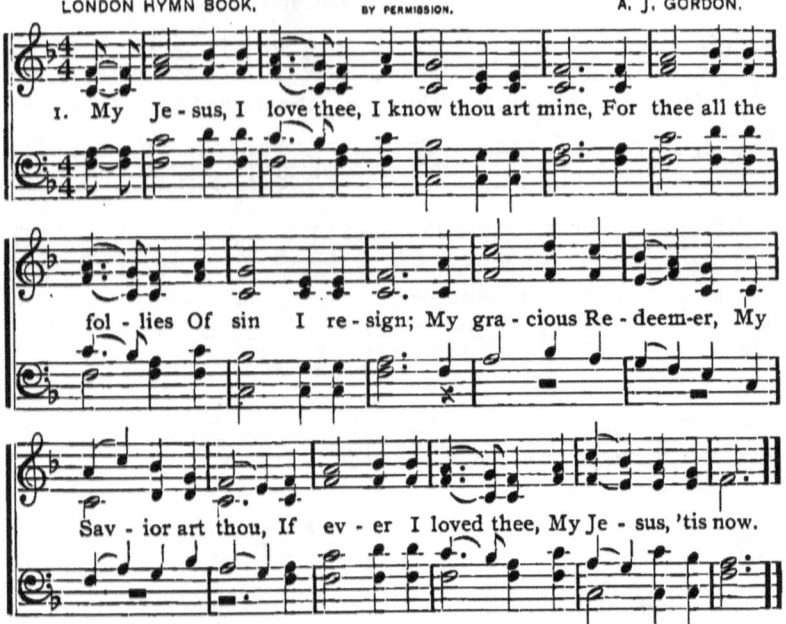

1. My Jesus, I love thee, I know thou art mine, For thee all the follies Of sin I resign; My gracious Redeemer, My Savior art thou, If ever I loved thee, My Jesus, 'tis now.

2 I love thee, because thou
    Hast first loved me,
And purchased my pardon
    On Calvary's tree;
I love thee for wearing
    The thorns on thy brow;
If ever I loved thee,
    My Jesus, 'tis now.

3 I will love thee in life,
    I will love thee in death,
And praise thee as long as
    Thou lendest me breath;
And say when the death-dew
    Lies cold on my brow,
If ever I loved thee,
    My Jesus, 'tis now.

4 In mansions of glory
    And endless delight,
I'll ever adore thee
    In heaven so bright;
I'll sing with the glittering
    Crown on my brow,
If ever I loved thee,
    My Jesus, 'tis now.

## No. 433. Love.

*Leader.*—For all have sinned, and come short of the glory of God.

*Response.*—But God commendeth his love toward us, in that while we were yet sinners, Christ died for us.

*Leader.*—And he is the propitiation for our sins; and not for ours only, but also for the sins of the whole world.

*Response.*—Behold, what manner of love the Father hath bestowed upon us, that we should be called the sons of God.

*All Sing*    1st verse, No. 432, My Jesus, I love thee, etc.

## Love: Concluded.

*Leader.*—For God so loved the world, that he gave his only begotten Son, that whosoever believeth in him should not perish, but have everlasting life.

*Response.*—Greater love hath no man than this, that a man lay down his life for his friends.

*Leader.*—We love him because he first loved us.

*All Sing.*    2d verse, I love thee because,

*Leader.*—Hereby perceive we the love of God, because he laid down his life for us: and we ought to lay down our lives for the brethren.

*All Sing.*    3d verse, I will love thee in, etc.

# No. 434. Jesus, I my Cross have Taken.

HENRY F. LYTE.  ELLESIDE. 8. 7. D. (M. H. 643.)  MOZART.

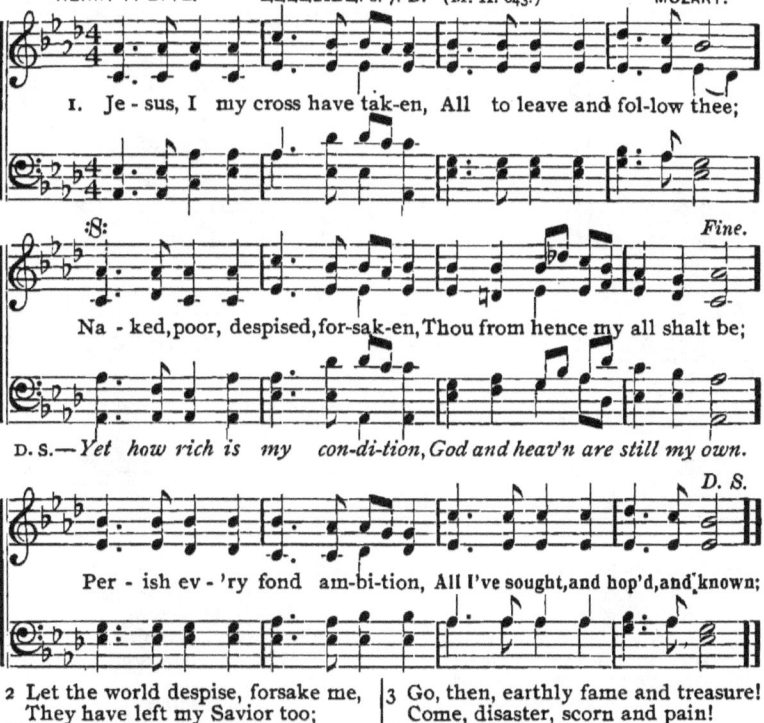

1. Je-sus, I my cross have tak-en, All to leave and fol-low thee;
Na-ked, poor, despised, for-sak-en, Thou from hence my all shalt be;
Per-ish ev-'ry fond am-bi-tion, All I've sought, and hop'd, and known;

D. S.—*Yet how rich is my con-di-tion, God and heav'n are still my own.*

2 Let the world despise, forsake me,
They have left my Savior too;
Human hearts and looks deceive me,
Thou art not, like man, untrue;
And, while thou shalt smile upon me,
God of wisdom, love and might,
Foes may hate, and friends may shun
Show thy face and all is bright. [me,

3 Go, then, earthly fame and treasure!
Come, disaster, scorn and pain!
In thy service, pain is pleasure;
With thy favor, loss is gain:
I have called thee, "Abba, Father,"
I have stayed my heart on thee; [er,
Storms may howl, and clouds may gath-
All must work for good to me.

---

## No. 435. Consecration.

*Leader.*—For the preaching of the cross is to them that perish, foolishness; but unto us which are saved it is the power of God.

*Response.*—Whosoever, therefore, shall confess me before men, him will I confess also before my Father which is in heaven.

*Leader.*—And he that taketh not his cross and followeth after me is not worthy of me.

*All Sing.* 1st verse, No. 434, Jesus, I my cross have taken, etc.

*Leader.*—And when he had called the people unto him, with his disciples also, he said unto them, Whosoever will come after me let him deny him-

## Consecration. Concluded.

self and take up his cross and follow me.

*Response.*—And whosoever doth not bear his cross, and come after me, can not be my disciple.

*Leader.* For whosoever shall save his life shall lose it, but whosoever shall lose his life for my sake and the gospel's, the same shall save it.

*All Sing.* 2d verse, Let the world, etc.

*Leader.* For what shall it profit a man, if he gain the whole world and lose his own soul?

*Response.* Or what shall a man give in exchange for his soul.

*All Sing.* 3d verse, Go, then, earthly, etc.

## No. 436. Come, Thou Almighty King.

CHARLES WESLEY.   ITALIAN HYMN, 6s, 4s. (M. H. 6.)   FELICE GIARDINI.

1. Come, thou Almighty King, Help us thy name to sing, Help us to praise! Father all glorious, O'er all victorious, Come, and reign over us, Ancient of days.

2 Come, holy Comforter,
Thy sacred witness bear,
In this glad hour.
Thou, who almighty art,
Now rule in every heart,
And ne'er from us depart,
Spirit of power.

3 To thee, great One in Three,
The highest praises be;
Hence, evermore;
Thy sovereign majesty
May we in glory see,
And to eternity
Love and adore.

### No. 437. Praise, No. 2.

*Leader.*—I am Alpha and Omega, the beginning and the ending, saith the Lord, which is, and which was, and which is to come, the Almighty.

*Response.*—O come, let us sing unto the Lord; let us make a joyful noise to the rock of our salvation.

*Leader.*—O sing unto the Lord a new song; sing unto the Lord all the earth.

*All Sing.* 1st verse, No. 436, Come, thou Almighty King, etc.

*Leader.*—Know ye not that ye are the temple of God, and that the spirit of God dwelleth in you.

*Response.*—Cast me not away from thy presence; and take not thy holy spirit from me.

*Leader.*—Restore unto me the joy of thy salvation and uphold me with thy free spirit.

### Praise, No. 2. Concluded.

*Response.*—Then will I teach transgressors thy way; and sinners shall be converted unto thee.

*All Sing.* 2d verse, Come, holy Comforter,

*Leader.*—Fear ye not, neither be afraid; have not I told thee from that time, and have declared it? ye are even my witnesses. Is there a God beside me? Yea, there is no God; I know not any.

*Response.*—For thou art great and doest wondrous things: Thou art God alone.

*Leader.*—He that overcometh shall inherit all things: and I will be his God, and he shall be my son.

*All Sing.* 3d verse, To thee, great One in,

## No. 438. Jesus Shall Reign.

WATTS. DUKE STREET, L. M. (M. H. 919.) JOHN HATTON.

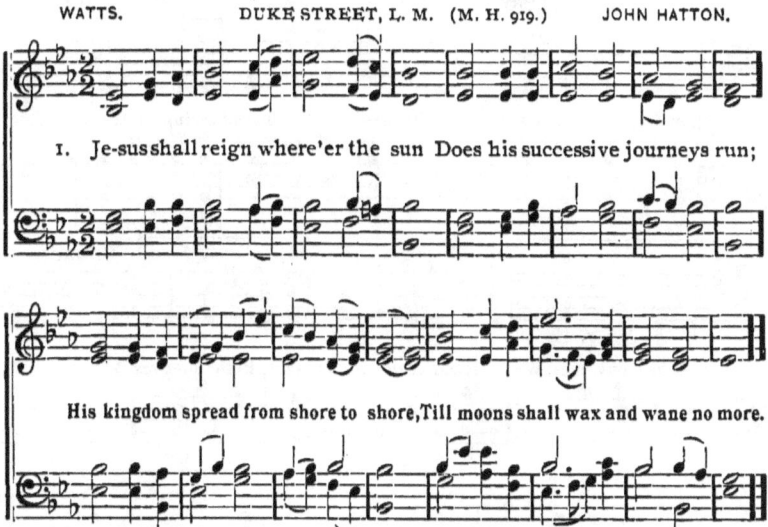

1. Jesus shall reign where'er the sun Does his successive journeys run;
His kingdom spread from shore to shore, Till moons shall wax and wane no more.

2 To him shall endless pray'r be made,
And praises throng to crown his head:
His name, like sweet perfume shall rise
With every morning sacrifice.

3 People and realms of every tongue
Dwell on his love with sweetest song;
And infant voices shall proclaim
Their early blessings on his name.

4 Blessings abound where'er he reigns,
The prisoner leaps to loose his chains;
The weary find eternal rest,
And all the sons of want are blest.

5 Let every creature rise, and bring
Peculiar honors to our King.
Angels descend with songs again,
And earth repeat the long amen.

---

## No. 439. Jesus Shall Reign.

*Leader.*—Behold the days come, saith the Lord, that I will raise unto David a righteous branch, and a king shall reign and prosper, and shall execute judgment and justice in the earth.

*Response.*—That as sin reigned unto death, even so might grace reign through righteousness unto eternal life by Jesus Christ our Lord.

*Leader.*—And he shall reign over the house of Jacob forever, and of his kingdom there shall be no end.

*All Sing.* 1st verse, No. 438, Jesus shall reign, etc.

*Leader.*—Evening and morning and at noon will I pray, and cry aloud; and he shall hear my voice.

## Jesus Shall Reign. Concluded.

*Response.*—And my tongue shall speak of thy righteousness and of thy praise all the day long.

*Leader.*—Continue in prayer, and watch in the same with thanksgiving.

*All Sing.* 2d verse, To him shall endless prayer, etc.

*Leader.*—My voice shalt thou hear in the morning, O Lord; in the evening will I direct my prayer unto thee and will look up.

*All.*—Let all those that put their trust in thee rejoice: let them even shout for joy, because thou defendest them: let them also that love thy name be joyful in thee.

*All Sing.* 3d verse, People and realms of,

## No. 440. Bringing in the Sheaves.

From "SONGS OF GLORY." GEO. A. MINOR.

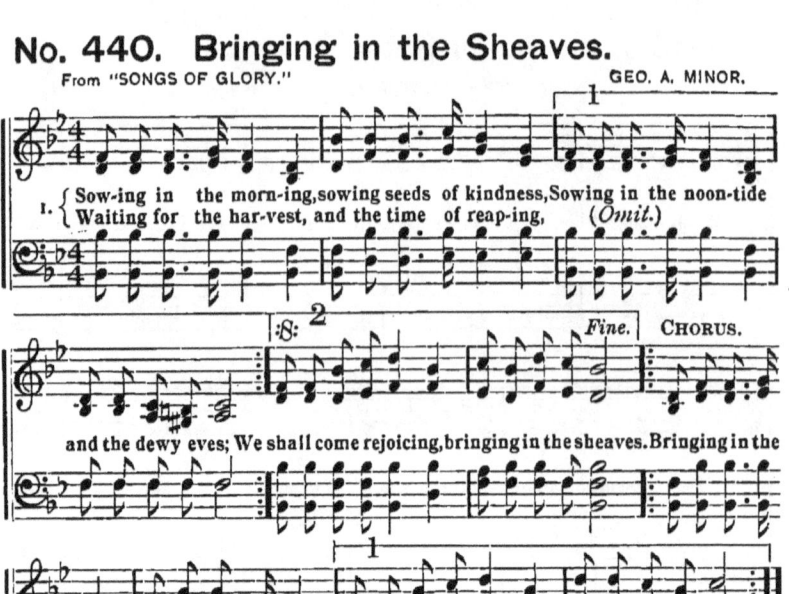

1. { Sow-ing in the morn-ing, sowing seeds of kindness, Sowing in the noon-tide
   Waiting for the har-vest, and the time of reap-ing, (*Omit.*) }
   and the dewy eves; We shall come rejoicing, bringing in the sheaves. Bringing in the sheaves, bringing in the sheaves, We shall come re-joic-ing, bringing in the sheaves.

2 Sowing in the sunshine, sowing in the shadows,
  Fearing neither clouds nor winter's chilling breeze;
  By and by the harvest, and the labor ended,
  We shall come rejoicing, bringing in the sheaves.

3 Go then, ever weeping, sowing for the Master,
  Though the loss sustained our spirit often grieves;
  When our weeping's over, he will bid us welcome,
  We shall come rejoicing, bringing in the sheaves.

---

## No. 441. Bringing the Sheaves.

*Leader.*—Be not deceived; God is not mocked; for whatsoever a man soweth, that shall he also reap.

*Response.*—For he that soweth to his flesh, shall of the flesh reap corruption; but he that soweth to the Spirit shall of the Spirit reap life everlasting.

*Leader.*—And the fruit of righteousness is sown in peace, of them that make peace.

*All Sing:* 1st verse No. 440, Sowing in the morning, etc.

*Leader.*—Say not ye, there are yet four months, and then cometh the harvest? behold I say unto you, lift up your eyes, and look on the fields; for they are white already to the harvest.

## Bringing the Sheaves. Concluded.

*Response.*—And he that reapeth receiveth wages, and gathereth fruit unto life eternal, that both he that soweth and he that reapeth may rejoice together.

*All Sing.* 2d verse, Sowing in the sun-

*Leader.*—In the morning sow thy seed, and in the evening withold not thine hand: for thou knowest not whether shall prosper, either this or that, or whether they both shall be alike good.

*Response.*—He that goeth forth and weepeth, bearing precious seed, shall doubtless come again with rejoicing, bringing his sheaves with him.

*All Sing.* 3d verse, Go then, ever, etc.

## No. 442. The Morning Light.

SAMUEL SMITH.     WEBB. 7s, 6s. (M. H. 932.)     GEO. WEBB.

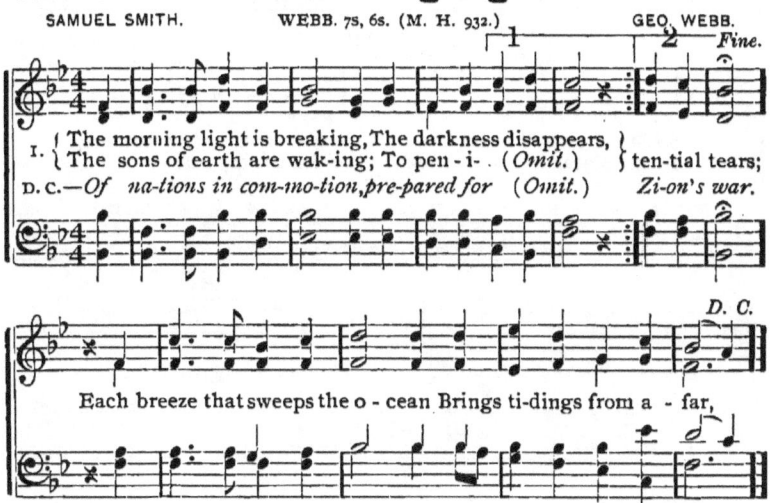

1. The morning light is breaking, The darkness disappears,
   The sons of earth are wak-ing; To pen-i- (*Omit.*) ten-tial tears;
   D.C.—Of na-tions in com-mo-tion, pre-pared for (*Omit.*) Zi-on's war.
   Each breeze that sweeps the o-cean Brings ti-dings from a-far,

2 See heathen nations bending,
Before the God of love,
And thousand hearts ascending,
In gratitude above;
While sinners, now confessing,
The gospel's call obey,
And seek a Savior's blessing,
A nation in a day.

3 Blest river of salvation,
Pursue thy onward way:
Flow thou to every nation,
Nor in thy richness stay.
Stay not till all the lowly,
Triumphant reach their home;
Stay not till all the holy
Proclaim, "The Lord is come."

---

## No. 443. The Morning Light.

*Leader.*—In the beginning was the word, and the word was with God, and the word was God. The same was in the beginning with God. All things were made by him; and without him was not anything made that was made. In him was life; and the life was the light of men.

*Response.*—I am the light of the world; he that followeth me shall not walk in darkness, but shall have the light of life.

*Leader.*—This then is the message that we have heard of him, and declare unto you, that God is light, and in him is no darkness at all.

*All Sing.* 1st verse No. 442, The morning light is breaking, etc.

*Leader.*—The people that walked in darkness have seen a great light; they that dwell in the land of the shadow of death, upon them hath the light shined.

### The Morning Light. Concluded.

*Response.*—Arise, shine; for thy light is come, and the glory of the Lord is risen upon thee.

*Leader.*—Look unto me, and be ye saved, all the ends of the earth; for I am God, and there is none else.

*All Sing.* 2d verse, See heathen nations bending, etc.

*Leader.*—And this gospel of the kingdom shall be preached in all the world for a witness unto all nations; and then shall the end come.

*Response.*—Go ye, therefore, and teach all nations, baptizing them in the name of the Father, and of the Son, and of the Holy Ghost: Teaching them to observe all things whatsoever I have commanded you; and, lo, I am with you alway, even unto the end of the world. Amen.

*All Sing.* 3d verse, Blest river of salvation, etc.

## No. 444. Savior, Like a Shepherd.

DOROTHY A. THRUPP.   SHEPHERD. 8, 7, 4. (M. H. 872.)   WM. B. BRADBURY.
BY PER. OF THE BIGLOW AND MAIN CO., OWNERS OF COPYRIGHT.

1. Savior, like a Shepherd lead us, Much we need thy tend'rest care,
   In thy pleasant pastures feed us, For our use thy folds prepare;
   Blessed Jesus, blessed Jesus, Thou hast bought us, thine we are;
   Blessed Jesus, blessed Jesus, Thou hast bought us, thine we are.

2 We are thine, do thou befriend us,
  Be the guardian of our way;
  Keep thy flock, from sin defend us,
  Seek us when we go astray;
  ||:Blessed Jesus, blessed Jesus,
  Hear, oh hear us when we pray.:||

3 Thou hast promised to receive us,
  Poor and sinful tho' we be;
  Thou hast mercy to relieve us,
  Grace to cleanse and power to free
  ||:Blessed Jesus, blessed Jesus,
  We will early turn to thee.:||

4 Early let us seek thy favor,
  Early let us do thy will;
  Blessed Lord and only Savior,
  With thy love our bosoms fill:
  ||:Blessed Jesus, blessed Jesus,
  Thou hast loved us, love us still.:||

---

## No. 445. Comfort.

*Leader.*—Know ye that the Lord he is God; it is he that hath made us and not we ourselves. We are his people and the sheep of his pasture.

*Response.*—I am the good shepherd and know my sheep, and am known of mine. As the Father knoweth me, even so know I the Father; and I lay down my life for the sheep.

*All Sing:* 1st verse, No. 444, Savior, like a shepherd, etc.

*Leader.*—The Lord is my shepherd, I shall not want; he maketh me to lie down in green pastures; he leadeth me beside the still waters.

*Response.*—He shall feed his flock

### Comfort. Concluded.

like a shepherd, he shall gather the lambs in his arms and carry them in his bosom, and shall gently lead those that are with young.

*All Sing.* 2d verse, We are thine, do, etc.

*Leader.*—All we like sheep have gone astray, we have turned every one to his own way, and the Lord hath laid on him the iniquity of us all.

*Response.*—And I will gather the remnant of my flock out of all countries whither I have driven them, and will bring them again to their folds, and they shall be fruitful and increase.

*All Sing.* 3d verse, Thou hast promised

## No. 446. Rejoice and be Glad.

2 Rejoice and be glad!
   It is sunshine at last!
   The clouds have departed,
   The shadows are past.
3 Rejoice and be glad!
   For the blood hath been shed;

Redemption is finished,
   The price hath been paid.
4 Rejoice and be glad!
   Now the pardon is free!
   The just for the unjust
   Hath died on the tree.

## No. 447. Rejoice and be Glad.

*Leader.*—Praise ye the Lord. Sing unto the Lord a new song.

*Response.*—For unto us a child is born, unto us a son is given: and the government shall be on his shoulder: and his name shall be called Wonderful, Counsellor, the Mighty God, the Everlasting Father, the Prince of Peace.

*Leader.*—O give thanks unto the Lord; call upon his name; make known his deeds among the people.

*All Sing.*  1st verse, No. 446, Rejoice and be glad, etc.

*Leader.*—Arise, shine; for thy light is come, and the glory of the Lord is risen upon thee.

*Response.*—For God, who commanded the light to shine out of darkness, hath shined in our hearts.

*All Sing:* 2d verse, Rejoice and be glad,

*Leader.*—Ye know that ye were not redeemed with corruptible things, as

## Rejoice and be Glad. Concluded.

silver and gold, but with the precious blood of Christ, as of a lamb without blemish and without spot.

*Response.*—For God so loved the world that he gave his only begotten Son, that whosoever believeth in him should not perish, but have everlasting life.

*Leader.*—In whom we have redemption through his blood, even the forgiveness of sins.

*All Sing.* 3d verse, Rejoice and be glad,

*Leader.*—Christ hath redeemed us from the curse of the law, being made a curse for us.

*All.*—Surely he hath borne our griefs and carried our sorrows. He was wounded for our transgressions, he was bruised for our iniquities, the chastisement of our peace was upon him; and with his stripes we are healed.

*All Sing.* 4th verse, Rejoice and be glad,

## No. 448. When I Survey.

ISAAC WATTS.   EUCHARIST. L. M. (M. H. 211.)   I. WOODBURY.

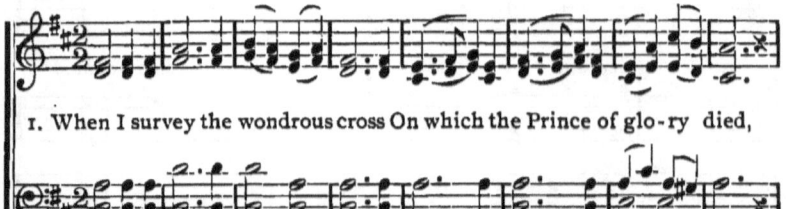

1. When I survey the wondrous cross On which the Prince of glo-ry died,

My richest gain I count but loss, And pour con-tempt on all my pride,

2 Forbid it, Lord, that I should boast,
  Save in the death of Christ, my God;
All the vain things that charm me most,
  I sacrifice them to his blood.

3 See, from his head, his hands, his feet,
  Sorrow and love flow mingled down;
Did e'er such love and sorrow meet,
  Or thorns compose so rich a crown?

4 Were the whole realm of nature mine,
  That were a present far too small;
Love so amazing, so divine,
  Demands my soul, my life, my all.

---

## No. 449. Consecration, No. 2.

*Leader.*—Blessed be the God and Father of our Lord Jesus Christ, who hath blessed us with all spiritual blessings in heavenly places in Christ Jesus.

*Response.*—In whom we have redemption through his blood, the forgiveness of sins, according to the riches of his grace.

*All Sing* 1st verse, No. 448, When I survey the wondrous, etc.

*Leader.*—And they that are Christ's have crucified the flesh with the affections and lusts.

*Response.*—But God forbid that I should glory save in the cross of our Lord Jesus Christ, by whom the world is crucified unto me, and I unto the world.

*All Sing.* 2d verse, Forbid it, Lord, etc.

*Leader*—Surely he hath borne our griefs, and carried our sorrows: yet we did esteem him stricken, smitten of God, and afflicted.

*Response.*—And when they had platted a crown of thorns, they put it upon his head, and a reed in his right hand: And they bowed the knee before him, and mocked him, saying, Hail, King of the Jews.

*All Sing.* 3d verse, See, from his head,

## No. 450. Prayer, No. 2.

*Leader:*—Enter into his gates with thanksgiving, and into his courts with praise.

*Response:*—I was glad when they said unto me, Let us go into the house of the Lord.

*Leader:*—They that wait upon the Lord shall renew their strength; they shall mount up with wings as eagles;

*Response:*—They shall run, and not be weary; they shall walk, and not faint.

*Leader:*—Blessed are they which do hunger and thirst after righteousness: for they shall be filled.

*Response:*—Blessed are the pure in heart: for they shall see God.

*Leader:*—Draw nigh to God, and he will draw nigh to you.

*Response:*—Ask, and ye shall receive; seek, and ye shall find; knock, and it shall be opened unto you.

*Leader:*—Let us therefore come boldly unto the throne of grace, that we may obtain mercy, and find grace to help in time of need.

*Response:*—O come, let us worship and bow down; let us kneel before the Lord our Maker.

*All Sing:* (See music No. 410.)

What a friend we have in Jesus,
  All our sins and griefs to bear!
What a privilege to carry
  Everything to God in prayer!
Oh, what peace we often forfeit,
  Oh, what needless pain we bear,
All because we do not carry,
  Everything to God in prayer!

## No. 451. Holy Spirit, No. 2.

*Leader:*—And it shall come to pass in the last days, saith God, I will pour out my Spirit upon all flesh.

*Response:*—And your sons and your daughters shall prophesy, and your young men shall see visions, and your old men shall dream dreams.

*Leader:*—And on my servants and on my handmaidens I will pour out in those days of my Spirit, and they shall prophesy.

*Response:*—But ye shall receive power after that the Holy Ghost is come upon you; and ye shall be witnesses unto me both in Jerusalem and in all Judea, and in Samaria, and unto the uttermost parts of the earth.

*Leader:*—And when the day of Pentecost was fully come, they were all with one accord in one place.

*Response:*—And suddenly there came a sound from heaven as of a rushing mighty wind, and it filled all the house where they were sitting.

*Leader:*—And there appeared unto them cloven tongues like as of fire, and it sat upon each of them.

*Response:*—And they were all filled with the Holy Ghost, and began to speak with other tongues, as the Spirit gave them utterance.

*Leader:*—Have ye received the Holy Ghost since ye believed?

*Response:*—Hereby know that we dwell in him, and he in us, because he hath given us of his Spirit.

*All Sing.* (See music No. 402.)

Holy Spirit, faithful guide,
Ever near the Christian's side,
Gently lead us by the hand;
Pilgrims in a desert land,
Weary souls, fore'er rejoice,
While they hear that sweetest voice
Whispering softly, "wand'rer come
Follow me, I'll guide thee home."

## No. 452. Praise, No. 3.

*Leader;*—Praise ye the Lord, sing unto the Lord a new song, and his praise in the congregation of saints.

*Response;*—For the Lord taketh pleasure in his people; he will beautify the meek with salvation.

*Leader;*—Praise ye the Lord. Praise God in his sanctuary; praise him in the firmament of his power.

*Response;*—Praise him for his mighty acts; praise him according to his excellent greatness.

*Leader;*—Praise him with the sound of the trumpet; praise him with the psaltery and harp.

*Response;*—Praise him with the timbrel and dance; praise him with stringed instruments and organs.

*Leader:*—Praise him upon the loud cymbals; praise him upon the high sounding cymbals.

*Response:*—Let everything that hath breath praise the Lord. Praise ye the Lord.

*All Sing.* (See music No. 457.)

Praise God from whom all blessings flow
Praise Him, all creatures here below;
Praise Him above, ye heavenly host;
Praise Father, Son, and Holy Ghost.

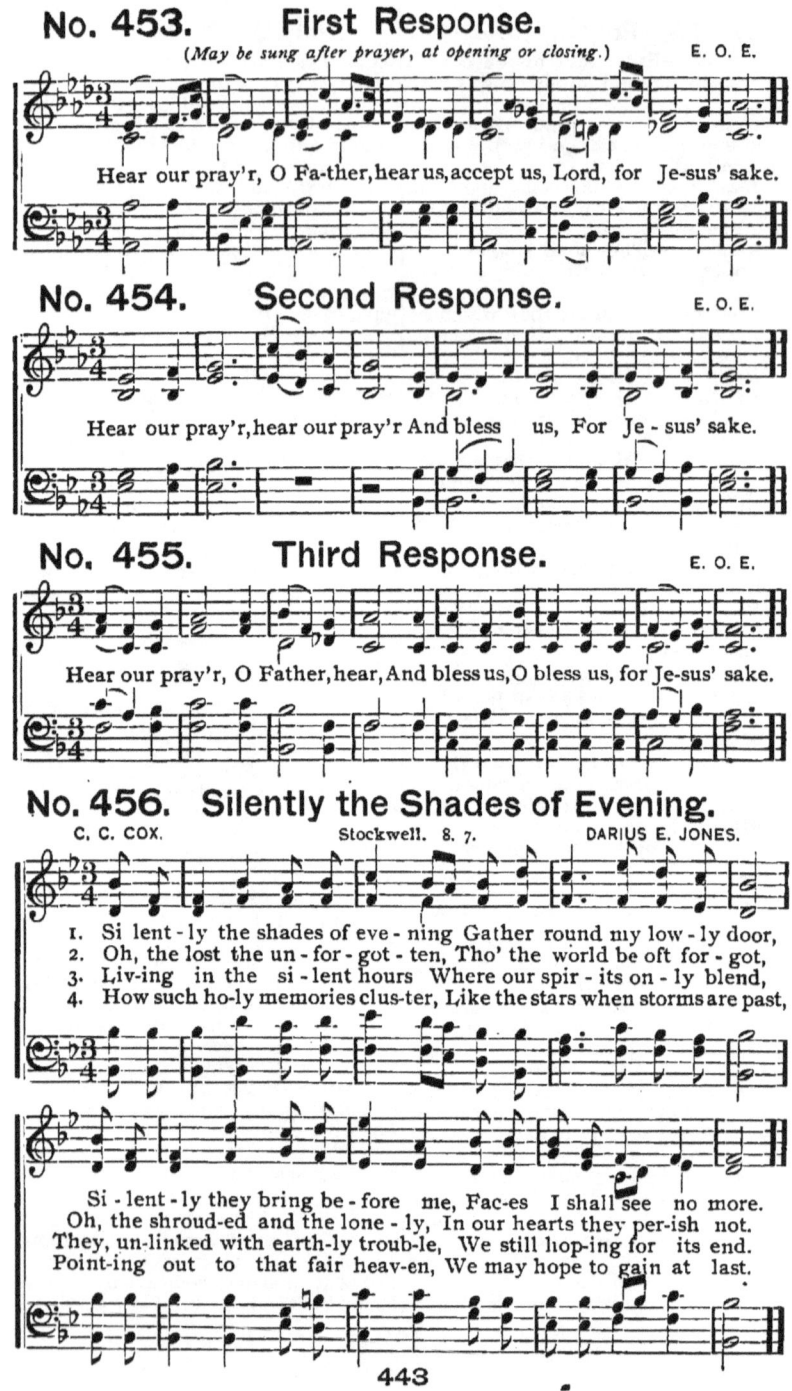

## No. 457. Doxology.
THOS. KEN.    OLD HUNDRED. L. M.    G. FRANC.

Praise God from whom all blessings flow; Praise Him, all creatures here below;
Praise Him a-bove ye heav'nly host, Praise Father, Son and Ho-ly Ghost.

## No. 458. Invitation to Worship.
*(See music above.)*

1 All people that on earth do dwell,
Sing to the Lord with cheerful voice:
Him serve with fear, His praise forth tell
Come ye before Him, and rejoice.

2 The Lord, ye know, is God indeed,
Without our aid He did us make;
We are His flock, He doth us feed,
And for His sheep He doth us take.

3 O enter then His gates with praise,
Approach with joy His courts unto:
Praise, laud, and bless His name always
For it is seemly so to do.

4 For why? the Lord our God is good,
His mercy is forever sure;
His truth at all times firmly stood,
And shall from age to age endure.
WILLIAM KETHE.

## No. 459. Doxology.
THOS. KEN.    SESSIONS. L. M.    L. O. EMERSON.

1. All people that on earth do dwell, Sing to the Lord with cheerful voice:
Him serve with fear, His praise forth tell, Come ye before Him and re-joice.

## No. 460. Gloria Patri.

1. Glory be to the Father, and to the Son, and to the Ho-ly Ghost:
2. As it was in the beginning, is now, and ev-er shall be, world without end. A-men.

# INDEX.

Titles in SMALL CAPS, First Lines in Roman.

| Title/First line | No. | Title/First line | No. | Title/First line | No. |
|---|---|---|---|---|---|
| A BETTER WORLD | 55 | BY AND BY, YES, BY | 128 | FROM GREENLAND'S | 172 |
| ABIDE WITH ME | 51 | By faith the Lamb | 336 | Gather them to us fro | 243 |
| ABUNDANTLY ABLE | 223 | By thy saving cross we | 64 | Gently Lord, O gently | 396 |
| A BURDEN BEARER | 215 | CALLING THEE AWAY | 19 | GLORIA PATRI | 460 |
| A doubly pious way | 20 | CALLING THE PRODIG | 233 | Glory be to the Father | 460 |
| After the joys of earth | 162 | CALL THEM IN | 243-366 | GLORY, GLORY TO | 232 |
| A great rock stands | 143 | CARRY EVERYTHING. | 212 | GLORY JESUS SAVES | 191 |
| ALAS AND DID MY SA | 391 | CHRIST IS ALL THE | 309 | GLORY TO HIS NAME. | 262 |
| A LITTLE TALK WITH | 296 | CHRISTMAS | 166 | GOD BE WITH YOU | 356 |
| All around on every | 161 | Christ the Lord on this | 27 | God is calling the | 233 |
| ALL FOR JESUS | 9-58 | CITY OF BEAUTY | 5 | GOD IS CALLING THEE | 85 |
| ALL HAIL THE POWER | 424 | CLEANSE ME FROM MY | 119 | GOD IS CALLING YET. | 34 |
| All people that on | 458-459 | Come and listen to | 323 | GOD IS EVER GOOD | 369 |
| All praise to Him who | 42 | Come and sit down to | 23 | GOD IS EVERYWHERE | 202 |
| ALL THE DAY LONG | 3 | Come, Christian sailor | 343 | GOD IS LOVE | 190 |
| All, yes all I give to Je- | 9 | Come contrite one | 87 | GO FORWARD CHRISTI | 227 |
| AMERICA | 131 | COME, HIS TABLE IS SP | 23 | GOOD NEWS | 304 |
| AM I A SOLDIER OF | 426 | COME HOLY SPIRIT | 150 | GOING DOWN TO THE. | 113 |
| ANGELS HOV'RING | 385 | COME LET US JOIN | 71 | GOLDEN GATES YE GL | 167 |
| AN HEIR TO THE KING | 273 | COME, SINNER COME | 334 | GO, SPREAD THE LIGH | 253 |
| A pardon is waiting | 59 | Come sinners to the | 252 | GRACIOUS PROMISES | 176 |
| ARE YOU DOING ALL. | 161 | COME THOU ALMIGHT | 436 | GUIDE ME, O THOU GR | 428 |
| Are you ready for the | 311 | COME THOU FOUNT | 100-372 | HAIL THOU ONCE DE | 395 |
| ARISE, HE CALLETH | 57 | COME TO JESUS | 383 | HAPPY DAY | 374 |
| A sinner was wand'rin | 277 | COME TO ME | 346 | HAPPY VOICES | 53 |
| AS WE GO | 110 | COME YE DISCONSOLA | 138 | HARK, TEN THOUSAND | 258 |
| AT THE FOUNTAIN | 390 | COME YE SINNERS | 382 | Hark, the herald ange | 324 |
| Awake my soul in joy- | 422 | COME YE THAT LOVE. | 380 | Hark, the voice of | 397 |
| AWAY THE BOWL | 305 | COMING TO-DAY | 240 | Hark, your captain | 21 |
| Back from the long a- | 32 | COMING UNTO JESUS | 333 | HAST THOU HEARD | 284 |
| BE ACTIVE IN THE | 201 | COMPANIONSHIP WIT | 362 | HAVE FAITH IN GOD. | 344 |
| BEAUTIFUL, BECKON- | 225 | CONSECRATION | 38 | Have you ever heard | 139 |
| BEAUTIFUL BETHLE- | 145 | Death bells tolling | 322 | Have you found a | 164 |
| BEAUTIFUL FACES | 61 | Depth of mercy | 190 | Have you heard the | 304 |
| BEAUTIFUL LAND OF | 69 | Down at the cross | 262 | HEALING | 88 |
| BEAUTIFUL ROBES | 347 | Do you hear the might | 213 | Heart of Jesus | 200 |
| BE CAREFUL WHAT | 94 | Do you hear those voi | 116 | Hear our prayer | 453-54-55 |
| Beckoning hands at | 225 | DOXOLOGY | 457-459 | Hear the gentle | 326 |
| BEHOLD A STRANGER | 371 | Drawing near to the | 159 | Hear the gospel | 209 |
| Behold how the fields. | 44 | DRAW ME CLOSER | 54 | HEAR THE MASTER | 341 |
| BEHOLD I STAND AT | 261 | ENDEAVOR | 175 | Hear the Savior | 366 |
| BEHOLD THE MAN | 127 | ENTIRE CONSECRATIO | 83 | Hear the temperance | 268 |
| Behold the Prince and | 127 | EVER WILL I PRAY | 270 | Heavenly portals ring | 107 |
| BE THOU MY GUIDE | 194 | Father, I am weak an | 70 | HEAVEN'S GATES WIL | 70 |
| Beyond the cares of lif | 19 | Father, in the mornin | 270 | HE CAME TO SAVE ME | 25 |
| BLESSED ASSURANCE. | 282 | Father, I stretch my | 381 | HE IS ABLE TO DELIV- | 169 |
| BLESSED BE THE NAM | 42 | FILL ME NOW | 17 | HE IS CALLING | 318 |
| BLESSED STRANGER | 103 | FIND SOMETHING TO | 332 | HE IS JUST THE SAME | 139 |
| Blessed words for | 234 | FOLLOW ALL THE WA | 189 | HE KEEPETH ME EVE | 306 |
| BLEST BE THE TIE TH | 170 | FOLLOW ME | 198 | HE LOVED ME SO | 336 |
| Blest rock of ages cleft | 2 | For all the Lord has | 192 | HE LOVES ME | 279 |
| BLOW YE THE TRUMP | 430 | Forever here my rest. | 394 | HERALDS OF JESUS | 155 |
| BOUNDLESS GRACE | 28 | FOR ME, AND FOR THE | 27 | HERE AM I | 256 |
| BRINGING IN THE SHE | 440 | For salvation are you | 198 | HE WEPT IN BLOOD | 82 |
| Brother, you have kno | 137 | FORWARD FOR THE | 21 | HIS BANNER IS LOVE. | 29 |
| BY AND BY | 114 | FROM ALL THAT DWE | 242 | Holy Father, freely | 180 |
| By and by the path | 128 | FROM EVERY STORMY | 300 | HOLY, HOLY, HOLY | 148-406 |

445

## INDEX.

| Title | No. | Title | No. | Title | No. |
|---|---|---|---|---|---|
| Holy one, holy one | 178 | In the time of peace | 45 | Let down your net to- | 68 |
| HOLY SPIRIT, FAITHF | 402 | IN THY LOVE | 70 | LET HIM IN | 18 |
| Hosannas now the peo- | 76 | INVITATION TO WORS | 458 | LET ME IN THE LIFE- | 343 |
| HOSANNA TO THE LA | 76 | I sat alone with life's | 171 | LET THEM COME TO ME | 326 |
| Hover o'er me Holy | 17 | I SHALL BE SATISFIED | 247 | LET US ALONE | 271 |
| HOW FIRM A FOUNDA | 398 | Is it there? writte | 120 | Let us rally | 363 |
| HOW GENTLE GOD'S | 404 | IS MY NAME WRITTEN | 56 | Like Jacob in his Beth | 342 |
| How I LOVE JESU | 269-384 | IT IS WELL | 84 | Like Samuel of old | 256 |
| How loving is Jesus | 231 | IT WILL NEVER GROW | 292 | LINGER WITH ME | 157 |
| HOW SWEET IS THE BI | 48 | I've a message from | 163 | LOOK AND LIVE | 163 |
| HOW THEY SING IN | 226 | I've two little hands | 81 | LORD FORGIVE | 180 |
| I acknowledge my tra | 119 | I want to be more like | 245 | LORD, WE COME BEFO | 73 |
| I ALWAYS GO TO JESU | 222 | I want to serve Jesus. | 193 | LOST BUT JESUS SAVE | 360 |
| I am coming to the | 104-377 | I WILL GO TO THE KIN | 294 | LOVING KINDNESS | 422 |
| I am coming unto Jes | 333 | I WILL LIFT UP MINE | 90 | LOYALTY TO CHRI | 64-229 |
| I am on my pilgrim | 108 | I WILL LOVE THEE | 236 | MERCY IS BOUNDLESS | 165 |
| I AM ON MY WAY TO | 108 | Jerusalem, my happy | 338 | MID SCENES OF CON- | 152 |
| I AM TRUSTING LORD | 377 | Jesus and shall | 368 | MIGHTY TO SAVE | 164 |
| I can hear my Savior | 244 | JESUS BIDS US SHINE. | 154 | MORE ABOUT JESUS | 181 |
| I CANNOT TELL WHY. | 187 | Jesus blest many | 279 | MORE LIKE JESUS | 184-245 |
| I COME TO THEE | 254 | Jesus came from heav | 179 | MOTHER'S PRAYER | 14 |
| I DO BELIEVE | 381 | JESUS FOR ME | 183 | My country, 'tis of | 134 |
| I do not ask for the | 120 | Jesus has offered the | 251 | MY FAITH LOOKS UP. | 408 |
| If beset by doubts and | 151 | Jesus, I bring to Thee | 38 | MY FATHER'S HOUSE | 278 |
| If I in thy likeness | 247 | JESUS I MY CROSS | 434 | MY HAPPY HOME | 338 |
| If in this world I have | 13 | JESUS IS BORN | 107 | My heart has found | 319 |
| IF I WERE A VOICE | 281 | JESUS IS CALLING | 251 | My heavenly home | 43 |
| If unrepentant you | 206 | JESUS IS PASSING | 87-230 | MY JESUS, I LOVE TH | 432 |
| I have a song I love to | 211 | Jesus is the light | 361 | My life, my love I | 328 |
| I have bathed in the | 191 | JESUS KNOWS | 72 | MY MOTHER'S HANDS | 135 |
| I HAVE LOOKED AND I | 149 | JESUS, LET THY PITY- | 142 | MY RESTING PLACE | 2 |
| I have no merit | 220 | Jesus Lord I come | 378 | My soul and I | 353 |
| I HAVE OFTEN HEARD | 259 | JESUS, LOVER OF | 8-414 | MY SOUL, BE ON THY | 123 |
| I have seen a mother | 52 | Jesus my all to heaven | 386 | My soul in sad exile! | 115 |
| I journey to the better | 196 | Jesus, my Lord, to thee | 31 | My soul is now united | 309 |
| I knew that God in | 289 | Jesus my Savior is a | 183 | My talents are few | 99 |
| I KNOW THAT MY RE- | 370 | JESUS SAVED OTHERS. | 340 | Naught we care for | 105 |
| I leave it all with Jesu | 72 | JESUS SAVES ME | 220-386 | NEARER THEE | 101-330 |
| I'LL BE THERE | 43 | JESUS SAVIOR PILOT | 214 | NEARER THE CROSS | 285 |
| I'll go to the King | 294 | JESUS SHALL REIGN | 438 | NEARER TO THEE | 32 |
| I'LL LIVE FOR HIM | 328 | JESUS THE LIGHT OF | 324 | No beautiful chamber | 60 |
| I'll sing of that beauti- | 69 | JESUS THINE ALL VIC | 388 | NO, NOT TOO LATE | 30 |
| I LOVE TO SING ABOUT | 182 | Jesus thou art the | 197 | NO ONE IS FORGOTT | 203 |
| I'm heir to the mansi | 273 | Jesus with you is plea | 334 | NO ROOM IN THE INN | 60 |
| I'M KNEELING AT TH | 387 | JOY COMETH IN THE | 234 | NOT ASHAMED OF JE- | 368 |
| I'M SEEKING THAT | 80 | JOY TO THE WORLD | 416 | Now I know the great | 6 |
| I'M TRUSTING IN | 210 | JUST AS I AM | 228 | O City of Beauty, I | 5 |
| In a world where sor- | 4 | JUST BEYOND THE | 313 | O DAY OF REST AND | 168 |
| I NEVER WILL CEASE | 192 | JUST OVER THERE | 78 | Of all the prayers that | 14 |
| IN HEAVENLY LO | 205-302 | Just to let thy Father | 50 | Of Him who did salva | 390 |
| IN HIS NAME | 105 | KEEP CLOSE TO JESUS | 249 | O for a closer walk | 393 |
| IN SIGHT OF THE CRYS | 171 | KIND WORDS CAN NE | 299 | O for a faith that will | 392 |
| In the army of the | 337 | KING OF KINGS | 379 | Often do my footsteps | 216 |
| In the Lamb's book of | 56 | Lamp of our feet | 65 | Oft in hours of pain | 176 |
| IN THE MORNING | 267 | LAND OF SONG | 280 | O GOD BE MERCIFUL | 351 |
| In the paths of sin I | 103 | LEAD ME, SAVIOR | 112 | O hallowed hour, when | 29 |
| IN THE SECRET OF | 327 | LEANING ON THEE | 216 | O happy day | 374 |
| In the service of the | 173 | LEAVE IT ALL TO JE- | 92 | O have you not heard | 292 |
| IN THE SHADOW OF | 283 | LEND A HAND | 339 | OH, BE READY | 311 |

# INDEX.

| Title | No. |
|---|---|
| Oh, blessed fellowship | 362 |
| OH, COULD I SPEAK | 420 |
| Oh, erring one | 30 |
| Oh Father, send me | 111 |
| OH, HOW HAPPY | 117 |
| Oh, if for me the cup | 47 |
| Oh, I love to think | 189 |
| Oh, now I see the crim | 389 |
| Oh, the Gospel story | 126 |
| Oh, those beautiful, han | 135 |
| Oh, turn ye, oh, | 188-399 |
| Oh, what shall it prof | 132 |
| O life-giving water | 11 |
| O LOVING JESUS | 231 |
| One of Christ's burden | 215 |
| ONLY | 248 |
| Only a word | 248 |
| Only waiting till | 357 |
| OLD TIME RELIGION | 102 |
| ON THE EVERGREEN | 160 |
| ONWARD | 345 |
| ONWARD AND UPWA | 316 |
| ONWARD CHRISTIAN | 125 |
| Onward still and | 316 |
| O sinner, God is call- | 96 |
| O the fountain stands | 373 |
| O the joy, the bliss | 288 |
| O they tell me of a | 237 |
| O TURN YE | 77 |
| Our Father which art | 260 |
| Our Father who art | 136 |
| Our youthful hearts | 305 |
| Out into the darkness | 84 |
| Out on the desert | 240 |
| Out where the reapers | 235 |
| Over Judea's rugged | 86 |
| OVER THERE | 308 |
| O where are the reape | 293 |
| PARDON IS WAITING | 59 |
| Patiently we toil alon | 280 |
| PEACE BE UNTO YOU | 275 |
| PILOT ME | 86 |
| Praise God from whom | 457 |
| PRAISE TO THEE | 364 |
| PRAYING FOR YOU | 310 |
| Pray when the days | 212 |
| Precious Savior, show | 264 |
| RAISE ME JESUS TO | 257 |
| RALLY! RALLY! RALL | 363 |
| RECRUITS FOR JESUS | 49 |
| REJOICE AND BE GLAD | 446 |
| RESCUE THEM | 22 |
| RESPONSES | 178-453, 454-455 |
| **RESPONSIVE SERVICES.** | |
| Bringing the sheave | 441 |
| Comfort | 445 |
| Consecration | 435-449 |
| Coronation | 425 |
| Faith | 409 |

| Title | No. |
|---|---|
| God's love | 401 |
| Great Physician | 419 |
| Guide me | 429 |
| Holy, Holy | 407 |
| Holy Spirit | 403-451 |
| Jesus shall reign | 439 |
| Joy | 417 |
| Love | 433 |
| Loving kindness | 423 |
| Missionary | 431 |
| Praise | 421-437-452 |
| Prayer | 411-450 |
| Refuge | 415 |
| Rejoice and be glad | 447 |
| Rock of Ages | 413 |
| Soldiers of the cross | 427 |
| The morning light | 443 |
| Wisdom | 405 |
| Psalm LIV | 67 |
| Psalm XCVI | 79 |
| Psalm CIII | 95 |
| Rest to the weary soul | 217 |
| Return, O wand'rer | 224 |
| REVIVE US AGAIN | 400 |
| RICHES UNSEARCHAB | 301 |
| RING OUT THE TIDING | 335 |
| RISE MY SOUL | 146 |
| ROCK OF AGES (new) | 74 |
| ROCK OF AGES | 272-276-412 |
| ROLL ON THE GOSPEL | 89 |
| Rows of cheerful faces | 106 |
| SAFELY THROUGH AN | 174 |
| SAILING | 159 |
| Sang the stars of morn | 53 |
| SATISFIED WITH CHRI | 41 |
| SAVED TO THE UTTER | 121 |
| SAVIOR BLESSED SAV | 288 |
| Savior, hear me while | 241 |
| Savior, lead me lest I | 112 |
| SAVIOR, LIKE A SHEP- | 444 |
| SAVIOR WASH ME IN | 124 |
| SAY, ARE YOU READY | 98 |
| SCATTER SUNSHINE | 4 |
| SCATTER GERMS OF | 321 |
| SCATTERING PRECIOU | 263 |
| SEEKING THE LOST | 286 |
| See the shining dew | 369 |
| SEND ME A LIFE-BOAT | 111 |
| SERVING JESUS | 198 |
| SHALL WE MEET BE- | 156 |
| SHELTERED IN THE CR | 264 |
| Should the death angel | 98 |
| Silently the shades of | 456 |
| SILENTLY THE SHAD | 320 |
| Silent the feet of the | 367 |
| SINCE I HAVE BEEN | 211 |
| SING IT WITH JOY | 36 |
| Sing me a song of the | 177 |
| Sing, O sing the dear | 303 |
| SING, THE LOVE OF | 303 |

| Title | No. |
|---|---|
| SINNER GO WILL YOU | 375 |
| SITTING AT THE FEET | 319 |
| SLEEP MY LITTLE ONE | 315 |
| SNOW FLAKES | 195 |
| Soft fell the mother's | 109 |
| SOLDIERS OF THE | 314 |
| SOME BLESSED DAY | 239 |
| Some day, but when | 239 |
| SOME SWEET DAY | 207 |
| SOMETHING FOR THEE | 99 |
| SOMETHING TO DO | 130 |
| Sowing in the morning | 440 |
| STANDING ON THE | 246 |
| STEAL AWAY TO JESU | 224 |
| STEER FOR THE LIGH | 186 |
| Step by step and day | 62 |
| STORY OF THE CROSS | 126 |
| SUN OF MY SOUL | 158 |
| SUNSHINE AND SHAD- | 12 |
| SUNSHINE IN THE SOU | 218 |
| SWEET AND LOW | 133 |
| SWEETLY SING THE LO | 40 |
| TAKE ME AS I AM | 31 |
| TAKE ME IN | 200 |
| Take my life and let | 83 |
| TAKE MY YOKE | 219 |
| TAKE THE WORLD | 265 |
| TELL IT ALL TO JESUS | 350 |
| TELL IT FAR AND WI | 185 |
| Tell it, let the people | 185 |
| TELL IT TO JESUS | 312 |
| TELL ME THE OLD, OL | 355 |
| TELL OF HIS LOVE | 179 |
| Thanks be to Jesus | 165 |
| THAT OLD, OLD STORY | 274 |
| THE ANGELS ARE LOO | 342 |
| THE ANSWERED PRAY | 109 |
| THE ASSURANCE | 10 |
| THE BEAUTIFUL LAND | 97 |
| THE BEAUTIFUL LIGH | 361 |
| THE BEAUTIFUL WAY | 39 |
| THE BIBLE | 65 |
| THE BLOOD IS ALL | 289 |
| THE CAUSE OF RIGHT | 37 |
| THE CHILDREN'S KIN | 116 |
| THE CLEANSING WAV | 389 |
| THE COMING OF THE | 213 |
| THE FOUNTAIN STAN | 373 |
| THE FOUR CALLS | 66 |
| THE GLAD GOOD NEW | 359 |
| THE GOLDEN SHORE | 1 |
| THE GOSPEL NET | 68 |
| THE GOSPEL PROCLA | 209 |
| THE GREAT PHYSICIA | 418 |
| THE GREAT REDEEM- | 6 |
| THE GUSHING RILL | 47 |
| THE HALLOWED SPOT | 35 |
| THE HARVEST | 44 |
| THE HAVEN OF REST | 115 |
| THE HEAVENLY GATE | 353 |

447

# INDEX.

| Title | No. | Title | No. | Title | No. |
|---|---|---|---|---|---|
| THE HEAVENLY LAND | 177 | Though the clouds are | 92 | WHAT LITTLE FOLKS.. | 24 |
| THE JUDGMENT........ | 367 | THOUGH YOUR SINS.. | 365 | WHAT SHALL IT PROF- | 132 |
| THE LAST CALL......... | 33 | Thro' all the changing | 184 | WHAT SINNER THEN. | 206 |
| The Lord of earth and | 16 | THROW OUT THE LIFE | 7 | What still.small voice | 85 |
| THE LORD'S MY SHEP | 118 | Tiny little snowflake. | 195 | WHAT THEN?............ | 162 |
| THE LORD'S PRAYER. | 260 | TIS FOR YOU AND ME | 250 | WHAT WILL YOU DO.. | 290 |
| The Master is coming. | 341 | 'TIS SWEET TO KNOW | 26 | WHEN I SURVEY...... | 448 |
| THE MORNING LIGHT | 442 | 'Tis the grandest them | 169 | When I walked with. | 12 |
| THE PENITENT'S PLEA | 241 | 'Tis the old time relig | 102 | When Jesus laid his... | 25 |
| THE PILGRIM'S SONG. | 13 | To-day if you will,... | 325 | When sorrow's cup.... | 82 |
| The precious book is.. | 317 | To my Savior clinging | 232 | When the burdened.. | 226 |
| THE SECRET OF A HAP | 50 | TO THE HIGHWAYS... | 137 | When the evening.... | 275 |
| THE SINNER'S CALL... | 96 | TO THE RESCUE........ | 322 | When the heart grows | 350 |
| The spirit came in..... | 66 | Trust thou in God..... | 344 | When the heart shall. | 78 |
| There are angels hove | 385 | TRUST THY FATHER.. | 129 | WHEN THE MISTS..... | 329 |
| There is a fountain (new) | 124 | 'TWAS RUM THAT SPO | 52 | WHEN THE ROLL IS.. | 204 |
| THERE IS A FOUNTAIN | 75 | TWO LITTLE HANDS... | 81 | When the trumpet.... | 204 |
| THERE IS A HAPPY LA | 358 | UNDER THE CROSS..... | 104 | When thou passeth... | 10 |
| There is a land of pure | 160 | UP AND BE DOING.... | 331 | When you hear the... | 221 |
| There is a name........ | 384 | Upon my heart I find. | 88 | When you start........ | 249 |
| There is another, bet- | 55 | Upon the western pla | 229 | WHEN WE ALL GET... | 141 |
| There is a spot........... | 35 | WAIT A LITTLE, YOU | 151 | WHEN WE ARE THER | 298 |
| There's a beautiful la | 97 | WAITING................. | 357 | WHERE ARE THE..... | 293 |
| There's a beautiful li | 186 | Waken a song to the La | 36 | WHERE ART THOU SO | 15 |
| There's a city bright.. | 313 | WAKE THE SONG..... | 291 | WHERE HE LEADS.... | 244 |
| THERE'S A GREAT..... | 266 | WALKING IN THE LIG | 197 | WHERE IS YOUR TRUS | 255 |
| THERE'S A HAND HEL | 140 | WASHED IN THE BLO | 378 | WHERE THE LIVING. | 217 |
| There's an end to all.. | 208 | WE ARE MARCHING... | 337 | WHERE WILL YOU.... | 93 |
| There's an uttermost. | 354 | We are marching to... | 37 | While shepherds watc | 166 |
| There's a pardon....... | 250 | We are workers for the | 147 | Whoever receiveth.... | 223 |
| There's a stranger at. | 18 | Weary and heavy lad | 351 | WHY I LOVE JESUS... | 307 |
| There's a voice soft... | 199 | Weary soul, by sin... | 346 | WHY NOT TO-DAY?... | 122 |
| There's a way that is | 39 | WEARY THE WAITING | 208 | WHY STAND YE HERE | 6? |
| THERE'S A WIDENESS | 144 | WE COME, COME AGAI | 295 | Why stand ye here... | 332 |
| There's a wideness..... | 318 | We come to worship.. | 295 | WHY WILL YE DIE?.. | 143 |
| There's a wonderful... | 274 | We come with banners | 49 | WILL YOU BE WITH... | 221 |
| There's sunshine in... | 218 | We go the way that... | 131 | WILL YOU COME....... | 199 |
| There's work for the.. | 130 | We hear the dear Mas- | 175 | WILL YOU HAVE THIS | 325 |
| There will be a wondro | 298 | Weighed by thy love.. | 348 | WILL YOU MEET ME | 46-196 |
| THE ROAD TO HEAVE | 376 | WEIGHED IN THE BA | 348 | WINE IS A MOCKER... | 352 |
| These are words of.... | 278 | WE'LL FOLLOW THEE | 62 | With an everlasting.. | 359 |
| THE SINNER AND THE | 277 | We'll meet again on.. | 238 | With bright banners.. | 91 |
| THE TEMPERANCE..... | 268 | We praise thee O...... | 400 | WONDERFUL LIFE-GI | 11 |
| THE UNCLOUDED DAY | 237 | WE'RE GOING HOME.. | 131 | WONDROUS GRACE.... | 16 |
| THE VERY SAME JESU | 252 | We shall be at home.. | 114 | Wondrous grace and.. | 28 |
| THE VOWS OF GOD.... | 297 | We shall have the flo | 267 | WON'T YOU TRUST HI | 153 |
| THE WONDERFUL....... | '317 | We shall hear the an- | 1 | WORKERS FOR THE... | 147 |
| THE WONDROUS STOR | 323 | We shall reach the.... | 207 | WORK FOR LITTLE SER | 173 |
| THE WORLD, THE FLE | 91 | WE SHALL STAND BE | 349 | WORK FOR US ALL... | 235 |
| They spake to him of | 57 | We shall walk with... | 347 | WORKING FOR THE... | 106 |
| They who seek the.... | 202 | We will give our heart | 110 | Would you know...... | 307 |
| They were singing..... | 101 | WE WILL REST IN THE | 45 | Yes, I am satisfied with | 41 |
| This is the season of.. | 230 | We will sing the praise | 141 | YES, WE WILL MEET.. | 238 |
| THIS UTTERMOST SAL | 354 | WHAT A FRIEND....... | 410 | Your mother is prayin | 310 |
| THOU ART MY SHEPH | 287 | What are you trusting | 255 | You think the house of | 122 |
| Thou art my strength | 254 | What if the watchma | 290 | | |